christine mcfadden

flour

a comprehensive guide

with photography by
Mike Cooper

ABSOLUTE PRESS

Absolute Press
An imprint of Bloomsbury Publishing Plc

50 Bedford Square   1385 Broadway
London   New York
WC1B 3DP   NY 10018
UK   USA

www.bloomsbury.com

First published 2018

British Library Cataloguing-in-Publication Data
A catalogue record for this book is available from the British Library.

Library of Congress Cataloguing-in-Publication data has been applied for.

ISBN   HB: 9781472945976
         ePDF: 9781472945969
         ePub: 9781472945952

2 4 6 8 10 9 7 5 3 1

Printed in China by C&C Offset Printing Co., Ltd.

Sincere thanks to my
late friend and poet Geoffrey Godbert,
and also to food writer Jenny Linford
for encouraging me
to write this book

6   introduction
8   how to use this book
8   flour notes
9   the recipes
10   ingredients
11   equipment

12   almond *flour*
16   amaranth *flour*
20   atta *flour*
24   banana *flour*
28   barley *flour*
32   black bean *flour*
36   buckwheat *flour*
44   cassava *flour*
52   chestnut *flour*
62   chickpea *flour*
68   coconut *flour*
74   coffee *flour*
78   corn*flour*
86   cornmeal
94   cricket *flour*
98   einkorn *flour*
102   emmer *flour*
108   fava bean *flour*
112   khorasan *flour*
116   lupin *flour*
122   maida *flour*
126   millet *flour*
132   mung bean *flour*

138   oat *flour*
142   pea *flour*
148   peanut *flour*
152   potato starch
158   quinoa *flour*
164   rice *flour*
172   rye *flour*
180   semolina
192   sesame *flour*
196   sorghum *flour*
202   soya *flour*
208   spelt *flour*
216   teff *flour*
222   tiger nut *flour*
226   water chestnut *flour*
232   wheat *flour:* fine
236   wheat *flour:* Italian 00
244   wheat *flour:* plain
256   wheat *flour:* self-raising
264   wheat *flour:* strong
270   wheat *flour:* whole
274   yam *flour*

278   bibliography
280   sources
282   index
288   acknowledgements

introduction

Researching and writing about flour has been an incredibly rewarding challenge. I have spent days deep in a floury haze of what often seemed to be hugely baffling information – the difference between flours, starches and meals; what is gluten and how does it make dough rise; what are 'falling numbers'; is there any difference between cereals, grains and seeds? I have learned the meaning of mysterious terms such as naked grains, autolysis and 'straight' and 'patent' flour. I have visited mills – thundering scary places where people stride about in steel-capped boots – and in doing so I have developed a fascination for paper flour sacks; I love the typography and sturdy white paper. The research has led me down rabbit holes that I didn't know existed – the intricacies of flours from Hong Kong and the Czech Republic for example. Whole books could be devoted to them.

I am lucky to live in a remote hamlet in Dorset, one of the UK's most bucolic counties. Arable farming is the norm, and there are plenty of grain fields to investigate, and friendly farmers happy to talk about crops. There are also millers and bakers who have generously shared valuable information. Through talking to these experts I have become much more aware of the natural rhythms of farming, the seasons when grains are sown and harvested, and the skill behind milling and professional baking.

Ferreting out accurate research has sometimes been frustrating. Barely five or six years ago, the term 'flour' implicitly meant ground wheat, and most major reference books didn't mention alternatives. *The Cambridge World History of Food*, for example, contains lengthy and learned entries on grains, nuts, pulses and starchy roots but doesn't touch on using them as flour. Neither flour nor grains are of consequence to the erudite Waverley Root, a respected authority on food. The flour entry in his hefty volume *Food* is curiously limited to 'the flour tree, whose beanlike fruit is fermented and used as a condiment throughout West Africa'.

I regularly resorted to perusing food science notes from my university days; I was so pleased I had kept them. Constants throughout were two trusty reference books: *On Food and Cooking: The Science and Lore of the Kitchen* by science writer Harold McGee, and the late Alan Davidson's enormous tome *The Oxford Companion to Food*. Both were permanently propped up next to my desk, appropriately in a director's chair, rather like unseen university tutors. Without them I would have been at a loss.

Though I love to cook, I am not a natural baker and I rarely eat sweet foods. Nor do I suffer from gluten sensitivity. Even though steep learning curves were involved as I honed my bread-making skills, learned to like cakes and got to grips

flour

with gluten-free dough, devising the recipes was such an enjoyable and satisfying process.

The first day of recipe testing happened to coincide with watching *Shrek 2* with my grandchildren. There is a memorable moment when Shrek bellows, 'We're gonna need flour, lots and lots of flour' – it brought about a frenzy of air-punching from me and my family. From that moment on, friends started sending me unusual flours, samples from mills arrived in the post and I became a flour junkie. That said, I haven't always been so flour fixated. I have childhood memories of a loathsome pot of flour-and-water paste and a bristly brush. I used it to laboriously paste scraps of paper round a light bulb to make a papier-mâché head for a doll, and I stuck treasured items into a paper scrapbook. I remember that the damp pages took ages to dry and left the entire scrapbook smelling faintly sour.

In what I call 'pre-book' days, my flours could be easily housed a single tub. Now I have a dedicated spare room lined with shelf after shelf of carefully labelled boxes. This has become the 'flour library' and I love to spend time there, occasionally plunging my hands into a particular flour, enjoying its softness and coolness. The flours have taken on anthropomorphic qualities – some seem gentle and accommodating, others need coaxing into submission. Some are pale and anaemic, others are robust and wholesome. Some are a cheerful yellow, others a mysterious blue or sombre grey.

Nowadays we are fortunate in having a cornucopia of flour at our disposal, gluten-free and otherwise, from all over the world, ground not only from grains and seeds but also from pulses, nuts, tubers, roots and even insects. I sometimes wonder if we have reached peak flour now that so many ingredients are ground to a powder and marketed as so-called 'flour'.

Flour has many roles, not just in baking but in weaving its way in and out of other ingredients in so many dishes. As Martial, the sharp-witted Roman, wrote in one of his pithy epigrams, 'You can list neither the virtues of fine flour, nor all its uses...' Responding to the challenge, I have made a point of including recipes that demonstrate the many ways in which flour can be used: in pancake batters, coating crisp fried foods, binding burgers and fritters, thickening sauces and stews, fortifying puddings and porridges, and more. The recipes in this book are a motley collection but there is something for everyone, including non-bakers. I hope you enjoy them.

Christine McFadden
October 2017

how to use this book

The forty-five flours in this book are listed in sequential A–Z format. This makes it easy to look up a flour that interests you rather than having to decide on a category in which it might be included. You will therefore find gluten-free flours listed with gluten-containing flours, flours from seeds listed with flours from nuts or tubers, and so on.

Each flour entry begins with a CV stating its source, Latin name, gluten and/or protein content, plus suggestions on ingredients or flavours that make good culinary partners, and ways in which it can be used.

The CV is followed by an in-depth description of the flour, including a brief historical or geographical background, interesting anecdotes, how it's produced, growing conditions, recipe suggestions, nutritional information, tips for the cook and where you can buy it. Following the description are one or more fully tested recipes showing good ways of using it.

Dispersed throughout the book are essays on flour-related topics. These include a simplification of the hard-core science of gluten, protein and resistant starch, an overview of wheat, a discussion of milling and a description of stone grinding at a traditional working watermill.

flour notes

With a cornucopia of alternative flours ground not only from grains but also from nuts, roots and pulses, there is a need for information about how to use, prepare and store them. Throughout the book you'll find this covered in detailed descriptions of each flour, but here are some basics.

Storing

All flours lose their flavour and nutrients over time, but they will last longer if properly stored.

- Buy only what you can use before it expires.
- Check the 'use by' date from time to time and throw out flour that is past its best.
- Don't add new flour to old.
- If not using quickly, decant an open packet into a sealed container.
- Store in a cool dry place. Don't use a cupboard that is close to hot water pipes or above the fridge.
- Store whole grain flours in a sealed container in the fridge or freezer. This will help prevent oil in the germ and bran from going rancid.
- If you find weevils, get rid of the flour and give your cupboard a good clean.

Measuring

Flour is one of the trickiest ingredients to measure. Always, always weigh rather than measure by volume. If you use a measuring cup or spoon, the weight will differ depending on the way the flour is added, how the surface is levelled and how much it is compacted.

Bear in mind that different flours may not weigh the same per cup – in other words a cup of wholemeal flour doesn't weigh the same as a cup of rice flour. Weighing is the only way to be consistently accurate.

Sieving

Experts might disagree, but I firmly believe that passing flour through a fine mesh sieve not only filters out lumps but more importantly introduces air. When mixing with other dry ingredients, sieve them with the flour to make sure they are evenly dispersed.

the recipes

The recipes give you an opportunity to experiment with a flour you may never have heard of, let alone used before. They also show you how to use a familiar flour in what might be an unfamiliar way – cornflour in Turkish Delight for example. There is a wide choice that brings to light the fascinating ways in which flour is used throughout the world, from Banana Flour Pancakes and Native American Fry Bread to Carrot and Cashew Samosas and Welsh Curd Cake.

Some are really quick and simple, others require more time, over a leisurely weekend perhaps.

Tips for success

Working with unfamiliar flours and other ingredients, and experimenting with new techniques mean that it's well worth spending time getting organized before you begin.

- Read the recipe all the way through, taking careful note of the total time needed, and also the time needed for pastry or batter to rest, dough to rise, ingredients to soak, chill, marinate and so on.
- Allow time for cakes and biscuits to cool to room temperature before icing or storing.
- Gather together your pans and utensils – that way you won't be frantically looking for something when the dish you're cooking needs urgent attention.
- Make sure you use the specified pan or dish size, or a close substitute. They are there for a reason.
- Sharpen your knives so you can chop and slice cleanly and quickly.
- Assemble all the ingredients, measure them accurately and put them in bowls or other containers ready for when you need them (see also Weighing and measuring).
- Position your oven racks before you preheat the oven.
- Allow time for the oven to reach the correct temperature (see also Oven temperatures).
- Clear up as you go along.

Weighing and measuring

In baking, accurate measuring is crucial for success. Use good-quality digital scales and a set of measuring spoons.

- All spoon measurements in the recipes are level unless specified otherwise.
- Use measuring spoons for volume but not for weight. Non-liquid items have different densities and don't necessarily weigh the same even if the volume is the same. For example, 2 tablespoons of cocoa powder weigh 15g/½oz whereas 2 tablespoons of granulated sugar weigh 25g/1oz.
- It is more precise to weigh larger amounts of liquids using digital kitchen scales rather than the calibrations on a measuring jug. Place an empty jug on the scales, then zero the scales. Gradually pour in the liquid until the scales register your chosen amount.

Oven temperatures

The temperatures given in the recipes are for fan and gas ovens. Bear in mind that no two ovens are alike and thermostats are rarely accurate. I have two fan ovens which each give different results for the same recipe. My advice is to get to know your oven and its quirks, and adjust the recipe timing accordingly.

A good-quality oven thermometer is essential for baking. As a test, put the thermometer on the middle rack of the oven and set the oven temperature to 200°C/Gas Mark 6. Check the thermometer every 10 minutes until it stops climbing. If the final temperature doesn't match the temperature to which you have set the oven, make a note of the discrepancy and remember it each time you bake. For example, when I set my oven to 200°C/Gas Mark 6, the thermometer registers 190°C/Gas Mark 5. I compensate by setting the oven temperature correspondingly higher.

ingredients

Success depends entirely on the quality of the ingredients – fresh flour, newly laid eggs from happy hens, good-quality oils and unsalted butter, plus top-notch fresh vegetables and fruit. Buy the best you can.

Some of the ingredients may be unfamiliar and aren't necessarily found in every supermarket. In some cases a substitute can be used, but it really is worth sourcing just small quantities of the more obscure ingredients so you can experience new flavours and expand your culinary repertoire. Nowadays it's really easy to buy ingredients online or you can enjoy rummaging in shops that sell Asian or African groceries. Good health food shops are another useful source.

Baking powder A raising agent made with alkaline bicarbonate of soda and a specific amount of an acid such as cream of tartar or tartaric acid. When exposed to moisture and/or heat, it produces carbon dioxide that makes batter or dough rise.

Bicarbonate of soda Also known as baking soda, an alkaline raising agent that releases carbon dioxide only when it comes in contact with acid ingredients such as cream of tartar, buttermilk, soured cream, vinegar or citrus juice. It has a harsh flavour that can be masked by using it with assertively flavoured ingredients such as ginger, chocolate and spices. Add it to batter or dough immediately before putting it in the oven, otherwise the gas will escape.

Butter In baking, you don't have an opportunity to test and check the seasoning, so always use unsalted butter unless specified otherwise. It has a cleaner flavour and puts you in charge of the salt.

Buttermilk Confusingly named, buttermilk contains no butter. Traditionally it was the acidic watery liquid or whey left behind after churning butter from milk. Nowadays it's a commercially cultured product made by adding friendly bacteria to milk. In baking, it produces carbon dioxide when mixed with bicarbonate of soda and acts as a leavener.

Cacao nibs Roasted cacao nibs are roasted cacao beans that have been separated from their husks and broken into small chips. On their own they have an ultra-intense chocolate flavour. They are best stirred into dough, batter or creamy desserts.

Chilli flakes Dried crushed chillies add zesty flavour to doughs and batters. My favourites are the slightly oily Turkish red flakes called *pul biber* and the dark smoky black ones called *urfa biber*.

Also good are Korean chilli flakes known as *gochugaru* and the chilli paste called *gochujang*. They're all easy to find online and in good supermarkets.

Chocolate Choose top-notch eating chocolate (not baking chocolate) with at least 70 per cent cocoa solids. It should have a good sheen and crisp snap.

Cream Use double, whipping or single cream as specified. I choose to buy organic cream as it is has a superior flavour and is relatively free from pesticide residues.

Eggs Choose organic or free-range eggs, or, even better, eggs from rare-breed hens. They have a fabulous fresh flavour, gloriously golden yolks and dense whites. Use medium-sized eggs unless otherwise specified.

Guar gum Made from guar beans and used as a binder and thickener in gluten-free baking. It has a lighter texture than xanthan gum (see below).

Herbs Herbs are fresh unless specified.

Milk Use semi-skimmed or whole milk as specified. I choose to buy organic milk as it is relatively free from pesticide residues.

Oils Groundnut oil is best for deep-frying as it has a high smoke point. Extra-virgin olive oil should be reserved for salads rather than frying as it burns at high temperatures. For frying and roasting use ordinary olive oil or all-purpose vegetable oils such as rapeseed or sunflower.

Salt Use fine sea salt or sea salt flakes as specified. I use fine sea salt for seasoning dishes where the salt dissolves during cooking, and sea salt flakes, either whole or lightly crumbled, for crunchy texture and delicious bursts of flavour on the tongue. Add them just before serving.

Seeds Cumin, dill and nigella seeds are good pantry staples. They add flavour to breads and crackers and help with digestion.

Spices Freshly ground whole spices, including pepper, are a must for bright zesty flavours. Pre-ground spices will have lost their distinctive aroma and flavour. Grind as needed using a mill for pepper, and a mortar and pestle for other spices.

Sugar Use the type of sugar specified in the recipes.

Granulated sugar is refined and is made from sugarcane or beets.

Caster sugar has smaller crystals that dissolve more easily, and is better for delicate mixtures.

Golden granulated and golden caster sugar are made from unrefined cane sugar. They add moisture and delicate flavour to baking and cream easily with fats.

Icing sugar is granulated sugar that has been crushed to a powder. It tends to clump, so needs sieving before use.

Jaggery or palm sugar is strongly flavoured unrefined dark sugar made from palm tree sap or sugarcane. It is available as a granular paste or a solid lump.

Coconut sugar or coconut palm sugar has a deep caramel flavour.

Wasabi Native to Japan, wasabi is a sought-after rhizome with a sinus-clearing aroma and flavour similar to horseradish. Available fresh or powdered from thewasabicompany.co.uk.

Xanthan gum A highly processed fermented product derived from corn, soya or wheat. Used as a binder and thickener in gluten-free baking. It is more powerful than guar gum (see above).

Yeast Baker's yeast creates the carbon dioxide gas needed to make dough rise. It comes in three forms:

Compressed fresh yeast: available in small lumps from bakers and good supermarkets. It has a limited shelf life of 7–10 days and must be stored in the fridge. Activated with sugar and tepid water.

Dried active yeast: sold in envelopes or tins. Activated with sugar and tepid water.

Dried easy-bake yeast: sold in envelopes or tins. Added directly to dry ingredients without activating.

Make sure dried yeast is well within the use-by date. Store in the fridge.

equipment

Having the right equipment is key to success in flour-based recipes. If you regularly cook, you're likely to have many of the items listed below. If you're just starting out, this is what you're likely to need. The list may look long but there is no need to buy everything all at once; build your 'batterie de cuisine' gradually as your cooking evolves.

Basics
Baking parchment
Baking sheets and trays
Baking dishes
Cake tins
Cutters, round
Dough scraper
Electric whisk
Flour sprinkler
Food processor
Graters
Greaseproof paper
Measuring jugs
Measuring spoons
Mixing bowls
Pastry brush
Pastry mat, non-stick
Rolling pins: long for pastry and pasta, short/narrow for flatbreads
Scales, digital
Sieves, large and small
Silicone sheets
Steamer
Spatulas: silicone and wood
Tart tins
Thermometers: sugar and oven
Timer
Tongs
Wire rack
Wooden spoons

Useful but not essential
Electric standing mixer

almond *flour*

plant source nut
aka almond flurry, almond powder
latin name *Prunus dulcis* var. *dulcis*
gluten none
protein 21%
goes with apricots, bananas, chocolate, cinnamon, citrus fruits, cream, milk, peaches, pears
uses bars, biscuits, bread, brownies, cakes, marzipan, muffins, pancakes, smoothies, thickener for curries and soups

Sweet and buttery almond flour works its special magic on so many delectable foods: moist cakes, puffy pancakes and creamy curries, to mention just a few. I first became aware of it in Sicily – home to the most exquisite cakes and pastries – where I came across it almost everywhere, packed in plain plastic bags, and sometimes in the most unlikely shops – ironmongers, for example. Invariably displayed alongside, also in plain plastic bags, were slabs of handmade marzipan, a clue to the culinary importance of almonds and sweetmeats in that part of the world.

Outside Sicily you'll find the flour in health food shops, specialist food shops and online. Confusingly, you'll also find almond flurry, almond powder, almond meal and ground almonds. The dividing line is thin. Almond flour, flurry and powder are the same thing, but almond meal is coarser since it's ground from almonds with skin. Ground almonds are coarse too, but skin-free.

Most almond flour is ground from blanched almonds. Cakes and other baked items made with it have a beautifully light crumb and a pale colour. Unblanched almond flour is available too, usually labelled 'raw'. It contains more fibre and produces a heavier, browner bake. It's useful for forgiving items such as biscuits and brownies where fluffiness and lightness aren't an issue.

Unlike most gluten-free flours, almond flour is usefully high in fat. This makes baked items moist and tender, and helps restore some of the strength and stretchiness that gluten would usually provide. The good news is that the fat is mainly monounsaturated, which means it's health-promoting in the same way as olive oil. The flour is also exceptionally high in protein and dietary fibre, and contains significant amounts of iron and calcium – almost as much as milk.

If you're not familiar with almond flour, it's a good idea to start off with recipes specifically designed for it. Try Sicilian Citrus and Almond Cake with Clementine Syrup (see page 14). Here, the flour is combined with semolina for extra texture, but it's fine to substitute a gluten-free flour if necessary – try tapioca starch or sorghum.

Otherwise, a useful rule of thumb is to substitute about a quarter of the main flour with almond flour. It's also a good idea to use a raising agent such as baking powder or bicarbonate of soda. In yeast-based recipes, almond flour works best for soft buns and rolls rather than crisp, chewy items such as pizza bases or crusty bread.

You'll discover that baked items made with almond flour tend to stick to baking trays and cake tins, so non-stick liners and cases are a must. If you're making scones and biscuits, dip the cutter in flour each time you make a cut to stop it sticking to the dough. And because almond flour is high in fat, baked items also tend to brown more quickly. Keep your oven temperature around medium and check regularly throughout the cooking time. If necessary, cover exposed areas with foil to prevent burning.

Moving on from baking, I love almond flour stirred into a smoothie or sprinkled over yogurt. It provides gentle sweetness and body, plus extra nutrients. If you like Indian food, try it in a creamy chicken korma; it will thicken the juices beautifully without making the flavour less savoury.

A drawback with almond flour, or any oily nut flour, is that it easily becomes rancid. To keep it fresh, store in an airtight container away from light and heat. It will last about three months in a cool dark cupboard, or longer in the fridge. You can freeze it too, but it will need defrosting before use.

sicilian citrus and almond cake with clementine syrup

almond flour 150g (5½oz)
fine semolina 100g (3½oz)
potato starch 50g (1¾oz)
baking powder 2 teaspoons
clementines 3, preferably
  organic
egg whites 5 (about
  150g/5½oz)
sea salt pinch
granulated sugar 200g (7oz)
unsalted butter 100g (3½oz),
  melted and cooled slightly
lemon finely grated zest of 1,
  preferably unwaxed
vanilla extract ½ teaspoon

for the topping
clementines 3–4, washed
  but not peeled
unrefined caster sugar 150g
  (5½oz)
water 200ml (7fl oz)

serves 8–10

Tangy citrus fruits and almonds bring back fond memories of Sicily where I first enjoyed this cake. Italian baking expert Ottavia Mazzoni kindly gave me her recipe.

The alchemy of almond flour and cloud-like egg whites makes the cake wonderfully light and moist. As Ottavia says, it will bring a ray of sunshine to your table during winter months. She suggests serving it as a dessert with very cold vanilla yogurt. It's good with ice cream too.

• • •

First make the topping. Slice the clementines thinly, keeping the juice but discarding the top and bottom. Put the sugar and water in a wide-based pan and bring to a boil over a medium heat. Add the clementine slices and the juice. Lower the heat, cover and simmer gently for 15–20 minutes, until tender but not disintegrating.

Meanwhile, grease and line a 25cm (10in) springform cake tin with baking parchment.

Using a slotted spoon, lift the clementine slices from the pan on to a plate. When they've cooled down, arrange them close together in a single layer in the bottom of the cake tin (this will eventually become the top of the cake).

Put the pan back on the hob and boil the juices until syrupy bubbles form – about 10 minutes, depending on the diameter of the pan. Set aside, ready to pour over the cooked cake.

Preheat the oven to 180°C/Gas Mark 4.

Put the almond flour, semolina, potato starch and baking powder into a sieve set over a bowl. Muddle with your fingers, then shake through the sieve. Sieve once or twice more until well blended.

Finely grate the zest from the clementines, taking care not to include the bitter white pith. Set the zest aside. Peel the clementines and break into segments, removing any pips. Put the segments in the bowl of a food processor, whizz to a pulp and set aside.

Using an electric whisk, beat the egg whites with a pinch of salt until droopy peaks form. Add the sugar and continue beating until the foam looks glossy.

Using a silicone spatula or large metal spoon, very lightly fold the foam into the flour mixture, alternating with

flour

the melted butter. Fold in the lemon zest, the reserved clementine zest and pulp, and the vanilla extract. Gently spoon the mixture into the prepared tin, levelling the surface with a wet palette knife.

Bake for 45–50 minutes, rotating the tin halfway through, until a skewer comes out clean. Remove from the oven on to a rack and leave for 10 minutes.

Invert the tin on to a serving plate and turn out the cake. Pierce the top in several places with a skewer and sprinkle over the reserved syrup. Leave to cool before serving.

amaranth *flour*

plant source seed
aka n/a
latin name *Amaranthus caudatus, Amaranthus cruentus, Amaranthus hypochondriacus*
gluten none
protein 14%
goes with bananas, berries, cheese, chillies, chocolate, coconut, corn, cream
uses biscuits, bread, brownies, cakes, coating for fried foods, crackers, desserts, pancakes

Amaranth is what I call a difficult flour. Though it has all the necessary credentials – nutritional powerhouse, gluten-free, 'super-grain', and so on – it hasn't quite managed to take centre stage, unlike its cousin quinoa (see page 158). Frankly, amaranth flour doesn't taste that great, It's also rather dense and gummy when used alone in baking. Putting aside these culinary inconveniences, it makes superb, highly nutritious cakes, breads and desserts that will appeal to wheat-eaters and gluten-avoiders alike.

Botanically, amaranth is a member of the goosefoot family, which includes beetroot and spinach. Since it's a seed rather than a cereal, it's more correctly called a pseudo-grain. Dozens of varieties exist but only a few are grown for edible seed. The plant is striking, with towering stalks and colossal flower heads in vibrant shades of red, purple, orange and gold. Weighing in at an impressive 1kg (2.2lb), each head contains around half a million microscopic seeds, and it's from these that the flour is ground.

Fine and free-flowing, amaranth flour is creamy white with a full-on earthy, grassy aroma and a faint hint of pea. Unusually for a plant food, amaranth contains a complete set of essential amino acids that make up protein (see page 59), putting it on a par with foods from animal sources. It also contains a significant amount of calcium, magnesium, iron and B-vitamins – all needed for good health. With such an impressive nutritional line-up, the flour is certainly a worthwhile option for gluten-eaters as well as those who need or choose to avoid it.

As far as the cook is concerned, it's best to combine amaranth with other flours and assertive ingredients to mask its challenging flavour. I successfully partnered it with chillies, cheese, plain flour and purple cornmeal in a tasty loaf (see page 19); replace the plain flour with a gluten-free one if you need to. A useful rule of thumb is to substitute about a quarter of the main flour with amaranth flour. You'll also need a raising agent if you're making bread.

flour

cheese and chilli purple cornbread

fleshy red or green chillies 2–3
amaranth flour 100g (3½oz)
plain flour 100g (3½oz)
purple or yellow cornmeal
    100g (3½oz)
baking powder 1 tablespoon
bicarbonate of soda
    1 teaspoon
sea salt 1 teaspoon
granulated sugar 50g (1¾oz)
mature Cheddar cheese 100g
    (3½oz), grated
buttermilk 250ml (9fl oz)
eggs 3, organic or free-range
unsalted butter 70g (2½oz),
    melted and cooled slightly

**makes one 23x10cm
    (9x4in) loaf**

Amaranth flour certainly ramps up the nutrients. It's strongly flavoured, however, and can be dense and sticky once cooked. To improve texture and flavour I've partnered it with plain wheat flour and purple cornmeal. Purple cornmeal is striking, but it's fine to use ordinary yellow cornmeal instead. For a truly colourful snack, spread the purple bread thickly with good butter and a topping of scarlet sweet chilli jam.

· · ·

Preheat the grill to very hot.

Put the chillies in a grill pan about 15cm (6in) from the heat source. Grill for about 10 minutes, turning regularly, until blackened and blistered on all sides. Put the chillies on a plate, cover with a clean tea towel and leave to stand for 10 minutes.

Meanwhile, grease and line a 23x10x7cm (9x4x2¾in) loaf tin. Preheat the oven to 200°C/Gas Mark 6.

Remove the skin and seeds from the chillies, then chop the flesh finely.

Put the amaranth flour, plain flour, cornmeal, baking powder, bicarbonate of soda and salt into a sieve set over a bowl. Muddle with your fingers, then shake through the sieve. Sieve once or twice more until well blended. Stir in the sugar and cheese.

Whisk the buttermilk, eggs and melted butter in another bowl, blending well. Make a well in the centre of the flour mixture and pour in all the buttermilk mixture. Combine with a fork, stirring from the centre and gradually drawing in the dry ingredients from around the edge. Once you have a soft dough, stir in the chillies, mixing well.

Spoon the mixture into the prepared loaf tin, pushing it into the corners. Bake for 40–45 minutes, rotating halfway through, until brown on top and a skewer inserted in the centre comes out clean. Remove from the oven on to a rack, then leave to cool in the tin for 10 minutes. Turn the bread out on to the rack and leave to cool completely.

atta *flour*

plant source grain
aka chapati flour
latin name *Triticum aestivum*
protein/gluten 10–14%
goes with anything
uses fried dough balls, Indian breads such as chapati, paratha, roti

Atta is an Indian wholewheat flour, milled from a particular type of hard durum wheat. It's a high-protein, high-gluten flour, which means that the dough made with it will be super-strong and stretchy. It can be rolled very thinly without tearing – perfect for Spiced Potato Puris (see page 22) and other flatbreads.

Atta is reasonably easy to find in the West, but bear in mind that Indian flours are often confusingly labelled according to how they're used, so you'll often find atta flour masquerading as chapati flour.

If you want to try your hand at Indian flatbreads, it's definitely worth using atta rather than regular wholewheat flour. It looks and behaves differently, and the flavour is different too. Atta is mostly stoneground, a process that generates heat, and this, in turn, gives the flour the faintly smoky flavour characteristic of Indian flatbreads. The flour is surprisingly fine with no evidence of husks, thanks to meticulous milling and sifting. It also absorbs more liquid than you might expect (see Cook's note, page 23).

Atta and other Indian flours are easy to buy online (see Sources, page 280), or you can enjoy a culinary adventure and rummage for them in shops that sell Indian groceries.

spiced potato puris

atta (wholewheat flour) 125g
(4½oz)
maida (plain flour) 125g (4½oz)
sea salt ½ teaspoon
bicarbonate of soda
¾ teaspoon
rapeseed oil 3 tablespoons
tepid water 100–150ml
(3½–5fl oz)
vegetable oil for deep-frying
pickles and yogurt to serve

for the potato stuffing
mashed potato 250g (9oz) or
mashed yam (see Yam Flour,
page 274)
cumin seeds 1 tablespoon,
crushed
red chilli 2 tablespoons,
finely chopped
green spring onion stalks or
garlic chives 2 tablespoons,
finely chopped
lime juice 1 tablespoon, or
to taste
sea salt ½ teaspoon

makes 16

There is a seemingly endless and fascinating menu of Indian breads. Some are puffy, some are flat. They can be grilled, deep-fried, stuffed or plain. These breads are unique and quite unlike Western breads, thanks to the flour (see Atta Flour, page 20 and Maida Flour, page 122) and expert kneading by Indian cooks. Here, I've made puris: deep-fried wholemeal flat breads that can be stuffed with spicy lentils, potato or other vegetables. I was taught to make them by the patient Mrs Moosa at her cookery school in Kerala, southwest India.

• • •

To make the dough, put the flours, salt and bicarbonate of soda into a sieve set over a bowl. Muddle with your fingers, then push through the sieve. Sieve once or twice more until well blended. Tip any bran remaining in the sieve back into the bowl.

Make a well in the middle of the dry ingredients, then pour in the rapeseed oil and most of the water (see Cook's note). Stir with a fork, drawing in the dry ingredients from around the edge. Once the dough starts to come together, tip on to a floured work surface and knead for 3–4 minutes until smooth and pliable. Cover with a clean damp tea towel and leave for 20 minutes.

While the dough is relaxing, put all the stuffing ingredients into a bowl and mix well. Check the seasoning and add more of anything as necessary. Divide the dough into 16 chunks weighing about 25g (1oz) each. Roll into smooth balls, then shape into 11–12cm (4¼–4½in) circles.

Put about 1 heaped tablespoon of stuffing into the centre of a circle, spreading it almost to the edge, leaving a 1cm (½in) margin all round. Dab the margin with water. Lightly gather up the edges and pinch together to enclose the stuffing (try not to create a thick wodge of dough). Turn over so the sealed side is underneath and gently roll into a 10cm (4in) circle. Repeat with the rest of the dough.

Pour the oil into a non-stick frying pan to a depth of 4cm (1½in). Heat over a medium-high heat until very hot, but not smoking – 180°C (350°F) on a thermometer, or until a cube of bread browns in 1 minute. Drop in three or four puris and fry for about 30 seconds, or until they float to the top. Turn them over, using tongs, and fry for another 30–60 seconds until deep golden and puffed up. Drain on paper towels and keep warm while you fry the rest. Serve immediately with your favourite pickles and some tangy yogurt.

flour

- To make puris without the stuffing, use 15g (½oz) of dough per ball. Roll out to 10cm (4in) circles and fry in hot oil as above.

cook's note
- The amount of water needed may vary, depending on humidity, room temperature or age of the flour, for example. Start with 100ml (3½fl oz), then gradually add more if the dough seems too dry. If it's too sticky after kneading, add a little more flour.

atta *flour*

banana *flour* (green)

plant source fruit
aka plantain flour
latin name *Musa acuminata*
gluten none
protein 3%
goes with allspice, cardamom, chocolate, cinnamon, citrus fruits, coconut, coffee, cream, ginger, honey, milk, orange-flavoured liqueur, vanilla
uses biscuits, bread, cakes, coating for fried foods, pancakes, smoothies, thickener for sauces and soups

At around twenty times the price of ordinary wheat flour, green banana flour isn't one you would use indiscriminately – for flouring the work surface, say. On the other hand, it's a nutritionally important flour, and especially worth considering if you're a coeliac or following a gluten-free diet. The flour has earned its stripes as a major source of 'resistant starch' (see page 205), which improves gut health.

Produced in the tropics, the flour is made by grinding the dried flesh of peeled green (unripe) bananas. It has the colour and texture of very fine sand, with a mild, neither sweet nor savoury banana flavour. Since it is mild, it goes well with most other ingredients. I like it with flavours that reflect its tropical origins such as allspice, aka Jamaica pepper, as in the pancake recipe (see page 27).

Though banana flour is expensive, a little goes a long way. Eke it out by sprinkling over breakfast cereal, or stirring a spoonful into a smoothie. It's also good for thickening a soup or sauce. You'll find batters made with it are thicker than usual, so you'll need less flour and more liquid. In baking, replacing just a quarter of the main flour with green banana flour will provide a significant nutritional boost.

When buying banana flour, check the wording on the packet and make sure you've got the green type. Don't confuse it with banana 'powder', which is typically made with ripe bananas rather than green, and doesn't contain the all-important resistant starch.

It's worth treating such a valuable flour with care. Keep it fresh by resealing the packet once opened, and storing it in the fridge or a cool, dry place.

You can buy green banana flour online (see Sources, page 280) or in good health food shops.

flour

banana flour pancakes with allspice and tangerine cream

green banana flour 150g (5½oz)
baking powder 1 teaspoon
sea salt ¼ teaspoon
coconut sugar or muscovado
    sugar 2½ teaspoons
allspice berries ½ teaspoon,
    crushed
eggs 2, organic or free-range,
    lightly beaten
milk 250ml (9fl oz), preferably
    organic
coconut oil or vegetable oil
    for frying
tangerine segments to
    decorate
clear honey for drizzling

*for the allspice and
tangerine cream*
whipping cream 150ml (5fl oz)
tangerine juice 4 tablespoons
    freshly squeezed (from about
    2 tangerines)
icing sugar 1 tablespoon
allspice berries ½ teaspoon,
    crushed

makes 6–8

Ground from dried green/unripe bananas, this flour has a mild banana flavour and makes delicious gluten-free pancakes. Here I've topped them with a cream flavoured with tangerine juice and allspice – a spice widely used in the Caribbean.

• • •

Put the flour, baking powder and sea salt into a sieve set over a bowl. Muddle with your fingers, then push through the sieve. Add the sugar and crushed allspice berries and stir to combine.

In a jug, whisk the eggs with the milk. Gradually pour this into the flour mixture, stirring until smooth. Set aside while you make the cream.

Using an electric whisk, whip the cream for 3–4 minutes until the beaters leave a distinct trail that doesn't disappear when you lift them from the bowl. Stir in the tangerine juice, icing sugar and allspice berries and leave in the fridge to chill while you make the pancakes.

Pour a little oil into a non-stick pancake pan and place over a medium heat. Pour in about three-quarters of a ladleful of batter. Tilt the pan and swirl the batter to form a thin circle, about 15cm (6in) in diameter. Cook for 1½–2 minutes, or until bubbles start to form on the surface and you can easily slip a spatula underneath. Flip the pancake over and cook the other side for another minute or so.

Slide the pancake on to a warm plate and cover with baking parchment or paper towel to prevent sticking. Repeat with the rest of the batter, adding more oil as necessary.

Top the pancakes with the cream, tangerine segments and a drizzle of clear honey.

barley *flour*

plant source grain
aka barley meal, bere (Scottish Orkney Islands)
latin name *Hordeum vulgare*
gluten/protein 5–8%
goes with bacon, beer, celery, cheddar cheese, lamb, mushrooms, oranges,
    spicy dishes
uses bannocks, bars, bread, cakes, flatbreads, muffins, pancakes, porridge, scones,
    thickener for sauces, soups and stews

Barley could do with some positive PR. Though it ranks fourth in world grain crops, it's unjustifiably overlooked, even though it's crammed with nutrients and tastes good. Strangely, barley often doesn't get a mention in cookbooks about grains. It once had gravitas, however. Dating back thousands of years, it was one of the first grains to be cultivated. Until the days of the Romans it was an important staple, used for bread, gruels, polenta-like porridge, and beer. Impressively, barley also formed the basis for today's imperial measuring system – Edward II decreed one 'ynce' (inch) to be three barleycorns laid end to end. Eventually, as bread-baking skills and wealth increased, barley was usurped by wheat and relegated to the grain of the poor.

One of the sturdiest of grains, barley tolerates environments as extreme as the Arctic and Africa. It's a staple in the Middle East and Morocco where cooks use it in delicious barley couscous and chewy breads. It's also been grown for centuries in Scotland's remote and chilly Orkney Islands. Here, the local barley is called 'bere' (pronounced 'bare') and is typically made into bannocks, an unleavened scone-like bread cooked on a griddle.

Barley flour is milled from dried grains. There are different types, but the one to go for is whole grain flour, sometimes called barley meal. The nutritious bran and germ are still intact, unlike the finer flour milled from pearl (or pearled) barley. There is also malted barley flour, which gives malt loaf its characteristic rich flavour, and the curiously named 'patent' barley flour, a finely ground product used in commercial baby foods.

Fine and free-flowing, whole grain barley flour is an attractive off-white with minute dark flecks. Dip your nose in the bag and you'll immediately get the delicious aroma of freshly baked bread. The flavour is also pleasant – mild and slightly earthy with an unexpectedly sweet after-taste. It blends well with both sweet and savoury dishes.

Nutrient-wise, barley flour ticks all the boxes. It has one of the highest dietary fibre levels of all grains. Better still, it contains a soluble type of fibre called beta-glucan, known to lower blood cholesterol and reduce the risk of heart disease. It also contains resistant starch (see page 205) which generally improves gut health.

Though barley flour contains gluten (see page 60), there's not enough to give baked items the necessary stretch and structure needed for rising. It's best to combine it with a high-gluten wheat flour – Canadian very strong wheat flour (see page 265), for example – or use ordinary wheat flour plus a raising agent such as baking powder or bicarbonate of soda. A useful rule of thumb is to replace a quarter of the regular wheat flour with barley flour, or up to half for biscuits and bread with a denser texture. If you get hooked on the flour, push the boat out and use 100 per cent. It should be fine for pancakes and quick breads.

barley and almond cake with cream cheese and orange frosting

unsalted butter 125g (4½oz),
plus extra for greasing
caster sugar 125g (4½oz)
eggs 3 large, yolks and whites
separated
barley flour 150g (5½oz)
baking powder 2 teaspoons
ground almonds 125g (4½oz)
orange 1 teaspoon finely
grated zest
ground cinnamon
⅛ teaspoon, plus extra
for dusting
orange thin strips of zest from
1, to decorate

*for the cream cheese and
orange frosting*
cream cheese 60g (2¼oz)
unsalted butter 2 tablespoons
vanilla extract 1 teaspoon
orange strained juice of ½
icing sugar 200g (7oz), sifted

serves 8–10

The combination of barley flour and ground almonds is a good one –
it gives the cake a mildly nutty flavour and keeps it moist. Egg whites
and baking powder are also important for keeping the mixture light.
This is a wheat-free cake, but it does contain a small amount of gluten
from the barley flour. The recipe was kindly given to me by my food
writer colleague Jenni Muir, author of my much-thumbed copy of
A Cook's Guide to Grains.

• • •

Grease a 22–23cm (8½–9in) springform cake tin with butter.
Line the base and sides of the tin with baking parchment,
then grease the paper too. Preheat the oven to 180°C/Gas
Mark 4.

Measure out the sugar and set aside 5 tablespoons to use in
the meringue. Tip the rest into a large mixing bowl with the
butter. Beat for a few minutes until the mixture is pale and
creamy. Beat in the egg yolks, then stir in the barley flour,
baking powder, ground almonds, grated zest and cinnamon
until well combined – the mixture will be quite stiff.

In a separate large bowl, whisk the egg whites until
soft peaks form when the whisk is lifted from the foam.
Gradually whisk in the reserved 5 tablespoons of sugar to
give a stiff meringue. Using a large metal spoon, fold in
about one-third of the meringue to slacken the dough, then
gradually fold in the rest. Tip into the prepared tin and
smooth the surface.

Bake for 30–40 minutes, or until a skewer inserted in the
centre of the cake comes out clean. Remove the cake from the
oven and leave to cool in the tin for 10 minutes. Remove from
the tin and place on a wire rack to cool completely.

To make the frosting, beat together the cream cheese,
butter, vanilla extract and orange juice until smooth and
fluffy. Gradually beat in the sifted icing sugar until the
frosting is well combined, creamy and light. Using a palette
knife, spread the frosting over the top and sides of the cake.
Decorate with the strips of orange zest and a dusting of
cinnamon powder.

black bean *flour*

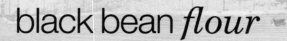

plant source pulse
aka n/a
latin name *Phaseolus vulgaris*
gluten none
protein 22%
goes with avocados, bananas, chillies, chocolate, cumin, sweetcorn, tomatoes
uses binding for burgers and meatballs, bread, brownies, dips, dumplings, filling
for tortillas, pancakes, sauces, thickener for soups and stews

Initially I had doubts about black bean flour. Most of the online recipes were for dips and soups, which seemed to limit its usefulness. I also questioned the benefits of using flour instead of the beans themselves. After all, once cooked the beans are easily mashed into a purée that can be used as a thickener in the same way as the flour.

Since then, and after several experiments, I've come around to it in a big way. I love the way a cement-coloured flour becomes an eye-catching aubergine purple as you stir it into hot liquid. I love its feisty flavour, its earthiness, and the fact that it doesn't have a bitter aftertaste – unlike some bean flours. And I now realize it's a really convenient way of incorporating beans into certain dishes – soups, stews and dumplings, for example. It takes the faff out of soaking and cooking dried beans, or even opening and draining a can of them.

The flour is ground from dried black beans, aka turtle beans, one of the main pulse crops in Central and South America. As such, it's perfect for Mexican-style dishes such as tamales (dumplings steamed in corn husks) or as a filling for enchiladas and burritos. Or try it in a robust soup (see page 34) topped with avocado, chilli and lime.

When combining it with other flours, a useful rule of thumb is to substitute about a quarter of the main flour with black bean flour. Bear in mind that it will darken the colour of whatever you're making, so it's best in biscuits and brownies where paleness isn't an issue, or combine it with chocolate or cocoa. Try adding a couple of spoonfuls to bread dough if you're after a dark and interesting look.

Health-wise, black bean flour packs a nutritional punch. It's also gluten-free, and as such offers interesting opportunities to the baker.

You probably won't find black bean flour in your local supermarket, but it's easy to buy online (see Sources, page 280) and in good health food shops. You might also find it in shops selling Asian groceries – look for black bean 'powder'.

Better still, if you have dried black beans in your store cupboard, and a milling attachment for a standing mixer, have a go at grinding the flour yourself. Grind in small batches so as not to overwork your mill. A NutriBullet is another option, but it produces a coarser flour that needs sieving to get rid of unwelcome bits and pieces.

flour

black bean and roasted tomato, garlic and onion soup

fleshy plum tomatoes 6
red onions 2, peeled and sliced
    into thick rings
garlic cloves 4 large, unpeeled
olive oil 1 tablespoon
coriander seeds 1 teaspoon,
    crushed
dried oregano 1 teaspoon,
    preferably Mexican or Turkish
cumin seeds ½ teaspoon,
    crushed
black peppercorns
    ½ teaspoon, crushed
good-quality chicken or
    vegetable stock 850ml
    (1½ pints), heated
black bean flour 6 tablespoons
lime juice 1 tablespoon
sea salt ½ teaspoon
soured cream to serve

to garnish
fresh coriander chopped
avocado ½, diced and tossed
    in lime juice
fresh red chilli slivers
lime segments

serves 6

This robust, spicy soup is a meal in itself, packed with feisty flavours and valuable nutrients. The vegetables are roasted rather than fried, which means the flavour is intensified and you'll need very little oil. Black bean flour is used to thicken the soup, which in some ways is easier than the usual method of cooking black beans and mashing them to a purée. The flour is easy to buy online (see Sources, page 280), or if you have a flour grinder you can grind the dried beans yourself.

• • •

Preheat the grill to hot. Arrange the tomatoes, onion rings and garlic in a single layer on a baking sheet. Grill for 12–15 minutes, turning occasionally, until charred. Slice the tomatoes in half, leaving on the charred skin. Slice the onion rings into chunks and peel the garlic. Put the vegetables in the bowl of a food processor and pulse briefly to a chunky purée.

Heat the oil in a large saucepan. Add the coriander seeds, oregano, cumin seeds and peppercorns. Fry over a medium heat for 30 seconds to flavour the oil. Add the vegetable purée and sizzle briefly to heat through.

Pour in the hot stock, then whisk in the black bean flour. Simmer for 5 minutes over a medium heat, stirring all the time. Stir through the lime juice and sea salt, then ladle into soup bowls, sprinkle over the garnishes and serve with soured cream.

buckwheat *flour*

plant source fruit seed
aka wheat, blé noir (French), Saracen wheat
latin name *Fagopyrum esculentum*
gluten none
protein 8–9%
goes with bay leaves, cheese, chocolate, coffee, ginger, hazelnuts, mushrooms, onions, walnuts
uses bread, brownies, cakes, coating for fried foods, dumplings, fritters, muffins, noodles, pancakes, pasta, pastry

The buckwheat chapter of *Vegetable Substances Used for the Food of Man*, published in 1832, tells us that when pigs are first fed buckwheat they 'exhibit symptoms of intoxication, so that they run squeaking and tumbling about in a grotesque manner'. I know how they feel. When I used buckwheat flour for the first time, I confess to excitedly clapping my hands and jumping up and down – it makes such a beautiful batter and dough. Admittedly, the robust flavour is an acquired taste, but this can be easily tamed with other ingredients.

Despite the name, buckwheat has nothing to do with wheat; it's related botanically to rhubarb and sorrel. The seeds, technically fruit, from which the flour is ground are triangular and look like mini-beechnuts – hence the old name 'beech flour'. The flour looks homely rather than exotic. The colour ranges from mousy beige to cement-grey flecked with microscopic fragments of husk. Despite the unpromising appearance, the flour is incredibly versatile and works well in both sweet and savoury dishes.

Buckwheat isn't fussy about where it grows. It thrives in cold climates and poor soils, so you'll come across it in parts of the world where wheat doesn't do well. Buckwheat noodles, or soba noodles, were a key food in the mountainous regions of Japan, for example, though nowadays they're enjoyed throughout the country. In Russia and Eastern Europe, plump buckwheat dumplings show up on restaurant menus everywhere. As light as a feather or hefty enough to sink a battleship, they perk up a soup or stew and make a meal go further. Try them in Hungarian Goose Soup (see page 38). There is also gorgeous buckwheat bread to be savoured. Food writer Lesley Chamberlain in *The Food and Cooking of Eastern Europe* aptly describes the dough as 'lustrous and silky like fine skin to touch, soothing as a mud pack and speckled like

a bird's egg'. In Italy's alpine Valtellina region you'll come across *pizzoccheri* – sturdy flat noodles topped with sage butter, garlic and grated local cheese, traditionally served with potatoes and cabbage – fortifying fodder for a cold climate. Another speciality is Sciatt (see page 40), meaning 'toad' – irresistible, crunchy cheese-filled fritters that do indeed resemble toads, albeit those you won't mind eating.

Buckwheat flour is probably best known for its use in pancakes, and most cuisines have their special version. There are Russia's fluffy little blinis – a tailor-made vehicle for caviar, smoked salmon and soured cream. Brittany, in northern France, boasts enormous savoury 'galettes' stuffed with melted cheese, ham, mushrooms or other titbits. The Belgians have their *boukètes* cooked with sliced apple and rum-soaked raisins. Canadians and the people of Maine, USA, pride themselves on 'ployes', a yeasted crêpe-style pancake either served with a special chicken stew, or drenched in maple syrup, molasses or brown sugar.

Buckwheat flour is gluten-free, so if you're using it for bread and cakes you'll need to combine it with wheat flour to give the dough structure. Use about two-thirds wheat flour to one-third buckwheat flour. If gluten is off-limits, combine it with other gluten-free flours plus xanthan gum or guar gum to help bind the dough. Be aware that buckwheat flour can make pastry slightly grey, but you can successfully mask this with cocoa powder, as in the Buttermilk and Bay Leaf Tart with Chocolate Pastry (see page 41).

Nutrient-wise, buckwheat flour is especially useful if you're vegetarian or following a gluten-free diet. It contains all the essential amino acids (see Protein, page 59), putting it on a par with foods from animal sources. Though gluten-free, the flour isn't always grown or milled in a gluten-free environment. If this is an issue, always check the label to make sure.

goose soup with buckwheat and bacon dumplings

good-quality goose, chicken or game stock 1.4 litres (2½ pints) (see Cook's notes)
carrot 1 small, quartered lengthways and diced
celery stalk 1 tender, destringed and diced
baby leek 1, quartered lengthways and diced
goose meat 250g (9oz), cut into bite-sized pieces (see Cook's notes)
sea salt to taste
flat-leaf parsley leaves to garnish

for the dumplings
buckwheat flour 110g (4oz)
plain flour 60g (2¼oz)
baking powder 2½ teaspoons
sea salt ½ teaspoon
freshly ground black pepper ¼ teaspoon
egg 1
milk 85ml (2¾fl oz)
pancetta 40g (1½oz), finely diced
flat-leaf parsley 3 tablespoons chopped

serves 4–6

I've wanted to recreate this soup ever since I ate it in Budapest a few years ago. It was so unusual to see a gooseneck submerged in an immaculate soup, a buckwheat dumpling bobbing on the surface and a slender goose leg elegantly placed on the rim of the bowl. In my part of the world we don't have excess goose pieces, so unless you have some left over from Michaelmas or Christmas, you can make this with canned goose confit or duck confit, or even a meaty chicken or duck carcass. It's essential to use good stock, either homemade (see Cook's notes) or from a pouch. Don't even think about stock cubes.

• • •

First make the dumplings. Put the buckwheat flour, plain flour, baking powder, sea salt and pepper into a sieve set over a bowl. Muddle with your fingers, then shake through the sieve. Sieve once or twice more until well blended.

Lightly beat the egg in a jug or bowl and add the milk. Stir this into the flour mixture, along with the pancetta and parsley. Knead lightly, then rest the dough for 30 minutes before dividing into six golf-ball-sized balls.

To make the soup, bring the stock to the boil in a large saucepan, then add the vegetables, goose meat, dumplings and salt to taste. Simmer briskly with the lid askew for about 15 minutes or until the dumplings are floating on top and are cooked through.

Ladle into soup plates or bowls, making sure everyone has some goose meat. Garnish with flat-leaf parsley leaves and serve immediately.

cook's notes
• To make goose or other poultry stock use a decent-sized carcass with a reasonable amount of meat for picking. Remove any chunks of meat and set aside for later. Put the bones in a large saucepan along with 2 quartered onions, 2 halved carrots, 2 celery sticks, 1 leek split lengthways, a small bunch of parsley and a few peppercorns. Pour in enough water to cover by about 6cm (2½in). Slowly bring to the boil, remove any scum, then gently simmer for 2 hours. Strain through a fine sieve and decant into lidded containers. Leave to cool, then chill or freeze.
• If using canned goose for the soup meat, drain the fat, remove the bones, then cut the meat into bite-sized chunks.

flour

buckwheat cheese fritters
(sciatt)

buckwheat flour 150g (5½oz)
plain flour 75g (2¾oz)
bicarbonate of soda
  ¼ teaspoon
sea salt ¼ teaspoon, plus extra
  flakes for sprinkling
freshly ground black pepper
beer 325ml (11fl oz), preferably
  Italian lager such as Moretti or
  Peroni Red
semi-soft cheese 100g (3½oz)
  such as Taleggio, or a cheese
  that melts easily
grappa, eau de vie or vodka
  1 teaspoon
groundnut oil for deep-frying
lemon wedges to garnish

to serve
bitter salad leaves such as
  Belgian chicory, radicchio or
  frisée
extra-virgin olive oil
white wine vinegar

**serves 4–6 as a light meal
  or starter**

A friend visiting Valtellina in northern Italy alerted me to these irresistible, crunchy, cheese-filled fritters, known locally as *sciatt*, meaning toad. Not the most inviting of names perhaps, but it undoubtedly refers to the haphazard shape of the batter as it hits the sizzling fat.

. . .

Put the flours, bicarbonate of soda, sea salt and a couple of grindings of black pepper into a sieve set over a bowl. Muddle with your fingers, then shake through the sieve. Sieve once or twice more until well blended.

Make a well in the centre of the flour mixture and gradually pour in the beer. Mix with a fork, stirring from the centre and gradually drawing in the dry ingredients from around the edge. Push the mixture through a sieve to get rid of any lumps. Cover and leave to rest for 1–2 hours, or overnight.

When you're ready to cook, cut the cheese into 2cm (¾in) cubes and drizzle with the grappa.

Pour enough oil into a deep pan (see Cook's note) to a depth of about 5cm (2in). Heat over a medium-high heat until very hot but not smoking – 180°C (350°F) on a thermometer, or until a cube of bread browns in 1 minute.

Dunk a few cheese cubes into the batter, turning them so they are completely coated. Using a large spoon, fish out a cube and a generous amount of batter. Tip the cheese and some of the batter into the hot oil, using a second spoon to help slide the cheese cube into the pan. Pour the batter remaining in the spoon over the cube so that it is covered in batter. Fry for about 1 minute each side until golden and crisp. Use tongs to lift your 'toad' on to a paper-towel-lined tray. Keep warm while you fry the rest.

Serve hot on a bed of chicory, radicchio or other bitter leaf salad, lightly dressed with extra-virgin olive oil and a splash of wine vinegar. Sprinkle the toads with a few sea salt flakes and garnish with a lemon wedge.

cook's note
· Once submerged in hot oil, the batter for each 'toad' spreads quickly and you will need to add more to cover the cheese. It's easiest to fry just two or three at a time. I use a small deep pan (20x8cm/8x3¼in) that doesn't need vast quantities of oil for deep-frying.

flour

buttermilk and bay leaf tart with chocolate pastry

buckwheat flour 200g (7oz)
unsweetened cocoa powder
    1½ tablespoons
caster sugar 25g (1oz)
sea salt ¼ teaspoon
unsalted butter 90g (3¼oz)
    chilled, diced
egg 1, lightly beaten
iced water 1–2 tablespoons

for the filling
buttermilk 280ml (9¾fl oz)
double cream 75ml (2½fl oz)
bay leaves 5 fresh tender
small orange small strips of
    zest from ½
eggs 3, organic or free-range
caster sugar 75g (2¾oz)
unsalted butter 25g (1oz),
    melted and cooled slightly
cornflour 1½ tablespoons

serves 6–8

Buckwheat flour has a rather worthy image, but here I have made it a bit edgier with chocolate pastry and a fragrant filling that reflects its Eastern European connections. The tart is best served at room temperature, so allow plenty of time for resting and cooling.

• • •

To make the pastry, put the buckwheat flour, cocoa powder, sugar and salt into a sieve set over a bowl. Muddle with your fingers, then shake through the sieve. Sieve once or twice more until well blended.

Tip the diced butter into the flour mixture. Rub the butter into the flour between the tips of your fingers and thumbs using a flicking movement – imagine you are playing castanets. Hold your hands well above the bowl so that the flour drifts down, incorporating air as it does so, and you can see any fragments of butter that still need rubbing in.

Using a fork, stir in the beaten egg. Sprinkle 1 tablespoon of iced water over the surface and stir until the mixture begins to clump. Sprinkle with a little more water if it seems dry. Gather the dough together and lightly knead for a few seconds, then form it into a thick disc, about 12cm (4½in) in diameter, ready to roll out. Wrap in greaseproof paper and chill for 30 minutes.

To make the filling, pour the buttermilk and cream into a saucepan and add the bay leaves and orange zest. Bring to a simmer over a medium-low heat (don't let it boil), then continue to simmer, stirring all the time with a wooden spatula and scraping the base of the pan, for about 5 minutes until slightly thickened. Remove from the heat, pour into a shallow dish and leave to cool for about 10 minutes (you can remove the zest and bay leaves at this point, but I prefer to leave them in: see Cook's note).

Meanwhile, grease a 24.5x2.5cm (9¾x1in) fluted metal tart tin, making sure the sides are well lubricated. Line the base with a circle of baking parchment and grease the paper too. Preheat the oven to 200°C/Gas Mark 6 and put a baking sheet in to heat.

Once the dough is chilled, remove from the fridge and allow it to return to room temperature before rolling out. Dust your work surface and rolling pin with flour. Roll out the pastry thinly to a 30cm (12in) circle and carefully lift it into the tin. Press the side of your index finger into the edge to even out

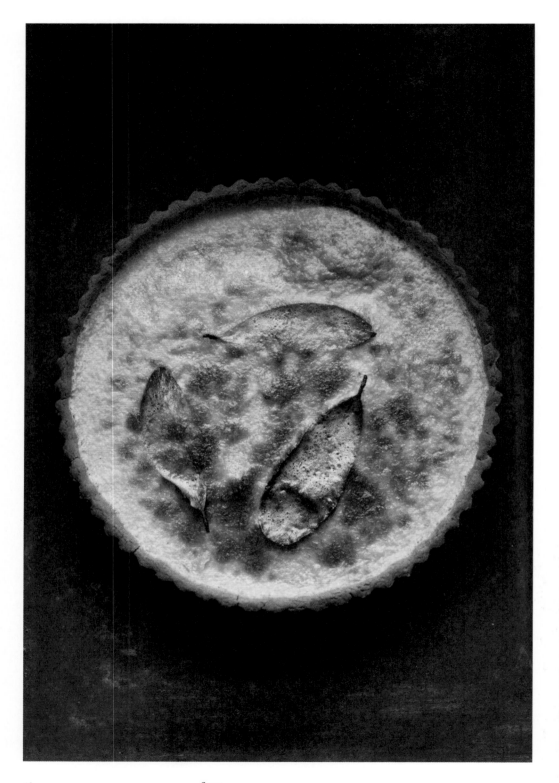

flour

the thick corners. Trim the top with a small sharp knife and use the offcuts to reinforce any weak areas.

Using an electric whisk, beat the eggs and sugar for the filling in a bowl for 4–5 minutes until pale and thick. Use a wire whisk to incorporate the cooled buttermilk mixture, the melted butter and the cornflour. Pour the mixture into the pastry-lined tin.

Place on the heated baking sheet and bake for 25–30 minutes, rotating halfway through, until the filling is golden in patches and a skewer inserted in the centre comes out clean. Transfer to a wire rack and leave for 15 minutes to settle. Carefully remove from the tin on to the rack and leave for an hour or so to cool and firm up. Serve at room temperature.

cook's note
· I have left the bay leaves and orange strips in the custard. They look attractive on top of the cooked filling and also give an indication of flavour, but it's fine to strain them out if you prefer.

cassava *flour*

plant source tuber
aka cassava meal, farinha de mandioca (Brazil, Portugal), gari (West Africa),
   manioc flour, povilho (Brazil, Portugal), tapioca flour, tapioca starch, yucca flour
latin name *Manihot esculenta*
gluten none
protein 0.0–0.3%
goes with beans, cheese, chillies, citrus fruits, coconut, fish, leafy greens, meat, nuts,
   poultry, tropical fruit
uses batters, biscuits, bread, brownies, cake, coating for fried food, crêpes, desserts,
   fritters, porridge, table condiment, thickener for pie fillings, sauces, soups
   and stews

My fascination with cassava began several years ago while researching a book on tropical roots and tubers. I mooched around some of London's food markets where African and Latin American foods were the norm, finding stall after stall piled high with this unprepossessing tuber, alongside yams, eddoes and other brown exotics. It's about the size of a very large parsnip with a bark-like brown skin. It doesn't travel well so it's usually protected with a wax coating.

Native to Central and South America, cassava has been used as food for thousands of years. There's evidence that it originated in the wild near the Amazon in Central Brazil, and was one of the first crops to be domesticated. In the sixteenth century Portuguese traders transported it from Brazil to parts of Africa, and from there it spread to the Philippines and Southeast Asia. It's reported to be one of the fastest expanding food crops, the fifth largest staple worldwide, ranking just two places behind wheat. In 2014 the largest cassava producer was Nigeria, followed by Thailand, Indonesia and Brazil.

So far so good, but when I search cookbooks and websites for information on cassava flour, I'm surprised at how it's excluded. At best it gets a line or two, while tapioca – though not quite the same product – gets more in-depth mentions. The reason for the lack of attention may be because cassava is looked on as a tropical crop, not especially relevant to the rest of the world. Brazilians, however, are proud of their cassava, or manioc as it's also known, so much so that the Ministry of Culture commissioned sociologist Maria Dina Nogueira to document every type of cassava flour produced in Brazil. It took her five years, during which she catalogued more than 4,300 varieties – a spectacular number for such an unacknowledged flour.

Though the number of producers is gradually dwindling, cassava remains a vital crop. It's easy to plant and harvest, it holds its own in poor soil and erratic weather, and it's apparently resistant to locusts. It can be left in the ground unharvested for long periods, making it an invaluable reserve crop during food shortages. It's also unique in being one of the very few plant foods from which an exceptional variety of different flours and by-products are made.

There are two main types of cassava tuber: bitter and sweet. Once it's peeled and washed, sweet cassava can be cooked and eaten like any other starchy vegetable. It has a soft texture and neutral flavour, similar to buttery mashed potatoes. Bitter cassava contains toxins that are removed by meticulous processing, which involves peeling, grating, pressing, toasting, sieving and drying, before it can be made into flour.

Nutrient-wise, the flour is worth considering if you're a coeliac or gluten-sensitive. Though it contains neither protein nor fat, it's particularly high in carbohydrate; in some parts of the world it provides up to 30 per cent of total daily calorie requirement. It also contains small amounts of calcium and vitamin C, and is a good source of resistant starch (see page 205), which generally improves gut health.

Cassava flour has many incarnations. You'll find it variously labelled as farinha de mandioca, manioc flour, yucca flour, tapioca flour, tapioca starch, povilho – the list goes on. The important thing to take on board is the difference between the coarse flour or meal, the fine flour and the starch. Bear in mind, too, that companies give the same product different names – tapioca, for example. Some market it as flour when in fact it's a starch. Here's what you need to know.

Cassava flour As far as the cassava novice is concerned, there are two main types of flour: the slightly crunchy meal labelled 'farinha de mandioca', and the regular fine-textured flour simply labelled 'cassava flour'.

Widely used in Brazil, farinha de mandioca is available raw (*cruda*) or toasted (*tostada*). Raw flour is a finely flecked creamy beige with a neutral flavour, while the toasted flour is slightly pinker and more savoury. The toasted flour tends to be used in dishes such as croquettes or stews, rather than baking, although it's basically up to the cook and the diners which type is used.

Farinha de mandioca is the key ingredient in Farofa (see page 51), a crunchy condiment that you'll find on most tables in Brazil, along with the pepper and salt. It's sprinkled over grilled meats, stews, fish and bean dishes to provide colour and crunch. I had my first taste when Brazilian friends served it with a wonderfully unctuous Oxtail and Black Bean Stew (see page 50). The texture and bright yellow colour of the farofa contrasted well with the tender dark meat, and it was perfect for sopping up meaty juices. Since then, I've kept a jar of it on the table ready for sprinkling.

As well as *farinha de mandioca*, there is an all-purpose cassava flour that looks and feels much the same as ordinary wheat flour. Bear in mind It's ground from the whole peeled tuber, so it's not the same as tapioca flour, which is a starch (see below). My brand of choice is Tiana (see Sources, page 280). There's also an identical product labelled 'wholemeal cassava flour', which again simply means it has been ground from the whole peeled tuber. It's white rather than the usual wholemeal brown.

All-purpose cassava flour is a popular gluten-free alternative to wheat flour and can be used in much the same way, in batters and dough, and for thickening sauces and stews. I used it in a spiced flour mix to thicken the Oxtail and Black Bean Stew (see page 50). If you're using it for baking it's best to combine it with another gluten-free flour, such as rice or sorghum flour, plus a raising agent if you're after a rise.

Sour starch (*povilho azedo*) This is fermented starch made from the liquid drained from mashed cassava pulp. The starchy slurry is left to ferment for several weeks before being spread out to dry in the sun. Unusually for starch, it has a slightly gummy texture when mixed with water. Rather like gluten, it produces an elastic

dough strong enough to hold its shape and rise, trapping gas bubbles in the process – miraculously without the help of yeast or a raising agent. Together with sweet starch (*povilho doce*), it's essential for Brazilian Cheese Puffs (see page 48), crisp and golden cheese puffs with a uniquely gooey centre.

Sweet starch (*povilho doce*) Marketed in the UK and the US as tapioca starch or flour, sweet starch is extracted from the liquid drained from mashed cassava pulp. Unlike sour starch (*povilho azedo*), the liquid is not left to ferment and the resulting starch is therefore flavourless. This makes it a popular thickener for sweet pie and tart fillings. It thickens at a lower temperature, and therefore more quickly, than cornflour, and it's transparent and glossy once cool – a more attractive option when you want to show off the colour of the fruit in your tart.

In gluten-free baking, it's best used in combination with other flours – it's a bit too gummy on its own. A mix of one part tapioca starch and three parts rice, sorghum or buckwheat flour works for yeasted breads and cakes, and non-yeasted items such as flatbreads and biscuits. A good mix for a crisp pastry is one part tapioca starch, two parts almond flour and a few spoonfuls of coconut flour. The only minor drawback is that it's so light it coats everything in sight, so be careful when opening the packet.

Tapioca pearls/granules These are made by extruding moist starch under pressure through a sieve. When heated and stirred in liquid, the starch cells in the pearls burst and soften, thickening the liquid. They are probably best known for old-fashioned tapioca pudding; try my tropical version with lime and mango (see page 47). They are also used in Southeast Asian desserts, and sweet drinks such as bubble tea.

To track down this cornucopia of cassava products, you'll need to look online (see Sources, page 280) or investigate health food shops and large supermarkets. Shops selling African, Portuguese or Braziliian ingredients are good hunting grounds for farinha de mandioca: Yoki is a well-known brand that's widely available.

tropical tapioca pudding with mango and lime

small tapioca pearls 60g
 (2¼oz)
cold water 175ml (6fl oz)
organic coconut milk 400g
 (14oz) can, stirred well
whole milk 150ml (5fl oz)
caster sugar 100g (3½oz),
 or to taste
mango 1 (weighing about
 650g/1lb 7oz), peeled
 and chopped
lime juice of 1

for decorating
lime very thin shreds of zest
coconut ribbons toasted

serves 6

You will need small tapioca pearls rather than flour to make this heavenly dessert. It's a combination of creamy tapioca, juicy mango, tangy lime and crunchy coconut flakes. You can make it ahead of time and chill until ready to serve.

. . .

Soak the tapioca pearls in the cold water for 30 minutes to soften, using the saucepan in which you will eventually cook the tapioca.

Add the coconut milk, whole milk and 2 tablespoons of sugar. Stir over a medium heat until gloopy bubbles start to plop on the surface. Reduce the heat to very low, then simmer, uncovered, for 6–7 minutes, stirring often, until the pearls are soft and the liquid has thickened enough to coat a wooden spoon. Tip into a bowl and leave to cool.

Meanwhile, whizz the chopped mango, lime juice and the remaining 75g (2¾oz) of sugar to a smooth purée. Sieve if necessary to get rid of any fibres. Tip into a bowl, cover and chill for an hour or two.

Divide the tapioca between serving bowls (glass bowls work well so you can see the layers) and top with the mango purée.

If serving right away, decorate with lime zest shreds and coconut ribbons. Otherwise, chill without the decorations and add these just before serving.

brazilian cheese puffs
(pão de queijo)

Parmesan cheese 150g (5½oz),
  freshly grated finely
eggs 2 large, organic or free-
  range
egg yolks 2 large, organic
  or free-range
cassava starch (*povilho azedo*)
  175g (6oz)
**tapioca starch/sweet cassava
  starch** (*povilho doce*) 100g
  (3½oz)
sea salt 2 teaspoons
whole milk 125ml (4fl oz)
water 125ml (4fl oz)
olive oil 100ml (3½fl oz)
freshly ground black pepper
  ¼–½ teaspoon
unsalted butter to serve
  (optional)

makes 20–25

Irresistible straight from the oven, these crisp and pleasantly chewy cheese-flavoured puffs are Brazil's favourite savoury snack. They're ideal for a drinks party or a pre-dinner snack. Although *pão* means bread, there is no yeast or wheat in the dough. The leavening comes from the mixture of naturally fermented sour cassava starch (*povilho azedo*), tapioca starch/sweet cassava starch (*povilho doce*) and cheese.

You can buy the starch in shops selling Brazilian groceries, or online (see Sources, page 280). Allow 2–8 hours for chilling the dough.

. . .

Put the Parmesan, eggs and yolks in the bowl of a food processor. Whizz for about 30 seconds or until you have a smooth paste, and set aside.

Carefully measure the starches (they're very fine and blow away easily) into a large bowl, or the bowl of a standing mixer fitted with a dough hook. Add the salt.

Pour the milk, water and oil into a saucepan and bring to the boil. Immediately pour the hot milk mixture into the starches. Whisk for about 2–3 minutes using an electric whisk or the standing mixer at low speed, until the dough is smooth.

Stir in the egg mixture and the pepper. Whisk for about 10–12 minutes until you have a pale yellow, sticky, lump-free paste. Cover with cling film and chill for 2–8 hours.

Preheat the oven to 180°C/Gas Mark 4. Line a couple of baking trays with silicone sheets.

Lightly coat your hands with oil or tapioca starch. Pinch off walnut-sized pieces of dough and roll between your palms. Place the balls on the baking tray, leaving about 5cm (2in) between them to allow for spreading. Bake for 12–15 minutes until puffed and golden brown. Rotate the tray halfway through to ensure even cooking.

Remove from the oven and leave to settle on a rack for a few minutes, resisting the urge to tuck in. Put in a basket lined with a napkin and serve warm, with butter if you like.

cassava *flour*

oxtail and black bean stew with farofa

black turtle beans 600g (1lb
  5oz), soaked for 8 hours (see
  Cook's notes)
oxtail 12 large thick pieces
  of, weighing about 2.3kg (5lb)
  in total
olive oil 6 tablespoons
good-quality meat stock
  1.5 litres (2¾ pints), heated
lime juice of 1
fresh coriander chopped,
  to garnish
farofa to serve (see page 51)

for the spiced flour
black peppercorns
  1 tablespoon
sea salt 2 teaspoons
dried thyme or oregano
  ½ teaspoon
red pepper flakes ½ teaspoon
allspice berries ¼ teaspoon
mustard powder 1 teaspoon
paprika 2 teaspoons
all-purpose cassava or plain
  flour 4 tablespoons

for the sofrito
olive oil 3 tablespoons
onions 3, roughly chopped
celery stalks 6, destringed
  and thickly sliced
bay leaves 4 fresh
cumin seeds 1 tablespoon,
  lightly crushed
garlic cloves 4 large, thinly
  sliced lengthways
tomato purée 2 tablespoons
red chilli flakes a good pinch
chopped tomatoes 400g
  (14oz) can
freshly ground black pepper
  1 teaspoon

serves 6

A dish not to be rushed – ideal for making with friends over a winter weekend. Meaty chunks of oxtail are dredged in a piquant mix of cassava flour and spices to thicken the juices. The meat is then stewed at a leisurely pace with the all-important *sofrito* (basic sauce) until it's falling off the bone. Serve topped with farofa, a crunchy cassava condiment that sops up the tasty juices.

· · ·

Drain the soaked beans, tip into a large saucepan and cover with fresh water. Bring to the boil for 15 minutes, then reduce the heat a little and cook for 30 minutes to 1 hour until tender but not breaking up. (The exact cooking time will depend on the age of your beans.) Drain and set aside.

Meanwhile, make the spiced flour. Grind the peppercorns, sea salt, thyme or oregano, red pepper flakes and allspice to a powder using a mortar and pestle or a clean electric coffee grinder. Mix with the mustard powder, paprika and cassava flour. Put the oxtail pieces and spiced flour in a large plastic bag and shake well until the meat is evenly coated. Shake off any residue.

Heat the 6 tablespoons of oil in a large frying pan over a medium-high heat. Add the oxtail in a single layer (in batches if necessary), and fry for 12–15 minutes, turning once, until lightly browned on both sides. Put the pieces on a plate as they brown.

While the meat is frying, make the sofrito. Heat the 3 tablespoons of oil in a large, wide-based casserole dish (see Cook's notes) over a medium heat. Add the onions, celery, bay leaves and cumin. Cover and gently fry for 10 minutes or until the onions are translucent. Add the garlic and fry for another minute, then add the tomato purée and chilli flakes and fry for 30 seconds. Stir in the chopped tomatoes and black pepper, and bring to a brisk simmer.

Preheat the oven to 150°C/Gas Mark 2. Add the oxtail to the sofrito, along with the cooked beans and all but a couple of ladlefuls of the hot stock. Deglaze the meat pan with the reserved stock, stirring the sediment with a wooden spoon. Pour this into the casserole. There should be enough liquid to almost, but not quite, cover the meat. Cover, bring to the boil, then put in the oven and cook for 1½ hours.

Using tongs, turn the oxtail pieces over and rotate the

flour

casserole. Cook for another hour, or until the meat is very tender. Stir in the lime juice and check the seasoning. Garnish generously with chopped coriander just before serving. Serve the farofa in a small bowl so people can help themselves.

cook's notes
- I have occasionally made this with drained and rinsed canned beans, adding them for the last hour of cooking, but they do taste sludgy compared with freshly cooked beans.
- You will need a sturdy wide-based casserole dish or Dutch oven, big enough to take the oxtail and the beans, as well as the sofrito.

farofa

dendê oil 3 tablespoons, preferably organic (see Cook's note)
onion 1 small, finely chopped
cassava meal (*farinha de mandioca cruda*) 200g (7oz)
sea salt ½ teaspoon, or to taste

A condiment found on every table in Brazil, farofa is made with lightly toasted cassava meal (*farinha de mandioca cruda*) ground from the cassava root. It's particularly good sprinkled over stews, providing the characteristic crunch typical of many Brazilian dishes. Farofa is so essential to Brazilian cuisine that there are specialists called *farofeiros*, renowned for their inventiveness. Here, farofa is fried Bahia-style with dendê oil (palm oil) that makes it an eye-catching yellow.

• • •

makes about 300g (10½oz)

Heat the oil in a large non-stick frying pan over a medium heat. Add the onion and gently fry for about 6 minutes or until translucent but not browned.

Stir in the cassava meal and salt. Reduce the heat to low and fry for about 5 minutes, stirring constantly, or until the mixture is crunchy. Be careful not to let it burn. Allow to cool, then store in a screw-top jar. It will keep for several months.

cook's note
- If you can't get any dendê oil, use olive oil or butter instead.

chestnut *flour*

plant source nut
aka farina dolce (Italian)
latin name *Castanea sativa*
gluten none
protein 4–6%
goes with brandy, chocolate, ginger, mushrooms, orange zest, pears, pumpkin, rosemary, walnuts
uses bread, cakes, fritters, pancakes, polenta, thickener for sauces, soups and stews

There was a time when I regularly rented a house in the Garfagnana region of Tuscany in Italy, a mountainous area densely wooded with sweet chestnut trees. Without fail I would bring back chestnut flour and proudly decant it into a storage jar, fully intending to cook with it. Inevitably, months would pass, enthusiasm would wane, and I'd open the jar to discover stale, sour-smelling flour.

An epiphany took place while researching this book. I discovered different types of chestnut flour with varying degrees of sweetness and smoke. I spent days making cakes and breads, polenta-like porridge and pastry. Some experiments ended in the bin, but others were surprisingly good. Chestnut Flour Fritters with Fennel and Orange (see page 54) were a real treat and so easy to make. The flour became a favourite and I now bake with it regularly.

I've always liked chestnuts, both roasted and raw. Peeling the inner skin is a challenge but it's this element of hard work that perhaps draws me to the nuts and to the flour. Unusually, the flour has a season. Autumn is when the nuts are at their glossiest best, and the end of November is the time for the new season's flour. It has a short shelf life and should be used within a few weeks.

Milled from pulverized dried chestnuts, the flour ranges in colour from chalky cream to a rich brown, depending on whether or not it's been roasted. The aroma and flavour are beautifully sweet and nutty, with a smoky hint of roasted chestnuts. I particularly like Amisa, a relatively mild organic brand (see Sources, page 280), though others are more rustic. Author Niki Segnit in *The Flavour Thesaurus* likens the aroma and flavour to 'somewhere between cocoa and silage', and the taste to 'the floor of a shepherd's refuge'. I'm not sure I agree, but brands certainly vary. It's a good idea to try a couple and see which you prefer.

Chestnut flour is unusually low in fat – most nut flours are quite oily – but it's high in carbohydrates and fibre and these make it quite heavy. This is fine for the traditional Italian Chestnut Cake with Rosemary (see page 55) – it's meant to be dense – but for most baking the flour needs lightening, either with wheat flour or a gluten-free flour.

Pastry made with chestnut flour particularly needs help. It's beautifully short and crisp, but will shatter unless mixed with other flours. I used tapioca starch and rice flour in the Pear Tart with Rosemary and Orange Syrup (see page 57) and it turned out perfectly.

Chestnut flour tends to clump, so it's a good idea to sieve it with other dry ingredients. The amount of liquid is also unpredictable – it depends on the quality and age of the flour. Add a little at a time until the dough is soft and pliable but not too sticky.

Though known in Italy as *farina dolce* (sweet flour), chestnut flour works well in savoury dishes too. Try it stirred into a robust polenta-like porridge – delicious with coarse spicy sausage or a strong cheese. It's also good in a rich dark bread, perhaps with some chopped chestnuts folded in, or an autumnal tart with a mushroom or pumpkin filling.

chestnut flour fritters with fennel and orange (fritelle dolce)

chestnut flour 150g (5½oz)
baking powder ¼ teaspoon
caster sugar 25g (1oz), plus
    extra for sprinkling
water 250ml (9fl oz)
fennel seeds 1 teaspoon,
    crushed
tangerine 1 teaspoon finely
    grated zest or ½ teaspoon
    finely grated orange zest
vegetable oil for deep-frying

makes about 14

Chestnut flour and things made with it tend to be somewhat austere, perhaps to reflect the hard work that goes into harvesting chestnuts and grinding the flour. But here is a delightful Tuscan recipe for lovely sweet fritters. I used to buy these freshly fried from a bakery in Lucca, and enjoy them with a lethal shot of espresso from a local bar. The fritters are not elegant – they're something of a raggle-taggle bunch – but totally delicious.

• • •

Put the chestnut flour, baking powder and caster sugar into a sieve set over a bowl. Muddle with your fingers, then push through the sieve. Make a well in the centre and pour in the water. Whisk from the centre, gradually drawing in the flour from around the edge. Stir in the fennel seeds and tangerine zest, and leave the batter to stand for 30 minutes.

Pour enough oil into a heavy-based non-stick pan to come to a depth of 2–3cm (¾–1¼in). Set over a medium-high heat until very hot but not smoking – 180°C (350°F) on a thermometer, or until a cube of bread browns in 1 minute.

Give the batter a stir, then pour 2 tablespoons per fritter into the oil. Use a fish slice to ease the fritters off the base of the pan when they first hit the oil. Fry in batches for 1–1½ minutes until puffed up and golden.

Drain on paper towels, then put in a warm serving dish and sprinkle with more caster sugar.

variations
• Leave out the fennel seeds and add a few sultanas to the batter instead.
• For a savoury version, leave out the caster sugar and orange zest. Serve with ricotta cheese sprinkled with sea salt, and a leafy salad.

italian chestnut cake with rosemary
(castagnaccio)

plump raisins 3 tablespoons
candied citrus peel 25g (1oz),
    diced (see Cook's note)
vegetable oil for greasing
chestnut flour 250g (9oz)
sea salt good pinch
caster sugar 2 tablespoons
extra-virgin olive oil
    3 tablespoons
pine kernels 3 tablespoons
freshly ground black pepper
    ¼ teaspoon
rosemary leaves from a
    large sprig
sea salt flakes 1 teaspoon

**makes one 20cm (8in) square
    cake**

Castagnaccio is a dense, flat and not very sweet cake made with chestnut flour, traditionally in the autumn to coincide with the chestnut harvest. It's particularly well known in Tuscany, but there are variations in other Italian regions where chestnuts are grown. I have departed from authentic recipes by adding black pepper to the batter and crunchy sea salt flakes to the usual topping of rosemary leaves. They add a welcome piquancy and crunch.

• • •

Put the raisins and diced candied peel in a bowl, cover with boiling water and set aside.

Preheat the oven to 200°C/Gas Mark 6. Grease and line the base and sides of a 20cm (8in) square shallow cake tin. Line the tin with baking parchment and grease the paper too.

Put the chestnut flour, sea salt and caster sugar into a sieve set over a bowl. Muddle with your fingers, then push through the sieve.

Drain the raisins and citrus peel in a sieve set over a measuring jug, so you can keep the liquid. Set the fruit aside and top up the liquid with water to make 300ml (½ pint). Add 2 tablespoons of the olive oil.

Make a well in the centre of the flour mixture and pour in all the liquid. Whisk from the centre, gradually drawing in the flour from around the edge. Stir in the raisins, candied peel, pine kernels and black pepper, mixing well.

Spoon the batter into the prepared tin, making sure the pine kernals are well submerged. Sprinkle with the rosemary leaves and sea salt flakes, and drizzle evenly with the remaining tablespoon of olive oil. Bake for 30–40 minutes until cracks appear on the surface and a skewer inserted in the centre comes out clean. Leave to settle in the tin for 10 minutes before turning out on to a wire rack. The cake is best eaten slightly warm or at room temperature.

cook's note
· Do the cake justice by using whole chunks of good-quality candied peel, rather than the pre-chopped mixed peel. It comes in tempting flavours – bergamot and citron and orange and lemon. You'll find it in Italian grocery shops, delis and some supermarkets.

flour

pear tart with rosemary and orange syrup

vegetable oil for greasing
elongated firm-fleshed pears
   3, such as Conference
granulated sugar
   2 tablespoons
peeled roasted chestnuts
   or skinless hazelnuts
   1 tablespoon, roughly
   chopped
thick cream to serve

for the pastry
chestnut flour 55g (2oz)
tapioca starch 55g (2oz),
   plus extra for dusting
rice flour 25g (1oz)
xanthan gum ½ teaspoon
sea salt pinch
unsalted butter 35g (1¼oz)
   chilled, diced
egg 1, organic or free-range,
   lightly beaten
iced water ½ tablespoon

for the syrup
golden granulated sugar
   150g (5½oz)
water 100ml (3½fl oz)
orange peel 5 short thin strips
   (without any bitter white pith)
rosemary 3–4 tender sprigs

serves 4–6

When used for pastry, chestnut flour needs a helping hand from other flours. Once baked it's wonderfully crisp and has a slight nutty flavour, as you would expect. The pastry really opened my eyes to the exciting possibilities of more tarts, both sweet and savoury. This one has an autumnal feel with pears and chestnuts doused in a rosemary syrup.

• • •

For the pastry, put the chestnut flour, tapioca starch, rice flour, xanthan gum and salt into a sieve set over a bowl. Muddle with your fingers, then push through the sieve. Sieve once or twice more until well blended.

Tip the diced butter into the flour mixture and rub it in between the tips of your fingers and thumbs using a flicking movement – imagine you are playing castanets. Hold your hands well above the bowl so that the flour drifts down, incorporating air as it does so, and you can see any fragments of butter that still need rubbing in. Once the butter has been completely rubbed in, mix in the beaten egg and water.

Tip the dough on to a floured work surface and form it into a thick narrow oblong (see Cook's notes), rather like a railway carriage, ready for rolling out. Wrap in greaseproof paper and chill for 30 minutes.

Preheat the oven to 220°C/Gas Mark 8. Grease the base and sides of an oblong metal tart tin measuring 35x10x2.5cm (14x4x1in).

Once the dough is chilled, remove from the fridge and allow it to return to room temperature before rolling out. Flour the work surface and your rolling pin. With the short side of the block of dough facing you, use your rolling pin to gently press it away from you in several places along its length. Repeat this two or three times so that the dough gradually begins to elongate and flatten. Roll it into a 41x16cm (16¼x6¼in) rectangle and carefully lift it into the tin, pressing it into the corners with the side of your index finger. Trim the edges with a sharp knife, using the trimmings to patch any cracks (see Cook's notes).

Slice the pears in half lengthways and remove the core and peel. Slice each half lengthways into three. Pack them tightly along the length of the pastry case, head to tail and rounded side facing down. Sprinkle evenly with the sugar.

Bake for 20 minutes, or until the pears are just tender and the tips beginning to blacken, rotating the tin halfway through. Protect the edges of the pastry with strips of foil if it browns too much.

Take the tart out of the oven and leave in the tin to cool to room temperature (see Cook's notes).

Meanwhile, make the syrup. Put all the ingredients in a saucepan over a medium heat. Once the sugar has dissolved, bring to the boil, then boil for 7–10 minutes until the bubbles look big and very syrupy. Remove from the heat and set aside until cool and thick, but still pourable.

Spoon the syrup over the pears and sprinkle with chopped nuts. Serve warm or at room temperature with a jug of thick cream.

cook's notes
- If you don't have an oblong tart tin, use a 20cm (8in) round tin instead. If you are using a round tart tin, form the pastry into a thick disc rather than an oblong.
- Scrupulously check the unfilled pastry case for any cracks. If there are any, patch them very carefully using any leftover pastry.
- The pastry is quite fragile so it's best to serve the tart in the tin in case the syrup leaks.
- Leave the rosemary and orange strips in the syrup when you pour it over the pears. They look lovely and give an appetizing hint of flavour.

protein

Some of us know that wheat contains gluten, and some of us know that gluten is a protein. What many of us perhaps don't realize is that there are proteins other than gluten in both wheat flour and non-wheat flour. It's complicated and gets more so.

There are literally millions of different types of protein but only a few are relevant to plant foods and flour. Of the many methods of classification, one is to divide them into storage proteins and structural proteins. Storage proteins are mainly gluten – the major protein in flour – and those within the gluten group (see Gluten, page 60). Structural proteins are involved with shaping cells, rather like a skeleton. They include globulins, albumins and enzymes.

Globulins make up 5–12 per cent of total flour protein. Though classified as a structural protein, they also function as a storage protein in plants. Soy beans, dried peas and whole grains are good sources. Albumins make up 6–12 per cent of total flour protein. They are found in developing seeds, and provide the embryo with nutrients and protection from insects and pathogens. Enzymes speed up biochemical reactions and break down compound molecules. They include amylases, proteases, lipases and oxidases. Though they constitute only a small percentage of total flour protein, enzymes significantly influence the way flour behaves in baking.

Proteins are also classified as soluble and insoluble. Globulins, enzymes and albumins are soluble, i.e. when mixed with water or a salt solution they dissolve and disperse. Gluten proteins are insoluble in water and form a stretchy network that gives wheat dough its characteristic texture and strength.

Protein is a particularly complex topic with regard to flour. Though the protein content is listed on the packet, it's very hard to find out exactly what these proteins are. The exception is wheat flour – the protein content refers to gluten, since millers and bakers tend to use the terms interchangeably. The protein/gluten content is shown as a percentage and this determines the flour's strength (see Wheat and heritage flours, page 262; Italian 00 Wheat Flour, page 236) and consequentially your choice for the item you want to bake. For bread you'll need strong flour with a high percentage of protein/gluten (about 14 per cent), and for cakes and pastry a soft or weak flour with a lower percentage (7–10 per cent).

If you're vegetarian or vegan it's worth getting to grips with the fact that all proteins are made up of chains of amino acids – often called the building blocks of protein. There are twenty amino acids in all, eight of which are classified as essential and must be provided by food since the body cannot make them for itself. Proteins in plant foods are usually missing one or more of the essential amino acids; as such they are sometimes called 'incomplete' proteins. However, when plant foods from different sources are eaten at the same time – pulses with grains, for example – the amino acids from one can compensate for deficiencies in another. Flour milled from quinoa (see page 158) and soya beans (see page 202) are exceptions since they contain a full complement of essential amino acids, making them a 'complete' protein on a par with foods from animal sources.

For more information, check out the following websites:
- nature.com/scitable/topicpage/protein-function-14123348
- thefreshloaf.com/node/17045/protein-content-flour

gluten

My favourite bakery, housed in a converted railway arch in Bristol, southwest UK, displays a prominent sign saying 'Eat More Gluten'. The bakery is invariably packed with gluten-guzzling hipsters and their offspring. Contrast this with an ever-growing battalion of gluten-shunners, and you have good reason to ponder the cause of such entrenched conflict.

As food writer Felicity Cloake stated in an article in the *Guardian*: 'For all its terrifying reputation, gluten is nothing more than a couple of proteins found in wheat and other cereals that help give bread, pasta and so on their characteristic structure and texture.'

The proteins to which Felicity is referring are glutenin and gliadin – insoluble storage proteins found in the starchy endosperm of wheat (see Protein, page 59; Wheat and heritage flours, page 262) and related grains such as spelt, khorasan, emmer and einkorn. They're also found to a lesser extent in the non-wheat grains rye, barley and oats.

In scientific terms, glutenin is made up of loose elongated molecules that are able to interact with other molecules, thanks to their sprawling nature. Gliadin molecules are the opposite – round and compact, described by UK-based baking expert Emanuel Hadjiandreou as resembling miniature metal bed springs. They form tightly knit circles that limit contact with other molecules. Of the two, glutenin is strong and elastic – it has what I call the 'ping-back' factor – whereas gliadin is soft and sticky, and has what physicists refer to as ductile strength. In other words it can be stretched into long strands before it eventually breaks.

Gluten is unique in that it forms a complex semi-solid stretchy substance when mixed with water. As such, it plays a crucial role in forming cohesive dough that will expand to accommodate the gases produced by yeast in risen bread dough, and raising agents in non-yeasted dough. The gases stretch the strands of gluten, rather like blowing a bubble into bubble gum. Once in the oven, the dough cooks and solidifies around the network of bubbles, producing appetizing open-textured bread, and airy cakes and muffins with a 'good crumb'.

Bread dough To develop gluten, bread dough must be kneaded until it's springy and satin-smooth, with absolutely no trace of cellulite-like graininess. Depending on the flour and the amount of moisture, kneading can take from about 10–20 minutes. Over-kneading is unlikely when you knead by hand, but it's certainly something to watch out for when using a bread machine or a standing mixer. The gluten strands may become so stretched that they break and the dough disintegrates into a soft runny mass. If using a machine, do so with care and stop kneading before it's too late.

When kneaded dough is left to ferment, or prove, gluten starts to break down – especially gliadin, the protein most likely to cause digestion problems. So the longer dough is left to ferment, the easier it will be to digest (see Gluten and health, page 61).

Pastry The aim here is to actually prevent gluten development by breaking up or 'shortening' the tangle of gluten strands and creating 'short' pastry – crisp and flaky, unlike bread dough. This is done by rubbing fat into flour before adding water. The coating of fat makes it difficult for water to penetrate and hydrate the flour – without it gluten proteins cannot easily develop. It's important not to overwork your dough as this breaks down the protective fat layer, as does warmth from your hands. Gluten proteins will, however, develop at some point no matter how light your touch or how cool your fingers. It's therefore a good idea to allow time for the dough to rest in the fridge so that the gluten strands relax and settle in their new arrangement. Once rolled, positioned in the tin and trimmed, the dough needs to relax again before it goes into the oven. This helps prevent shrinkage during baking.

Gluten and health There are several disorders triggered by gluten, namely coeliac disease, gluten sensitivity, wheat allergy and wheat sensitivity. Coeliac disease is a serious autoimmune condition in which the small intestine becomes inflamed, resulting in debilitating symptoms such as chronic diarrhoea, bloating, nausea, vomiting, loss of appetite and poor absorption of nutrients. The only cure is a life-long gluten-free diet. Non-coeliac gluten sensitivity causes similar symptoms that improve when switching to a gluten-free diet, but, unlike coeliac disease, isn't potentially life-threatening. Wheat allergy is a reaction that causes sneezing and wheezing within minutes of consuming wheat. It can be diagnosed with a simple skin-prick test. Wheat sensitivity produces symptoms, such as diarrhoea and bloating, that start more slowly than an allergy – usually several hours after eating wheat. There is currently no method of diagnosis but an exclusion diet, in which wheat is removed then gradually reintroduced, is said to be helpful in identifying the condition.

The number of people who believe they have gluten-related health problems has risen dramatically in recent years – so much so that it has become something of a hyper-trend for people to exclude gluten simply because they think it is healthier, rather than for a specific medical reason. Among the causes implicated are the growing westernization of diet, replacement of rice by wheat in Asia, the Middle East and North Africa, increasing use of wheat-based foods, and higher amounts of gluten in mass-produced bread and bakery products to compensate for cut-backs in the time allowed for fermentation.

It's hard to know how many people are truly affected but let's get the statistics out of the way. Several research studies indicate that coeliac disease affects no more than 1–2 per cent of the population, and gluten sensitivity only 6–10 per cent. These figures are not intended to undermine sufferers; they are simply to put things in perspective.

Given the crucial and beneficial role of gluten in baking, and indeed the importance of bread throughout the world, the strident anti-gluten backlash seems baffling. As Doctor Stephen Jones and Bethany Econopouly, research assistant at The Bread Lab (Washington State University–Mount Vernon Research Center), wrote in a recent article for *Gastronomica* magazine, 'Journalists, writers, film-makers, lobbyists, retailers and scientists have jumped on board to get to the bottom of, make us feel better (and worse) about, and personally gain from this out-of-control food movement.' They go on to point out, 'The upside is that it has aimed the spotlight on wheat, formerly just a mundane commodity crop, now magically transformed into something tragically hip.' I am not sure if the terms 'tragic' or 'hip' apply to the encouraging interest increasingly shown in growing better-quality wheat, and milling it with care (see The miller's tale, page 187).

Another important upside is that there has been an improvement in the quality of gluten-free products, along with a wider choice – a marketing opportunity certainly not to be missed.

chickpea *flour*

plant source pulse
aka besan flour, garbanzo bean flour, gram flour
latin name *Cicer arietinum*
gluten none
protein 22–28%
goes with cheese, chillies, fish, ginger, harissa sauce, mint, mushrooms, peas, pickles, poultry, seafood, tomatoes
uses batter, binder, biscuits, cakes, chips, coating, crispbread, flatbreads, fritters, Indian confectionery, pakoras, pancakes, polenta-like porridge, thickener for sauces, soups and curries

Of all the gluten-free flours, chickpea flour must be the most amenable. It's used all over the world, from southern Europe to North Africa, from India to China and beyond. It has a satisfying mellow flavour, albeit highly redolent of peas, and a cheerful sunny cream colour. It's nutrient-rich – loaded with protein, dietary fibre and resistant starch (see page 205), easy to buy, and there's an enormous choice of things to make with it.

As food historian Ken Albala points out in *Beans: A History*, the chickpea is actually a bean rather than a pea. Albala prefers the Spanish term 'garbanzo bean', used in the US, which he understandably feels is 'a rather robust and dashing name, befitting this sturdy bean'. The pea/bean debate may arise from the fact that the flour is also milled from Indian split yellow peas (*channa dal*) as well as dried chickpeas. The split pea flour is usually called besan or gram flour, but the two plant species are closely related botanically, and the flours can be used interchangeably.

Both the beans and the flour have been around for thousands of years. They were always looked down on as food for the rural poor, as the Greek physician Galen says in his treatise *De Alimentorum Facultatibus* (*On the Properties of Foodstuffs*), written in the first century AD. In a whole chapter devoted to chickpeas he states, 'It is not very usual for people in the towns to make soup from chickpeas, but in the country I have sometimes seen this take place, as indeed I have also seen chickpea flour cooked in milk.'

Indian cooks have also used the flour for centuries. It goes into anything from crisp fried pakoras and pancakes, to savoury snacks, luscious desserts and fudgy sweetmeats. A favourite is 'ladu' – a hard-to-resist concoction of besan flour sizzled in ghee and palm sugar then rolled into sweet syrupy balls. Also good is 'sev', aka Bombay mix – crisp golden threads of dough extruded through a decorative perforated disk and deep-fried in oil.

The late Dharamjit Singh, erudite author of *Indian Cookery*, applauds the use of the flour in batter, especially for fish, 'where it acts like blotting paper, absorbing superfluous oils and the fishy odour'. The Spanish are also devotees. They pride themselves on a fail-safe tempura-style batter in a dish charmingly called Prawns in Raincoats (see page 66).

Moving round the Mediterranean, chickpea flour is the key ingredient in utterly addictive Sicilian *panelle* (see page 64), and large egg-free pancakes known as *socca* in Provence and *farinata* in neighbouring Italy.

It also makes what I call the chip to excel all chips. Mix one part chickpea flour with two-parts water and stir over a medium heat. Once you have a lump-free polenta-like porridge, tip it into an oiled shallow rectangular tin and leave to cool to a thick slab. Slice into slim batons and fry in piping hot oil. Your chips will be golden crisp on the outside and superbly creamy within. Alternatively, do as the Burmese do and slice the cooled slab into cubes of 'tofu', to serve as a snack. It can be mixed with turmeric for a more intense colour. Food writer Naomi Duguid calls this one of the great unsung treasures of Southeast Asia.

If you're cooking for vegans, it's worth remembering what must be one of the best-kept culinary secrets: chickpea flour is an invaluable egg substitute, containing the nutrients normally supplied by eggs, plus the yellow colour. It's makes beautiful, lacy, egg-free crêpes, especially good seasoned with nigella seeds or cumin, and topped with shredded courgettes, carrots and slivers of toasted coconut.

The beauty of chickpea flour is that unlike most gluten-free flours, you can substitute it 100 per cent for wheat flour in items that don't need to rise very much. For cakes, muffins and popovers, it's best to combine it with 25 per cent wheat flour plus a raising agent. If gluten is off-limits, use tapioca flour or sweet sorghum flour instead.

The flour is easy to find online, in supermarkets and shops specializing in Asian or Middle Eastern groceries. It contains fat and therefore has a limited shelf life of about six months. Empty it into an airtight container rather than leaving it in an opened packet. Store in the fridge or another cool, dry place.

sicilian chickpea fritters
(panelle)

chickpea flour 110g (4oz)
boiling water 500ml (18fl oz)
sea salt ½ teaspoon, plus sea
  salt flakes to garnish
freshly ground black pepper
  ½ teaspoon
flat-leaf parsley 2 tablespoons
  chopped, plus sprigs to
  garnish
vegetable oil for deep-frying
lemon wedges to garnish

makes about 16

Chickpea flour imparts its warm, mellow flavour to these totally addictive fritters. I first ate them strolling along the quay in Ortigia, the island off Syracuse. Perfect street food, but so easy to make at home.

• • •

Sieve the flour into a bowl. Pour the water into a large, heavy-based, non-stick saucepan, add the salt and bring back to the boil. Slowly add the flour, trickling it through your fingers like sand and whisking all the time to prevent lumps. Add the pepper and parsley, then cook over a medium heat for 15–20 minutes, still whisking, until the mixture is very thick and comes away from the sides of the pan.

Tip the mixture on to an oiled surface and roll it into a log measuring about 20x5cm (8x2in). Wrap loosely in greaseproof paper and leave to cool completely (see Cook's note).

Slice the log into rounds about 1cm (½in) thick. Pour enough oil into a heavy-based pan to come to a depth of 3–4cm (1¼–1½in). Heat over a medium-high heat until very hot but not smoking – 180°C (350°F) on a thermometer, or until a cube of bread browns in 1 minute. Fry the fritters a few at a time for 5–6 minutes until beautifully crisp and craggy.

Drain on paper towels, tip into a warm serving dish and garnish with a sprinkle of sea salt flakes, parsley sprigs and lemon wedges.

cook's note
• If you don't want to fry the panelle right away, chill the log for up to 24 hours, or freeze it in slices.

spiced pancakes with mint, chilli and apple relish *(besan ka chilla)*

cumin seeds 1 teaspoon
chickpea flour 250g (9oz)
mild chilli powder
   1–2 teaspoons
water 300–325ml (10–11fl oz)
red onion 1 large, diced
green chillies 1–2, deseeded
   and finely chopped
coriander 2 tablespoons
   chopped
ginger root 25g (1oz), grated
tomato 1, diced
vegetable oil for frying
full-fat yogurt to serve

for the mint, chilli and
apple relish
mint leaves 1 large handful,
   tough stalks discarded
Bramley apple 1, chopped
caster sugar 1 tablespoon
ground cumin ¾ teaspoon
ginger root 25g (1oz), chopped
garlic clove 1 large, chopped
green chilli 1, deseeded and
   chopped
lime juice of 1

makes 8

This recipe was kindly contributed by food writer Roopa Gulati. Roopa recalls how, when she lived in India, Sunday brunches began with the toasty, nutty scent of chickpea flour pancakes cooking on the stove. She loved the sizzling sigh as the onion-flecked batter hit the hot griddle and was smoothed into shape with the base of an obliging ladle. As Roopa says, this is finger food at its best, and the enjoyment is in ripping the almost too-hot-to-handle chilla and using it to scoop up cooling yogurt and zesty mint chutney.

· · ·

Blend all the ingredients for the mint relish in a liquidizer (or use a stick blender) with a dash of hot water until you have a thick, fragrant paste. Aim for a sweet and tangy flavour, adding more sugar or lime juice if needed. Set aside while you make the pancakes.

Heat a small frying pan over a medium heat and roast the cumin seeds for a few seconds, stirring all the time, or until they release their nutty aroma. Tip them on to a plate.

Sieve the chickpea flour and chilli powder into a bowl and add the cumin. Gradually beat in the water – enough to make a smooth batter with the consistency of single cream. Stir in the onion, green chilli, coriander, ginger and tomato. Leave to rest for 20 minutes (see Cook's note).

Heat a heavy-based 20cm (8in) non-stick frying pan or griddle over a high heat. Pour a thin film of oil over the base of the pan, then pour a ladleful of batter into the centre, and spread it out in a circular movement until it's about 15–18cm (6–7in) in diameter and as thin as possible.

Lower the heat to medium-high and cook the pancake for about 2 minutes, or until brown at the edges. Drizzle a little more oil around the pancake, flip it over and continue cooking for another 2 minutes until golden. Serve straight away with mint relish and yogurt on the side.

cook's note
· The batter tends to thicken on standing so you may need to add more water just before cooking.

prawns in raincoats
(gambas in gabardinas)

olive oil for deep-frying (see
    Cook's notes)
raw headless peeled prawns
    250g (9oz) (see Cook's notes)
cocktail gherkins or caper
    berries to garnish
lemon wedges to garnish

for the batter
chickpea flour 125g (4½oz),
    plus extra for dredging the
    prawns
paprika 1 teaspoon
egg 1, organic or free-range
iced water 110ml (3¾fl oz)
sea salt ¼ teaspoon
freshly ground black pepper
    ¼ teaspoon

serves 3–4

Chickpea flour makes beautiful tempura-style batter that's both light and crisp at the same time – perfect for dunking juicy prawns in their so-called 'raincoats' without imprisoning them in a heavy coating. The dish is popular in Madrid where it's served in the city's tapas bars.

• • •

To make the batter, sieve the flour and paprika into a bowl. Whisk in the egg, then slowly pour in the water, whisking all the time, until the batter is smooth but fairly thick. Season with the salt and pepper, and leave to rest in the fridge for an hour or two.

Pour enough oil into a heavy-based pan to come to a depth of 2–3cm (¾–1¼in). Place over a medium-high heat until very hot but not smoking – 180°C (350°F) on a thermometer, or until a cube of bread browns in 1 minute.

Have ready a shallow dish of flour for dredging the prawns. Stir the batter again. Using tongs, dip the prawns in the flour, shake to remove any excess, then dunk in the batter. Lift up and let the batter drip back into the bowl, then dunk in the hot oil. Fry for 2 minutes until the prawns are no longer pink.

Drain on paper towels and tip into a warm serving dish. Garnish with cocktail gherkins or caper berries, and wedges of lemon. Serve hot or warm.

cook's notes
· Don't use extra-virgin olive oil. It isn't suitable for heating to the high temperature needed for deep-frying.
· Though the prawns need peeling, they look best with the tails left on, and are easier to pick up and eat with your fingers.

coconut *flour*

plant source nut
aka n/a
latin name *Cocos nucifera*
gluten none
protein 19.3%
goes with chocolate, citrus, pineapple, rum, tropical flavours, warm spices
uses binding burgers and meatballs, biscuits, cakes, coating for fried foods,
   pancakes, pastry, smoothies, thickener for sauces, soups and stews

Gluten-free, high-protein, high-fibre and low-carb, coconut flour certainly ticks all the right health boxes. These credentials aside, it's the flour I'm drawn to when I feel the urge to experiment with baking. I love its smell, its tropicality, its faint sweetness. That said, it's also the flour I found the most challenging, particularly during my early days of gluten-free baking. Still memorable is a whole morning spent trying to produce acceptable coconut flour pastry for a tart. Five attempts later, with a bin full of trashed tart shells, I was ready to give up.

My mistake was trying to create something similar to wheat pastry dough using flour with very different properties. Instead of going with it I was fighting it. Once I had accepted that the dough was going to be very moist and sticky, that I had to press it into the tin instead of rolling it, I was able to appreciate the end result: a slightly soft coconut-flavoured crust that would appeal to people with allergies or following a gluten- or wheat-free diet.

Coconut flour is a natural by-product of the coconut milk industry – it's ground from defatted, dried coconut flesh. (Don't confuse it with coconut powder for making coconut milk.) As such, it's particularly high in fibre and incredibly dry. It's a hydrocolloid, which to you and me means that it absorbs an excessive amount of liquid. Therein lies the chief difference between coconut flour and wheat flour.

In baking, replacing wheat flour or other grain-based flour with the same amount of coconut flour simply won't work; the finished product will be horribly dense and dry. It needs combining with another gluten-free flour, such as sorghum, to make the dough easier to handle. You will need extra eggs to compensate for the lack of gluten (see page 60). The flour will absorb what seems like far too much moisture, but the eggs will help bind the ingredients and stop your pastry from crumbling. A spoonful of clear honey or maple syrup also helps bind the mixture, as does a little xanthan gum.

An easier option is to use a tried-and-tested pastry recipe specifically designed for coconut flour. Try Piña Colada Tart with Rum Custard and Caramelized Pineapple (see page 72). Be aware that brands of flour vary in the amount of fibre and/or protein they contain, so if you switch you may get different results from the same recipe. I get the best results from Tiana, an organic fair-trade brand (see Sources, page 280).

Though baking with coconut flour involves a steep learning curve, using the flour in other ways is relatively trouble-free. It makes terrific chocolate cake, muffins and – best of all – pancakes. Try the Coconut Flour and Lime Pancakes on page 71.

You can also stir a spoonful into a smoothie or gravy to thicken it, or use it instead of breadcrumbs to bind meatballs or burgers, or as a gluten-free coating for fried foods. In these cases it's fine to substitute the same amount of coconut flour for ordinary flour or cornmeal.

flour

coconut flour and lime pancakes

coconut flour 2 tablespoons
(see Cook's notes)
rice flour 2 tablespoons
eggs 3, organic or free-range,
lightly beaten
organic coconut milk 100ml
(3½fl oz), whisked until smooth
(see Cook's notes)
ground turmeric ¼ teaspoon
sea salt ⅛ teaspoon
vegetable oil for frying

to serve
granulated sugar
lime juice
lime thin slivers of zest

makes 6

Coconut flour makes superb gluten-free pancakes. Here, it is combined with rice flour to tame its tendency to sop up liquid. The batter is seasoned with a dash of turmeric to brighten the colour. The pancakes are naturally slightly sweet – delicious sprinkled with sugar, lime juice and ultra-thin slivers of lime zest.

· · ·

Put the flours, eggs, coconut milk, turmeric and salt in the bowl of a food processor and whizz until smooth. Decant into a jug, leave for a few minutes, then stir.

Spray a non-stick pancake pan with oil and place over a medium heat. Pour in about half a ladleful of the batter. Tilt the pan and swirl the batter to a thin circle, about 15cm (6in) in diameter. Cook for 30–40 seconds, or until the edge and bottom are starting to colour and you can easily slip a spatula underneath. Flip the pancake over and cook for another minute or so.

Slide the pancake on to a warm plate and cover with baking parchment or paper towel to prevent sticking. Repeat with the rest of the batter.

Serve warm, sprinkled with sugar, lime juice and a few very thin slivers of lime zest.

cook's notes
· Coconut flour brands vary. I get the best results from Tiana coconut flour, an organic fair-trade brand (see Sources, page 280).
· It is essential to use organic coconut milk without any additives. The batter will not work with non-organic coconut milk.

piña colada tart with rum custard and caramelized pineapple

coconut flour 140g (5oz) (see
    Cook's notes)
sorghum flour 75g (2¾oz)
sea salt ½ teaspoon
xanthan gum ½ teaspoon
unsalted butter 110g (4oz)
    chilled, diced
eggs 3 large, organic or free-
    range, lightly beaten
clear honey 1 tablespoon
vegetable oil for greasing
cornflour for dusting
lime 4 thin slices, quartered, to
    decorate
rum for sprinkling

for the rum custard filling
egg 1, organic or free-range
egg yolks 4, organic or free-
    range
caster sugar 75g (2¾oz)
cornflour 4 tablespoons
salt pinch
organic coconut milk 400g
    (14oz) can, stirred if separated
    (see Cook's notes)
unsalted butter 25g (1oz)
rum 1 tablespoon

for the pineapple
pineapple 1 medium ripe,
    peeled and cored
sugar 85g (3oz)
water 125ml (4fl oz)
limes finely grated zest of 2

serves 8

This gorgeous gluten-free tart is just right for a special occasion when you're feeding people who follow a gluten- or wheat-free diet. The recipe is long, but if you break it down – pastry, filling and pineapple – it's easier than you think. That said, it's worth reading the recipe all the way through before you begin.

· · ·

Using a large dinner plate or frying pan as a template, draw a 30cm (12in) circle on a piece of baking parchment at least 38cm (15in) square, and set aside. Grease a 25x3cm (10x1¼in) deep non-stick fluted tart tin, making sure the sides are well lubricated. Place a circle of baking parchment in the base and grease the paper too.

To make the pastry, tip the flours, sea salt and xanthan gum into a sieve set over a bowl. Muddle with your fingers, then shake through the sieve. Sieve once more. Get your fingers nice and cold – I hold mine under running water. Tip the diced butter into the flour mixture and rub it in between the tips of your fingers and thumbs using a flicking movement – imagine you are playing castanets. Hold your hands well above the bowl so that the flour drifts gently down, and you can see any fragments of butter that still need rubbing in.

Once the butter has been completely rubbed in, mix in the beaten eggs and honey. The dough will feel alarmingly wet but don't panic – the coconut flour will gradually absorb the liquid. Gather the dough into a ball, then flatten it into a thick disc about 12cm (4½in) in diameter, ready for when you roll it out. Wrap in greaseproof paper (not cling film) and set aside for 15 minutes. Do not chill, otherwise the pastry will be hard to roll.

Preheat the oven to 180°C/Gas Mark 4. Dust your rolling pin with cornflour, then dust the baking parchment on which you drew a circle. Place the disc of dough on the parchment and roll it into a rough-and-ready 30cm (12in) circle. Place your tart tin upside down over the circle. Lift up the four corners of the parchment and fold them over the underside of the tin towards the middle. Using both hands, hold the corners in place and quickly turn the tin over, allowing the dough to flop into the base of the tin. There will be inevitable cracks – just press the dough together.

Place a 23cm (9in) diameter piece of parchment over the dough in the base. Working from the middle to the outer edge, press with a flat-bottomed implement – the side of your

flour

fist, or a smooth meat pounder will do. The aim is to make the dough as thin as possible and at the same time ease it up the sides of the tin. Press the side of your index finger into the edge of the base and the fluted sides to even out the thickness. Trim the top with a small sharp knife. Use the offcuts to reinforce any weak areas.

Bake for 10–12 minutes, rotating halfway through, or until the crust looks slightly golden. Protect the edge with foil strips if it starts to look too brown. Remove from the oven and put on a rack. Leave the crust in the tin for 30 minutes to firm up, then carefully ease it out of the tin and leave on the rack to cool.

For the rum custard filling, put the whole egg, yolks, sugar, cornflour and a pinch of salt into a bowl. Whisk for 3–4 minutes until the sugar has dissolved. Gently heat the coconut milk until just simmering. Whisk a little into the egg mixture. Whisk again then pour the egg mixture into the saucepan. Whisk over a medium heat for about 5 minutes until thickened and no longer tasting floury. Whisk in the butter, followed by the rum. Pour into a shallow dish, cover with cling film and leave to cool to room temperature.

Cut the prepared pineapple horizontally into four slices about 1cm (½in) thick. Cut the slices in half, then cut each half into thirds, so you end up with six segments per slice.

Put the sugar, water and lime zest in a small frying pan over a gentle heat. Once the sugar has dissolved, boil hard for 1–2 minutes or until the bubbles look big and syrupy. Add the pineapple segments in a single layer, in batches if necessary. Fry over a high heat until the edges are starting to caramelize and the syrup is very bubbly. Tip into a shallow dish and leave to cool to room temperature.

To assemble the tart, pour the filling into the pastry case, spreading it out with a palette knife. Scatter the pineapple segments over the top, along with any sticky residue. Tuck in the lime slices here and there, sprinkle with a splash of rum and serve right away.

cook's notes
- Coconut flour brands vary. I get the best results from Tiana coconut flour, an organic fair-trade brand (see Sources, page 280).
- It is essential to use organic coconut milk without any additives. The batter will not work with non-organic coconut milk.

coffee *flour*

plant source seed
aka n/a
latin name *Coffea arabica, Coffea robusta*
gluten none
protein 1.5%
goes with bananas, chocolate, cinnamon, ginger, molasses, nuts, oranges, sea salt, vanilla
uses bread, biscuits, brownies, cakes, ice cream, sauces

As someone who likes to start the day with a punchy espresso, I was delighted to hear about coffee flour and had hopes of caffeine-rich pastry. Sadly, research reveals that it's milled from the dried 'cherry' – the skin and pulp surrounding the coffee bean – rather than the bean itself, where most of the caffeine is located. The flour does contain a little caffeine but not enough to keep you awake at night.

Coffee flour was initially produced as a way of using leftover cherry pulp after the beans had been harvested. Though some of the pulp is recycled as fertilizer for coffee trees, much of it is apparently left to rot. Coffee flour innovators argue that using this by-product for flour provides an answer to the hot topic of food waste, as well as producing extra revenue for the farmers. Others argue that turning more of the pulp into fertilizer would be a better bet, invaluable for small producers, and that the cost of milling, packaging and exporting the flour outweighs the benefits.

Moving on from political debate, the flour certainly has credentials. It's high-fibre, low-fat, and rich in iron, potassium and antioxidants. It has a lovely aroma – chocolatey, floral and fruity. Surprisingly, it doesn't taste of coffee, even though the dark colour suggests it might.

For the cook, coffee flour is a versatile ingredient and interesting to experiment with. As a high-fibre flour it needs 10–25 per cent more liquid than most others. Even though I followed a supposedly tried and tested recipe, my first batch of brownies was as dry as volcanic dust. Remember, too, that the flour's brown colour means baked items will look even darker while baking. Don't be tempted to take them out of the oven too soon.

Coffee flour is gluten-free so you'll need to pair it with other flours when baking. Start by substituting 10–15 per cent with coffee flour, then increase to 20 per cent once you're familiar with how it behaves. Remember to sieve the flours and other dry ingredients together to make sure they're evenly mixed before you add liquid ingredients. If you're pairing coffee flour with other gluten-free flours, add a little xanthan gum or guar gum to help bind the dough.

At the time of writing, coffee flour hasn't reached supermarket shelves, but it's easy to find online (see Sources, page 280).

triple chocolate brownies

plain flour 60g (2¼oz)
coffee flour 10g (¼oz)
unsweetened cocoa powder
   2 tablespoons
freshly ground black pepper
   ½ teaspoon
dark chocolate 140g (5oz)
   (at least 75 per cent cocoa
   solids), broken into small
   pieces
unsalted butter 110g (4oz),
   diced
eggs 2, organic or free-range
golden caster sugar 150g
   (5½oz)
split vanilla pod seeds from 1
sea salt pinch
cacao nibs 4 tablespoons

makes 16

Coffee flour adds significant depth of flavour to these chocolate-rich brownies. The batter may seem sloppy, but the coffee flour absorbs more liquid than other flours because of its unusually high fibre content.

• • •

Preheat the oven to 180°C/Gas Mark 4, positioning the rack just below the middle of the oven. Grease the base and sides of a 20cm (8in) square cake tin. Line the tin with baking parchment and grease the paper too.

Put the flours, cocoa powder and black pepper in a sieve set over a bowl. Muddle with your fingers, then push through the sieve. Repeat once or twice more until the mixture is a uniform colour.

Place the chocolate and butter in a bowl, and melt in the microwave or over a pan of boiling water (see Cook's note).

Put the eggs, sugar, vanilla seeds and salt in a large bowl. Whisk lightly for about 20 seconds, then stir in the melted chocolate mixture. Using a wooden spoon, gently fold in the flour mixture and the cacao nibs until just combined – it's important not to overmix.

Pour the mixture into the prepared tin, levelling the surface with a wet palette knife. Bake for 20–25 minutes, rotating the tin every 10 minutes, until a skewer inserted in the centre comes out with a small amount of crumbs sticking to it, rather than completely clean. If there is wet mixture sticking to it, bake for another 3 minutes and check again.

When you take the tin out of the oven, tap it on the work surface to release air from under the crust. This helps the surface to dry and the mixture underneath to have the desired fudgy texture. Leave in the tin to cool completely before turning out on to a wire rack.

cook's note
· Melt the chocolate and butter by microwaving on medium for 3 minutes, stirring every 30 seconds. Alternatively, melt in a bowl set over boiling water.

flour

corn*flour*

plant source grain
aka cornstarch (US, Canada)
latin name *Zea mays*
gluten none
protein 0.3%
goes with anything
uses batter, binder, biscuits, bread, cakes, coating for fried foods, ice cream,
   meringues, sweetmeats, thickener for desserts, pie and tart fillings, sauces, soups

Any discussion of cornflour is likely to be fraught with culinary conflict, so let's get the semantics straight. Confusingly, 'corn' is a universal term for cereal crops; it can mean wheat in the UK or oats in Scotland, for example. In the US the term more correctly refers to maize, aka 'corn'. Even though cornflour is a starch, here in the UK we call it 'cornflour'. As far as Americans are concerned, 'cornflour' means flour ground from cornmeal, an entirely different ingredient, so they rightly call it 'cornstarch'.

Cornflour is an American invention dating back to the mid-nineteenth century. It's said to be one of the most widely used ingredients in food processing and baking. It's what I call culinary wallpaper – always there in the background, incredibly useful but lacking in wow-factor.

Like most starches, cornflour is dazzlingly white with a talcum powder-like texture. It's odourless, flavourless and squeaks when you rub it between your fingers. When removed from the bag, it has an irritating tendency to cover nearby surroundings with fallout.

For a blow-by-blow account of how cornflour is produced, check out the Danish International Starch Institute – yes, really (see Selected websites, page 279). To explain the process more simply: kernels from dent corn (a non-sweet variety) are soaked for several hours in a mildly acidic solution. The main part of the kernel – the endosperm – is separated and pulverized while still wet. The resulting slurry goes through a centrifuge to remove detritus and the extracted starch is then washed, dried and ground to a very fine powder.

For the home cook, cornflour is used mainly to thicken pie and tart fillings, custard, gravy, stews and certain Oriental sauces. It's the key ingredient in milky desserts such blancmange, and in Turkish Delight (see page 83). It's also useful in baking, and makes a rather good crisp batter for fish, meat and tempura-style vegetables.

Thickening a liquid with cornflour isn't always straightforward, so it's helpful to understand what's going on under the microscope. Like all starches, cornflour is made up of tightly knit chains of molecules. When heated in liquid to 62–70°C

(143–158°F) they expand and collide with each other, and in doing so form a mesh that thickens the liquid – a process called gelatinization. Thickening is a slow process that requires patience and a wooden spatula. You may have experienced this when stirring custard or a lemon meringue pie filling. Nothing seems to be happening then suddenly the mixture at the bottom of the pan starts to feel different and gradually the whole thing changes from a liquid to a gel.

If you're flavouring with sugar, or acids such as lemon juice, wine or vinegar, be aware that these can prevent starch granules from swelling. Wait until the mixture has thickened before adding them, and be sure to do so while the mixture is still hot rather than when it's cooled and solidified.

When adding cornflour to a hot liquid – to gravy, say – it's essential to first make a smooth slurry with equal parts cornflour and a cold liquid such as water, stock or wine before adding it. If you add neat cornflour directly to hot liquid it will form lumps that are almost impossible to smooth out.

In baking, cornflour works its magic on texture and structure. For super-light sponge cakes, replace 1–2 tablespoons of plain flour with cornflour. Cornflour is also an option for shortbread (see page 81). The texture is significantly melt-in-the-mouth and delicate, rather than crunchy as when made with rice flour.

Moving on from baking, cornflour is an excellent binder for fishcakes and burgers, and it makes an appetizingly crisp coating for fried pieces of meat or fish – useful when catering for people who don't eat gluten.

Though it has a reasonably long shelf life, cornflour can lose some of its thickening ability if exposed to air over long periods. It's best to keep it in a sealed container rather than leaving it in an opened packet. If you're using cornflour that's been on the shelf for a while you may need to use more than the recipe specifies.

Cornflour gets a bad press because it's often made with genetically modified corn. If you want to avoid GM foods, check the label and go for an organic brand, or one that's guaranteed GM-free.

flour

alda o'loughlin's shortbread

butter for greasing
plain flour 100g (3½oz)
cornflour 50g (1¾oz)
salted butter 100g (3½oz), at
   room temperature, cubed
golden caster sugar 50g
   (1¾oz), plus extra for dredging

makes 8

This recipe comes from Marina O'Loughlin, one of my favourite restaurant reviewers. It is her mother's recipe, which Marina rates as the best shortbread in the world. Mixed with plain flour, cornflour produces wonderfully short shortbread. As Marina writes, 'It may be simple, but it's a thing of utter beauty, so crisp, so buttery, so perfectly short: a cup of tea was never so finely accessorized.'

• • •

Preheat the oven to 150°C/Gas Mark 2. Butter the base and sides of a shallow 19cm (7½in) loose-bottomed cake tin.

Tip the plain flour and cornflour into a sieve set over a bowl. Muddle with your fingers, then push through the sieve. Sieve once more until well blended.

Put the cubed butter in a bowl and beat with a wooden spoon, or an electric whisk, to soften it. Add the sugar and beat for a few minutes until light and fluffy. Add the flour mixture, working it in with a wooden spoon and pressing to the side of the bowl. Finish mixing with your hands until you have a smooth dough.

Tip the dough on to a lightly floured work surface. Roll it into a circle, giving it a quarter turn as you roll, to about the same diameter as your tin. Lightly press the dough into the tin and prick all over with a fork. Press the tines of the fork all round the edges to create 'petticoat tails'.

Bake on the middle shelf of the oven for 25–30 minutes until firm in the middle. Remove from the oven and use the edge of a palette knife to mark out eight wedges. Leave in the tin until completely cold. Cut into wedges, dredge with more of the golden caster sugar, and store in an airtight container.

belly dancer's jelly with cardamom brittle (*balouza*)

cornflour 70g (2½oz)
organic whole milk 1 litre
  (1¾ pints)
caster sugar 100g (3½oz)
vanilla pod 1, split
mastic crystals 2 (optional),
  crushed with 1 teaspoon
  granulated sugar (see
  Cook's notes)
rose water 1 tablespoon

for the cardamom brittle
caster sugar 200g (7oz)
cardamom seeds from 10 fat
  pods

serves 6

Delicate milky desserts such as this are popular in the Middle East, and refreshing to eat at any time of day. They are often scented with rose water or orange blossom water and thickened with rice flour or semolina. Here, cornflour is used as the thickener – it makes the dessert a beautiful opalescent white. Once unmoulded, it trembles like a jelly – hence the name.

• • •

Mix the cornflour to a smooth paste with a little of the milk. Pour the rest of the milk into a large saucepan, along with the sugar, then stir in the paste. Add the split vanilla pod and mastic, if using. Slowly bring to the boil, stirring all the time, then immediately reduce the heat to medium-low, and continue to stir until the mixture thickens – 10–12 minutes. You'll feel it thickening at first on the base of the pan, so be sure to scrape the base regularly to prevent catching and burning. Keep patiently stirring for another 12–15 minutes until the mixture coats the back of a teaspoon, or a drop remains solid on a chilled plate.

Fish out the vanilla pod, and stir in the rose water. Pour into a bowl or mould, leave to cool, then cover with cling film and chill for a couple of hours.

Meanwhile, make the cardamom brittle. Line a baking sheet with a sheet of silicone. Pour the sugar into a heavy-based saucepan over a medium heat. Let the sugar melt without stirring, shaking the pan occasionally until all the sugar has dissolved. Increase the heat slightly and bring to the boil. Let it bubble away for a few minutes until evenly golden. Stir in the cardamom seeds and boil for a few more seconds. Pour on to the silicone-lined baking sheet, tilting it so that the brittle spreads in a very thin layer. Once it's set solid, break into shards or small fragments.

When ready to serve, turn out the balouza on to a beautiful serving plate and scatter with shards of brittle.

cook's notes
- Mastic is dried crystals of sap from the mastic tree. A popular ingredient in the Middle East, it adds a certain something to the texture of desserts and ices. It's easy to buy online and in shops selling Middle Eastern groceries.
- When making the brittle, watch the bubbling sugar like a hawk. It can burn very quickly.

almond and bergamot turkish delight

vegetable oil for greasing
sugar 450g (1lb)
cream of tartar or citric acid
  ½ teaspoon
mastic crystals 3 (optional),
  crushed with 1 teaspoon
  granulated sugar (see
  Cook's notes)
water 800ml (27fl oz)
cornflour 110g (4oz), plus extra
  for dusting
orange food colouring a few
  drops
orange blossom water
  1 tablespoon
whole almonds 90g (3¼oz),
  roughly chopped
candied bergamot peel 100g
  (3½oz), or other flavour, diced
  (see Cook's notes)

makes about 500g (1lb 2oz)

Though full of Eastern promise, Turkish Delight can be a challenge, especially if you live, like I do, in a damp part of the world. That said, once you get to grips with the essentials, it really is a delight. You can play with flavours, colours and add-ins to your heart's content. Cornflour plays its usual role as a thickener, this time in a sugar-and-water syrup. It also has an important role in drying the cubes of jelly. Ideally, you'll need a 32-cup silicone ice cube tray to use as a mould. Failing that a small roasting pan will do.

• • •

If using a silicone ice cube tray, lightly spray it with vegetable oil, then wipe off any excess with paper towels. Otherwise, generously grease a small 23x18cm (9x7in) roasting pan and line the base with baking parchment, then grease the paper too.

Put the sugar, cream of tartar and crushed mastic, if using, in a heavy-based saucepan. Pour in 600ml (1 pint) of the water. Bring just to the boil, stirring to dissolve the sugar. Keep stirring over a medium-low heat until the mixture reaches 120°C (250°F) on a sugar thermometer.

Meanwhile, put the cornflour in a saucepan with 200ml (7fl oz) of the water. Whisk to a smooth milky liquid, then put the pan over a medium-low heat. Keep whisking until the mixture thickens to a smooth paste – about 8 minutes.

Take the sugar pan off the heat and stir a ladleful of the syrup into the cornflour paste. Next, slowly pour the cornflour mixture into the syrup, stirring all the time. Put the pan over a low heat and keep stirring. After about 5 minutes it will start to thicken from the base. After about 10 minutes it will become quite transparent. Keep stirring, for about 40 minutes in total, or until the mixture plops and spurts like a geyser and you can see the base of the pan when you draw a spoon through the mixture. The longer you cook it, the firmer your Turkish Delight will be.

Now the fun begins. Stir in a few drops of food colouring, the orange blossom water, chopped nuts and candied peel. Pour the mixture into your prepared mould, levelling the surface with a wet palette knife. Leave in a cool, dry place (not the fridge) for several hours to cool down and set.

Turn out on to a tray. If you have used a roasting pan rather than an ice cube tray, slice the block into small cubes. Dust generously with cornflour to prevent sticking. Store in an airtight container, in layers divided with baking parchment. Eat within a few days, occasionally dusting with more cornflour to keep the sweetmeats dry.

cook's notes
- Mastic is dried crystals of sap from the mastic tree. A popular ingredient in the Middle East, it adds a certain something to the texture of desserts and ices. It's easy to buy online and in shops selling Middle Eastern groceries.
- It's well worth using whole chunks of good-quality candied peel, rather than the pre-chopped mixed peel sold in supermarkets. It comes in tempting flavours – bergamot and citron as well as orange and lemon. You'll find it in Italian grocery shops, delis and the better supermarkets.

cornflour

cornmeal

plant source grain
aka cornflour (US), maize flour, masa (Spanish), masarepa, masa harina, polenta
latin name *Zea mays var. indentata*
gluten none
protein 7–9%
goes with avocados, bacon, berries, black beans, cheese, chillies, chorizo, citrus fruits, coconut, eggs, honey, mushrooms, nuts, seafood, stone fruits, tomatoes
uses arepas (patties), batter, binder, biscuits, bread, cakes, chips, coating for fried foods, empanadas (pasties), fritters, muffins, pancakes, polenta, tamales, tortillas

As with cornflour, let's get semantics out of the way and clarify what corn and maize actually mean. Confusingly, corn may be used in a general sense to describe a staple crop – wheat in England and oats in Scotland, for example – whereas maize usually refers to corn-on-the-cob or even cattle fodder. It's complicated and gets more so. In the UK, finely ground cornmeal is often called maize flour. Americans call this cornflour, and as far as they're concerned it's an entirely different product from cornstarch – our term for cornflour in the UK (see page 79). And then there is polenta, which may be yellow or white, fine or coarsely ground. Strictly speaking, this should be called cornmeal since polenta refers to a porridge-like dish popular in northern Italy.

The list goes on. From Central America there is *masa harina* ('dough flour' in Spanish) made from white, blue or yellow corn kernels. These are soaked in a highly alkaline solution of water and slaked lime (calcium hydroxide, not the citrus fruit) to soften the hulls – a process called 'nixtamalization'. Once softened, the hulls are removed and the remaining kernel is ground to a very fine powder. This, in turn, has to be reconstituted with a relatively large amount of water before it becomes dough. In Mexico and elsewhere, you'll see cooks expertly slapping and pounding the dough to make tortillas (see Blue Cornmeal Tortillas, page 90), tostadas, enchiladas and many other corn-based dishes.

Not to be confused with *masa harina* is *harina de maiz precocida* or *masarepa*, non-nixtamalized, precooked cornmeal for making arepas (see page 93). These delicious soft corn patties are popular in Venezuela and Colombia, served plain or stuffed with tasty morsels of whatever is to hand.

Regular, non-nixtamalized cornmeal is an exceptionally versatile alternative to wheat flour, so it's a good choice if you're a coeliac or gluten-sensitive. It contains useful amounts of protein, iron, antioxidants, carotenoids and other vitamins. Whole grain cornmeal contains valuable dietary fibre and resistant starch (see page 205), beneficial for gut health.

Ground from non-sweet 'dent' or 'field corn', cornmeal has a mild flavour and, as you might expect, a pleasant aroma of corn. It happily holds its own with assertive ingredients such as chillies, citrus fruits and aromatic herbs and spices. It's also much appreciated for the appetizing crunch and tasty crisp edges it gives to baked items.

Cornmeal is essential for polenta, a deeply comforting dish that's often dismissed as bland mush, though it is exactly what's needed to go with strongly flavoured dishes. It's easy to make but requires patience – mix one part cornmeal with five parts water and stir over a gentle heat while it plops and thickens. This could take 30–40 minutes, but it allows you to exercise your upper arms and dream at the same time. ('Instant' polenta is a no-no as far as I'm concerned.) Once it's reached a porridge-like consistency, you can serve it wet, like mashed potato, or cooled, cut into shapes and grilled or fried until crisp. Polenta chips are a not-to-be-missed treat, especially when flavoured with plenty of freshly ground black pepper.

Combined with strong wheat flour, cornmeal makes the best-ever sunshine yellow bread (see page 89). And for a colourful gluten-free loaf, combine it with amaranth flour, cheese and chillies in Cheese and Chilli Purple Cornbread (see page 19). You can use cornmeal instead of breadcrumbs as a crisp coating for fried fish fillets, slivers of chicken or vegetable chunks. It's also handy for sprinkling inside cake tins or over a pizza peel to stop the dough from sticking.

Regular cornmeal is easy to find in supermarkets and health food shops. Make sure it's labelled whole grain rather than degermed. If you want to avoid GM foods, check the label and buy an organic brand. You'll find *masa harina* and *masarepa* online, or you can have fun rummaging in shops specializing in Latin American, Caribbean or Mexican groceries.

Degermed cornmeal, *masa harina* and *masarepa* will keep for up to one year without going rancid. Whole grain cornmeal has a shorter shelf life – two or three months in a sealed container in a cool room, or six months in the fridge. It's best to buy it in small quantities and use it right away.

flour

polenta village bread

yellow cornmeal (polenta) 175g
(6oz), plus extra for sprinkling
sea salt 1 tablespoon
boiling water 250ml (9fl oz)
unsalted butter 40g (1½oz),
melted
granulated sugar 2 teaspoons
tepid water 150–175ml
(5–6fl oz)
active dried yeast 1 tablespoon
extra strong white bread flour
450g (1lb), such as Canadian
(see wheat flour: strong,
page 262)
oil for greasing
sea salt flakes

makes 2 loaves

This has to be my favourite bread, inspired by a recipe for Greek
village bread by gifted baker Emmanuel Hadjiandreou. The loaves
are cooked directly on a baking sheet rather than in a tin, which gives
them a wonderful crust.

• • •

Tip the cornmeal and salt in to a large saucepan. Over a
medium heat, gradually whisk in the boiling water, making
sure there are no lumps. Continue to whisk vigorously for
about 3 minutes until the water is absorbed and the mixture
starts to look a little smoother. Stir in the melted butter,
remove from the heat and allow to cool for 10 minutes, or
until the mixture no longer burns when you insert a finger.

Meanwhile, dissolve the sugar in 75ml (2½fl oz) of the tepid
water in a small bowl. Sprinkle with the dried yeast and
leave in a warm place for about 10 minutes until frothy.

Once the cornmeal mixture is tepid, whisk in the yeast
mixture. Gradually add the bread flour, alternating with
tablespoons of the remaining tepid water. Add as much of the
water as necessary to bring the dough together into a clump.

Tip the dough on to a generously floured work surface and
form into a ball. The dough will be sticky, so add more flour
if necessary. Knead for 10–15 minutes, or use a stand mixer
fitted with a dough hook if you have one. Once the dough is
elastic, divide it in half, form into balls, and place in lightly
oiled bowls. Cover with oiled cling film and leave in a warm
place to rise for 2 hours or until doubled in size.

Tip both balls of dough on to a baking tray lined with a sheet
of silicone. Form into two round loaves and lightly sprinkle
with cornmeal. Cover with cling film and leave for 45–60
minutes, or until doubled in size again.

Meanwhile, preheat the oven to 240°C/Gas Mark 9. Put a
large roasting pan in the bottom of the oven.

Slash the top of the dough, sprinkle with sea salt flakes and a
little more cornmeal. Pour some water into the roasting pan
and reduce the oven temperature to 220°C/Gas Mark 7. Bake
on the middle shelf for 25–35 minutes, rotating the baking
tray halfway through, or until the bread sounds hollow when
you tap the bottom. Leave the loaves to cool on to a wire rack.

blue cornmeal tortillas with tomato, avocado and chilli salsa

cornflour for dusting
vegetable oil for greasing
masa harina azul 200g (7oz)
  (see Cook's notes)
hot water 280ml (9½fl oz) (not
  boiling), plus extra cold water
  as needed

for the salsa
tomatoes 7 firm ripe
red onions 2 small, diced
mild green chillies 1–2, such as
  Poblano, deseeded and diced
fresh hot red chilli 1, such as
  Cayenne (optional), deseeded
  and diced
avocado 1, cut into 1cm (½in)
  chunks
limes juice of 2
sea salt flakes to taste
coriander small bunch, tough
  stalks discarded, leaves sliced

to serve
soured cream
hard cheese coarsely grated
black beans cooked
chicken cooked morsels

makes about 12

These tortillas are made with *masa harina* ('dough flour' in Spanish), a type of specially treated cornmeal used for tortillas and tamales. It's easy to find online (see Sources, page 280) and in some delis and supermarkets. *Masa harina* comes in blue (*azul*), yellow or white. The blue is more popular in New Mexico, where I learned to make these tortillas.

• • •

If you have a tortilla press, cut two squares of polythene (I use a thick plastic bag) a bit bigger than the round plates of the press. Otherwise, flour your work surface and a rolling pin – preferably a small, slim one for rolling flat breads. You'll also need to lightly grease a heavy-based smallish non-stick frying pan (about 18cm/7in across the base).

Sieve the masa harina into a bowl. Mix any husks left in the sieve back into the bowl. Stir in the hot water. Use your hands to mix to a smooth, stiff dough that feels like Play-Doh. Cover with a damp tea towel and leave for 30 minutes.

While the dough is resting, make the salsa. Halve the tomatoes crossways and scoop out the seeds and juice (use these in another dish). Place the halves cut-side down on a board. Using a sharp serrated knife, cut into 5mm (¼in) slices, holding the slices tightly together. Then slice neatly crossways to create 5mm (¼in) dice. Tip into a serving bowl. Add the diced red onion, chillies and avocado. Stir in the lime juice, sea salt flakes and coriander leaves. Leave to stand at room temperature for at least 30 minutes to allow the flavours to develop.

Returning to the dough, you may find it feels a bit drier. Use your hands again to work in a little more water, a tablespoon at a time, until it is softer but not sticky (see Cook's notes). Weigh the dough and divide into 12 chunks. Roll into smooth golf-ball-sized balls and cover with a damp tea towel while you work.

Place one ball on the bottom plate of your plastic-lined tortilla press and press it into a 12cm (4½in) circle about 2mm (⅟₁₆in) thick. Otherwise, roll it out on a well-floured surface.

Spray your pan with oil and place over a medium to medium-high heat. Once hot, drop in the tortilla. Shake the pan to prevent sticking, then fry the tortilla for 1–2 minutes, or until the underside is lightly flecked with brown and the

cornmeal

top, hopefully, is starting to look puffy in places. Flip it over and cook the other side for a minute or two. Keep warm on a paper-towel-lined plate while you cook the rest. Spray the pan with oil as necessary.

Once you've cooked all the tortillas, stack them in a basket lined with a nice cloth. Cover them with the cloth and leave for 10 minutes to relax and finish cooking. Top with the salsa and any of my other serving suggestions.

cook's notes
- If you can't get hold of blue masa harina, it's fine to use yellow or white instead.
- The amount of water needed for the dough depends on all sorts of variables: the humidity and temperature of the room, the age of the masa, the temperature of your hands, for example. You may not even need to add any more. You'll know when the dough feels just right.
- Put the salsa and the other serving suggestions in bowls and let your guests help themselves.

arepas

arepa flour (*harina de maíz precocida*) 140g (5oz)
sea salt ½ teaspoon
water 250ml (9fl oz)
Cheddar cheese 50g (1¾oz), grated (see Cook's note)
vegetable oil for shallow frying
lime wedges to serve

makes 8 as a snack

A Latin American favourite, these flat corn cakes are made with finely ground white or yellow cornmeal (or 'corn flour' as fine cornmeal is known in the US). It's a particular type of pre-cooked flour, known as *masarepa* or *harina de maíz precocida*. It's easy to buy online (see Sources, page 280) or you can find it in shops selling Latin American groceries. Arepas are really easy to make and addictively delicious, so it's well worth getting hold of the flour. Recipes vary depending on country, region, community or even family. Arepas can be thin and crispy, as here, or thick enough to split open and stuff with whatever you have to hand – a combo of cooked chicken, avocado, red onion and black beans is good.

• • •

Sieve the arepa flour and salt into a large bowl. Make a well in the centre and pour in all the water. Mix with a fork, stirring from the centre and gradually drawing in the dry ingredients from around the edge. Once you have a soft dough, stir in the cheese, mixing well. Set aside for 15 minutes, or longer, to allow the flour to absorb the liquid.

Divide the dough into eight balls, then flatten into discs measuring 80x5mm (3¼x¼in) – it's easiest to do this on a sheet of silicone so they don't stick.

In a large non-stick pan, heat enough oil for shallow frying over a medium-high heat. Add the arepas, in batches if necessary. Give them a little shunt to make sure they don't stick to the pan. Lower the heat to medium, then fry for 6–8 minutes, turning once, until golden and crisp on both sides.

Arrange in a serving dish and garnish with lime wedges. Serve hot, warm or at room temperature.

cook's note
· As an alternative to Cheddar, use any cheese that melts unctuously – mozzarella or Gruyère, for example.

cricket *flour*

plant source insect
aka cricket powder
latin name *Acheta domesticus, Gryllodes sigillatus*
gluten none
protein 56–57%
goes with chocolate, citrus, dried fruit, nuts, warm spices
uses biscuits, brownies, cakes, pastry

Even though humans have been eating insects for hundreds of years, it takes a giant leap of faith for most of us to overcome hard-wired distaste. I have to say I approached cricket flour with some trepidation, despite my usual openness to new ingredients.

Made from roasted ground crickets, the flour is a relative newcomer to the market. Containing a massive amount of high-quality protein (see page 59), the flour is considered by some to be a feasible answer to unsustainable meat-eating and the food shortages predicted for the coming decades. Price is an issue, however. While basketloads of edible insects sell very cheaply in parts of Africa and Asia, in the West the flour currently costs over 150 times more than plain wheat flour.

As I quickly discovered, there are differences between brands of flour and varieties of cricket. A brand made with *Acheta domesticus* resembled clumpy soil with an unpleasant whiff of fish food. On the other hand, one made with *Gryllodes sigillatus* was free-flowing, warm brown and twinkling with what looked like specks of fool's gold – ground cricket wings, perhaps? The aroma was malty, redolent of old-fashioned milky bedtime drinks, and the flavour pleasantly savoury.

The advice for baking is to replace 10 per cent of the flour with cricket flour, or 5 per cent of the overall ingredients. With this in mind, I developed a recipe for a rum-flavoured spicy fruit cake (see page 97) on the basis that other ingredients would be robust enough to prevent possibly unwelcome cricket flavours from dominating. The cake was surprisingly good and I would certainly make it again.

At the time of writing, cricket flour hasn't reached supermarket shelves, but it's easy to find online (see Sources, page 280).

flour

rum-soaked prune and sultana cake

soft pitted prunes 250g (9oz)

raisins or large sultanas 85g (3oz)

rum 150ml (5fl oz) (see Cook's notes)

oil for greasing

self-raising flour 100g (3½oz)

wholemeal self-raising flour 100g (3½oz)

organic cricket flour 25g (1oz), such as Crobar

mixed spice 1 tablespoon

sea salt ¼ teaspoon

rapeseed oil 2 tablespoons

eggs 2, lightly beaten

egg whites 4

apple juice concentrate or clear honey to glaze

skinless toasted hazelnuts 40g (1½oz), halved

good-quality candied citrus peel 40g (1½oz), such as orange, bergamot or lemon, diced

makes one 23cm (9in) cake

If you are curious about cricket flour, try it first in this low-fat cake. A relatively small amount is combined with wheat flour, sweet spices, rum-soaked prunes and sultanas. The flour adds extra protein, making this a particularly nutritious cake. Allow plenty of time for soaking the prunes and sultanas.

• • •

Soak the prunes and raisins in the rum for 3 or 4 hours, or overnight. Drain, reserving the liquid, chop the prunes roughly and set aside.

Grease the base and sides of a 22–23cm (8½–9in) loose-bottomed cake tin. Line with baking parchment and grease the paper too. Preheat the oven to 170°C/Gas Mark 3.

Put the three flours, mixed spice and the salt into a sieve set over a bowl. Muddle with your fingers, then shake through the sieve. Sieve once or twice more until well blended.

In a large bowl, beat together the oil, 100ml (3½fl oz) of the reserved rum and the whole eggs. Stir in the prunes and raisins, followed by the flour mixture.

Beat the egg whites in a separate bowl until stiff but not dry. Fold about one-third of the whites into the batter to slacken it, then gently fold in the rest. Pour into the prepared cake tin.

Bake for 50–60 minutes, rotating every 20 minutes, until a skewer inserted in the centre comes out clean. Leave in the tin for 10 minutes before turning out on to a wire rack. Paint with the apple juice concentrate while still warm, then strew with hazelnuts and candied citrus peel. Leave to cool completely before slicing.

cook's notes
· For an alcohol-free cake, use apple juice instead of rum.
· The sweetness comes from the prunes and raisins. If you would like a sweeter cake add 2 tablespoons of muscovado sugar.

einkorn *flour*

plant source grain
aka petit épeautre (French), piccolo farro (Italian)
latin name *Triticum monococcum*
protein/gluten 10–14%
goes with anything
uses biscuits, bread, cakes, pancakes, pastry, thickener for sauces, soups and stews

As a newcomer to einkorn flour, and a tad sceptical about rave reviews, I was genuinely astonished by the difference the flour made to my baking, and to my digestion. Pastry made with it was exceptionally crisp and well flavoured, and I had no bloating or sleepiness after eating einkorn bread. The flour is also attractive to look at – a sunny golden cream – with an enticing aroma of sweet hay.

Meaning 'one grain', and so-called because of the single grain attached to the stem rather than the usual cluster of four, einkorn is said to be the purest and most ancient form of wheat. Unlike modern wheat, it hasn't been hybridized, which, in simple terms, means that it hasn't been crossbred with another variety. Domesticated in southern Turkey about 10,000 years ago, einkorn spread through the Balkans to Central and Northern Europe. For a while it was a staple grain, but as other wheat varieties evolved – emmer (see page 102) and spelt (see page 208), for example – einkorn gradually disappeared off the culinary map.

Einkorn flour isn't easy to harvest and mill. It's not as tall as modern wheat, which makes mechanized harvesting more difficult. The grains are noticeably smaller and they have tough, tightly clinging husks that cause problems with threshing. The yields are about one-fifth of modern wheat, so it's not popular with profit-seeking farmers. And yet, despite the not insignificant drawbacks, einkorn has been enjoying a recent renaissance. It's being produced by niche farmers in Italy; books, magazine articles and recipes proliferate, and the flour has become easy to find online, in supermarkets and health food shops.

The driving force behind this upturn is undoubtedly the gluten issue. For sure, einkorn contains gluten, so coeliac sufferers should steer clear of it. On the other hand, a significant number of the gluten-sensitive find einkorn far easier to digest. The reason for this is that it contains less gliadin and glutenin (see Gluten, page 60), the proteins responsible for elastic dough and well-risen bread.

For non-scientists, this may be a hard concept to grasp. The difference, however, becomes more obvious when kneading bread dough – normally a lengthy process designed to activate gluten and make the dough more elastic. Since einkorn flour is low in gluten, kneading doesn't significantly alter the stickiness, whereas in other wheat flours, kneading reduces stickiness and makes the dough more elastic. So, if you're making bread with einkorn flour, accept the stickiness, and remember to knead by hand rather than with a mixer.

In pastry-making the situation is reversed. The aim is not to develop the gluten, so kneading should be minimal, otherwise your pastry will be tough rather than crisp. The lower levels of gluten in einkorn flour are therefore an advantage. Try the pastry in Spiced Pumpkin Pie (see page 100) and see for yourself.

In general, when substituting einkorn flour for ordinary flour, it's fine to use the same amount. Be aware that einkorn flour absorbs liquids more slowly, so if your cake or bread dough seems too wet at first, be patient and don't be tempted to add more flour. Remember, also, that dough made with einkorn flour doesn't rise as exuberantly as dough made with ordinary wheat flour. When adapting recipes you may need to compensate by adding a raising agent such as baking powder or bicarbonate of soda.

spiced pumpkin pie

pumpkin or winter squash
   900g (2lb) unpeeled (see
   Cook's note)
vegetable oil for greasing
granulated sugar 100g (3½oz)
ginger root 1½ teaspoons,
   grated
ground cinnamon ½ teaspoon
nutmeg ⅛ teaspoon, freshly
   grated, plus extra
   for sprinkling
ground cloves good pinch
salt ¾ teaspoon
double cream 175ml (6fl oz),
   preferably organic
whole milk 175m (6fl oz),
   preferably organic
eggs 2 large, organic or
   free-range
egg yolks 2 large
vanilla extract ¾ teaspoon
icing sugar for sprinkling
whipped cream to serve

for the pastry
einkorn flour 200g (7oz)
sea salt ¼ teaspoon
unsalted butter 100g (3½oz)
   chilled, diced
iced water 2 tablespoons plus
   1 teaspoon
egg white 1, lightly beaten,
   for brushing

serves 8

Even though it's wholemeal, einkorn flour makes a beautifully crisp pastry case that contrasts so well with the trembling filling.

. . .

Preheat the oven to 180°C/Gas Mark 4. Leaving the peel in place, cut the pumpkin into large chunks and scrape out the seeds. Place skin-side down in a roasting pan, cover tightly with foil and bake for 45–55 minutes until soft. Once cool enough to handle, remove the peel. Whizz the flesh in a food processor until reasonably smooth. You should end up with about 425g (15oz) of purée.

Meanwhile, make the pastry. Sift the flour and salt into a roomy bowl. Add the diced butter and rub in between the tips of your fingers and thumbs. Hold your hands well above the bowl so that the flour drifts down, incorporating air as it does so, and you can see any fragments of butter that still need rubbing in. Sprinkle most of the water over the surface and stir until the mixture begins to clump together. Sprinkle with a little more water if the dough seems dry. Gather it into a ball then flatten to a thick disc ready for rolling out. Wrap the dough in greaseproof paper and leave to rest at room temperature for 15 minutes.

Lightly grease a 23cm (9in) diameter, 4cm (1½in) deep, loose-based tart tin. Roll the dough out to a 32cm (13in) circle and carefully lift it into the tin. Using the side of your index finger, press the dough into the fluted edge so that it is slightly higher than the rim. Patch any cracks and paint the base with lightly beaten egg white. Chill for 15 minutes.

Increase the oven temperature to 200°C/Gas Mark 6. Line the pastry case with foil, and weigh down with baking beans, making sure they go to the edge. Bake for 15 minutes, then remove the foil and beans, rotate the tin and bake for 6–8 minutes more, until the pastry is light brown and the base is cooked. Remove from the oven and keep warm.

While the pastry is baking, combine the pumpkin purée, sugar, ginger, cinnamon, nutmeg, cloves and salt in a heavy-based saucepan. Simmer over a medium heat, stirring constantly, for 5 minutes. Remove the pan from the heat.

Whisk the cream, milk, eggs, yolks and vanilla together in a bowl, then whisk this into the pumpkin mixture in the pan. Strain through a sieve set over a bowl, pressing hard with the back of a wooden spoon to extract as much liquid

flour

as possible. Briefly whisk again and pour into the warm pastry case. Return to the oven and bake for 10 minutes, then reduce the oven temperature to 150°C/Gas Mark 2 and continue baking for 30–40 minutes, or until the filling is set. Cover the pastry with strips of foil if it browns too much.

Remove from the oven and put the tin on a wire rack. Loosen the pastry with the tip of a knife, then leave to cool in the tin. Carefully move the pie to a serving plate and dust with icing sugar and a little nutmeg. Serve at room temperature with whipped cream.

cook's note
- Roasting the pumpkin rather than steaming or boiling brings out the flavour and gets rid of excess liquid. Don't even think about canned pumpkin pie filling; it may be convenient but it has very little flavour.

einkorn *flour*

emmer *flour*

plant source grain
aka farro media (Italian)
latin name *Triticum dicoccum*
protein/gluten 12–14%
goes with chocolate, cheese, Mediterranean vegetables
uses biscuits, bread, brownies, pasta, pastry, pizza base, thickener for sauces, soups and stews

If you look up emmer wheat in a cookbook or reference book, be prepared for a can of worms. Frequently you'll be redirected to 'farro', or you might find it called 'true farro', or *farro media* in Italian, or 'hulled wheat', 'starch wheat' or 'rice wheat'. As the erudite historian Andrew Dalby sensibly suggests in *Food in the Ancient World*, 'These terms are confusing and best avoided'.

Emmer was one of the first crops to be domesticated. The Roman naturalist Pliny the Elder wrote that emmer was the oldest wheat – even in his day (AD 23–79). As such it's been fittingly called 'the mother-ship of flour'. There is a rather pleasing account on archaeological websites of an Egyptian pregnancy test dating back to around 1350BC. The theory goes that emmer and barley grains will germinate if a pregnant woman urinates on them; if she isn't pregnant they won't. The test also predicted gender – germinated barley signified a boy, emmer a girl. Interestingly, archaeologists replicated the test in the 1960s and apparently found it 70 per cent accurate.

Like most ancient grains, emmer is pest- and drought-tolerant, it thrives without fertilizers, but is not easy to harvest and mill. It grows to an inconvenient 2 metres (6½ feet), and the grains are tightly enclosed in a tough glume or husk that makes threshing difficult. In the past, the grains were extricated by heavy-duty pounding with a massive pestle and mortar – a backbreaking task that was allocated to convicts as hard labour. Mechanized milling eventually took over, but inevitably emmer was gradually abandoned in favour of wheat varieties that were easier to process.

Compared with modern wheat, emmer grains are unusually flat and pointed, with creamy stripes running along the length. The flour itself is what I think of as an old-style Birkenstock type of flour – worthy, easy to use, but unprepossessing. It's fine-textured, free-flowing and, being naturally whole grain, it contains the nutritious bran.

The flour has an unexpectedly feisty flavour that belies its understated looks. Robust, nutty and slightly sweet, it's a natural partner for equally robust ingredients such as chocolate, cheese and Mediterranean vegetables. Try it in Mushroom, Artichoke and Tomato Pizza (see page 105) or the irresistibly crunchy Salted Cacao Biscuits (see page 107).

Emmer has always been popular in parts of Italy, particularly Tuscany and Umbria. There, the grain shows up in appetizing salads, side dishes and hearty soups, while the flour goes into somewhat chewy but nevertheless delectable bread. In the rest of Europe, emmer has made a significant comeback, spearheaded by chefs and food writers, an increasingly health-conscious public, and dedicated farmers and millers.

A likely reason for this newfound popularity is that many people find emmer flour easier to digest. Though it's not gluten-free, the gluten (see page 60) has a weaker structure and breaks down more easily, which could account for the tolerance. It's also high in protein and fibre and a good source of resistant starch (see page 205), which generally improves gut health.

Emmer flour works well as an alternative in any recipe specifying wheat flour. It's excellent for biscuits and brownies, or other baked items that don't need to rise very much. For bread and pizza dough, it's best to combine it with strong wheat flour – about one-third wheat to two-thirds emmer. Bear in mind that emmer dough is denser than ordinary wheat dough, and absorbs more moisture. To compensate, gradually add about 25 per cent more liquid, and perhaps an extra egg.

You'll also find that bread dough will be stickier because of the weaker gluten. No amount of kneading will improve this, nor will adding extra flour. It's best to accept the stickiness and knead just enough to make the dough soft and pliable rather than super-stretchy. It's a good idea to do this by hand, rather than in a mixer, so you have more control over texture. It's also worth baking your loaf in a well-greased tin rather than freeform on a baking sheet.

Because emmer is a naturally whole grain flour, it contains more fat and therefore has a shorter shelf life. Decant it into an airtight container rather than leaving it in an opened packet, and store in the fridge or another cool, dry place.

flour

mushroom, artichoke and tomato pizza

for the dough (for three pizza bases)
sugar 1 teaspoon
warm water 300ml (10fl oz)
dried active yeast 1 tablespoon
emmer flour 450g (1lb)
strong wheat flour 150g (5½oz)
sea salt 2 teaspoons
olive oil 1 tablespoon, plus
    extra for greasing and painting
    the edges of the pizza

for the topping (for one pizza)
olive oil 2 tablespoons
chestnut mushrooms 300g
    (10½oz), sliced
dried oregano 2 teaspoons
passata 5 tablespoons
oil-cured bottled artichokes
    3–4, drained and quartered
baby plum tomatoes 9, halved
    lengthways
garlic cloves 2 fat, thinly
    sliced lengthways
mozzarella cheese 125g
    (4½oz), shredded (see
    Cook's note)
sea salt and freshly ground
    black pepper

makes three 30cm (12in) pizza
    bases

Emmer flour is wholemeal, but it makes a beautifully light pizza base with a distinctive nutty flavour. It's best with a robust topping, as here. The dough makes three pizza bases – it's not really worth making a smaller quantity. If you want to make one pizza only, divide the spare dough into two portions and freeze it before you let it rise. The topping is enough for one pizza. Treble it if cooking for a crowd, or try some of my other topping suggestions overleaf.

• • •

First make the dough. In a small bowl, dissolve the sugar in 150ml (5fl oz) of the warm water. Sprinkle with the yeast and whisk thoroughly. Leave in a warm place for 15 minutes until the surface is covered with froth.

Meanwhile, put the two flours and sea salt into a sieve set over a bowl. Muddle with your fingers, then shake through the sieve. Sieve twice more until well blended. Tip the bran remaining in the sieve into the flour in the bowl. Mix in the yeast mixture, the rest of the warm water and the olive oil. Knead for at least 10 minutes until silky smooth and springy. Shape into a ball and put in a lightly oiled bowl. Cover with cling film and leave to rise in a warm place for 2 hours or more, until doubled in size.

Divide the dough into three. Freeze two balls if you don't want to use them right away. Alternatively, store them in the fridge for up to 24 hours, covered with cling film. Punch the air out of the dough you are going to use. Put on a baking sheet and cover with cling film.

Preheat the oven to 240°C/Gas Mark 9, or the highest setting. Grease a perforated pizza pan.

To make the topping, heat the olive oil in a large frying pan over a medium-high heat. Add the mushrooms, oregano, and sea salt and freshly ground black pepper to taste. Fry for 6–7 minutes or until the mushrooms release their juices, then drain thoroughly.

Flatten a ball of dough on a floured surface, prodding with your fingertips to remove the air. Roll out to a 30cm (12in) circle and lift on to the pizza pan. Spread with your fingers to make a slightly thicker rim. Spread the passata over the base, using your fingertips. Arrange the drained mushrooms, artichokes, tomatoes and garlic on top. Season with sea salt and freshly ground black pepper, then sprinkle with the mozzarella cheese. Paint the edges with olive oil.

emmer *flour*

Bake for 5 minutes, then rotate the pan and bake for 2–3 minutes more, or until the cheese is bubbling and the edges are crisp. Remove from the oven and leave to rest for a few minutes to allow the oil to soak into the base.

topping variations
- Pre-grilled aubergine slices, piquillo peppers, tomatoes, olives
- Chicory, gorgonzola, walnuts
- Pancetta, red onions, goat cheese, caper berries

cook's note
- It's best to use pre-grated mozzarella or 'cooking' mozzarella (mozzarella *cucina*), sold in a block. Fresh mozzarella gives off too much liquid for a pizza topping.

salted cacao biscuits

coconut sugar or muscovado
   sugar 100g (3½oz)
unsalted butter 75g (2¾oz)
milk 1½ tablespoons
vanilla extract 2 teaspoons
emmer flour 100g (3½oz)
baking powder ¼ teaspoon
sea salt ⅛ teaspoon, plus extra
   for sprinkling
cacao nibs 4 tablespoons

makes 12

Emmer flour makes wonderfully light, crisp biscuits, particularly irresistible studded with cacao nibs – mini-nuggets of melted chocolate deliciousness – and topped with crunchy sea salt flakes. It's well worth making double the quantity.

• • •

Preheat the oven to 190°C/Gas Mark 5. Line a baking tray with a sheet of silicone.

Tip the sugar and butter into a large deep bowl. Using an electric whisk, cream for 4–5 minutes until pale and fluffy. Beat in the milk and vanilla extract.

Put the flour, baking powder and sea salt into a sieve set over a bowl. Muddle with your fingers, then shake through the sieve. Add to the butter mixture, combining with a fork. Fold in the cacao nibs, mixing well.

With well-floured hands, divide the mixture into 12 walnut-sized lumps and arrange them on the silicone-lined baking tray. Flatten into 4cm (1½in) discs, leaving about 5cm (2in) between them. Sprinkle very lightly with sea salt flakes.

Bake for 10–12 minutes, rotating the tray halfway through, or until the edges begin to darken. Remove from the oven and put the tray on a wire rack. Leave for 5 minutes while the biscuits firm up. Remove the biscuits from the tray and arrange directly on the rack. Leave to cool completely.

fava bean *flour*

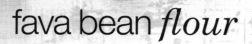

plant source pulse
aka broad bean flour
latin name *Vicia faba*
gluten none
protein 27%
goes with cheese, eggs, Mediterranean vegetables, onions, pickles
uses batter, bread, dips, flatbreads, fritters, pancakes, pasta, pastry, pizza, thickener
    for sauces and soups

The first time I sampled fava bean flour was in 'deluxe medieval pottage', an unexpected concoction of almond milk, ginger, fava bean flour, honey and rose petals, rustled up for lunch by Josiah Meldrum of Hodmedod, a pioneering company dedicated to growing and marketing British-grown pulses and grains. On a sweltering day, the pottage, or soup, was beautiful and cooling, and it tasted remarkably good, too.

As Josiah pointed out, fava beans, or dried broad beans, were eaten long before fresh broad beans. They date back to the Iron Age in the UK, and are still a major farm crop. Experts disagree as to whether the bean originated in Mediterranean/Middle Eastern countries, or in western Asia and beyond. Needless to say, it has a long history and may have been one of the earliest beans to be domesticated.

Fava beans get surprisingly few mentions in cookbooks and other reference books. This may be because the tough skin and mealy texture of mature beans are not to everyone's liking. Or because they are flatulence-inducing. Or perhaps it's because of persisting superstitions: the Egyptians regarded the beans as unclean, while the Greek philosopher Pythagoras wouldn't go near them. There was also a belief that the souls of the dead might migrate into the beans, and it would therefore be wrong to eat them. Sicilians call them *fave dei morti*, 'Beans of the dead'.

Superstition aside, the flour itself is milled from a small, hard variety of field bean. These are more strongly flavoured than fresh broad beans, and are left in the field until completely dry before harvesting. Once harvested, they're cleaned, mechanically split, skinned, and then milled to a fine, creamy, gluten-free flour.

Nutritionally, the flour is exceptionally high in protein, although like all pulses, it doesn't contain the essential amino acid methionine (see Protein, page 59). It's high in fibre, well endowed with vitamins and minerals, and a good source of resistant starch (see page 205), which generally improves gut health.

The flour certainly has a feisty flavour. Lick a flour-dipped finger and you'll get earthiness and a slightly bitter aftertaste – rather like mature raw peas. It works best in savoury items combined with other robust flavours. Try it with emmer flour in Mushroom, Artichoke and Tomato Pizza (see page 105). For an extra hit of nutrients, use it as a binder for burgers and fritters, or stir a spoonful or two into sauces and soups to thicken them.

The flour really comes into its own as a natural flour improver. Though it's gluten-free, it contains certain enzymes which indirectly lengthen the gluten proteins in wheat flour (see Gluten, page 60), and this helps speed up the rise in bread dough. Try replacing about 25 per cent wheat flour with fava bean flour, as in Bean Flour Wholemeal Bread (see page 110) and you'll be pleasantly surprised at the difference. You can also use the flour to make superb pasta, either on its own or blended with a little wheat flour to provide gluten and make it easier to work. Pancakes can made entirely with fava bean flour, but let the batter rest for an hour before frying. If gluten is off-limits, mix it with another gluten-free flour such as sorghum (see page 196), which will also tame the assertive flavour. You'll also need a raising agent for bread dough, and a binder such as xanthan gum or guar gum when making pastry.

The flour hasn't yet hit many supermarket shelves, but you can buy it in farm shops, health food shops or online from Hodmedods (see Sources, page 280). To keep it at its best, empty it into an airtight container rather than leave it in the opened packet, and store in the fridge or another cool, dry place.

For super-fresh flour, try milling your own using split dried fava beans. They're easy to find online and in shops selling Middle Eastern groceries. Use a milling attachment for a standing mixer, and grind in small batches so as not to overwork your mill. A NutriBullet is another option, but it produces coarser flour that needs sieving to get rid of unwelcome bits and pieces.

fava bean flour wholemeal bread

fava bean flour 125g (4½oz)
vegetable oil for greasing
strong wholemeal bread flour
 500g (1lb 2oz)
sea salt 1 teaspoon
sugar 1 teaspoon
easy-bake dried yeast
 1¾ teaspoons
warm water 350–400ml
 (12–14fl oz)
rapeseed oil 2 tablespoons

makes 1 loaf

This recipe is adapted from one given to me by Carol Kearns, creator of the beautiful illustrations on Hodmedod's packaging for bean flours and pulses (see Sources, page 280). Carol was pleasantly surprised by the difference fava bean flour makes to bread made with wholemeal flour. She says, 'The finished loaf has a much lighter texture [something much prized in a wholemeal loaf] and the crust has a divinely nutty taste.' Combined with strong wholemeal bread flour, bean flour does indeed make an impressive loaf. The bread makes substantial sandwiches and terrific toast.

• • •

Preheat the oven to 180°C/Gas Mark 4.

Spread the fava bean flour on a small baking tray, and toast in the oven for 10–15 minutes until it just starts to change colour and give off a beany fragrance. Watch the flour with an eagle eye – it can burn very quickly. Tip into a large mixing bowl and leave to cool.

Meanwhile, thoroughly grease the base and sides of a 20x10x6cm (8x4x2½in) loaf tin. Line with baking parchment and grease the paper too.

Tip the wholemeal flour, fava bean flour, sea salt, sugar and yeast into a large sieve set over a bowl. Muddle with your fingers, then push through the sieve two or three times until well mixed. Return to the bowl any bran left in the sieve.

Make a well in the centre, then pour in enough of the water to bind the ingredients together. Using a wooden spoon, gradually draw in the dry ingredients from round the edge to form a soft dough. Leave it for 5 minutes to absorb the moisture, then mix in the rapeseed oil.

Turn out on to a floured work surface and form into a ball. Knead for 5–10 minutes until smooth. Put into a lightly greased bowl, cover with greased cling film and leave in a warm place for 1 hour or until doubled in size.

Turn out and knead again for 7 minutes. Form the dough into a rectangle with the short end nearest to you. Pull the edge furthest away over to fold the dough in half. Pinch the edges together. Put in the greased loaf tin and slash the top in three or four places. Cover and leave in a warm place for another hour until well risen.

Preheat the oven to 220°C/Gas Mark 7. Bake the loaf on the middle shelf for 30–40 minutes, rotating halfway through, or until it sounds hollow when you rap the base of the tin. If it's not quite cooked, take it out of the tin and put it back in the oven, lying on its side, and bake for another 5 minutes. Remove from the oven and leave to cool on a wire rack.

khorasan *flour*

plant source grain
aka Kamut®
latin name *Triticum turgidum,* subsp. *turanicum*
protein/gluten 12–18%
goes with bananas, cheese, nuts, oranges
uses biscuits, brownies, dessert toppings, pastry, pizza, quick breads, scones,
   thickener for sauces, soups, stews

It took me a while to figure out that kamut and khorasan are basically the same ancient variety of wheat. Kamut® is the brand name for khorasan, trademarked in the US and Canada by Kamut International, a company founded by Montana-based farmer Bob Quinn and his father, who wanted to protect the quality and genetic purity of the wheat. To be called Kamut®, the wheat must meet their mega-stringent criteria, otherwise it's simply classified as khorasan. The somewhat exotic names kamut and khorasan are respectively derived from the ancient Egyptian word for 'wheat', and the Khorasan province of northeast Iran where this particular variety of wheat originated.

As an ancient grain, probably descended from emmer wheat (see page 102), khorasan isn't picky about where it grows. Like emmer, it's drought- and pest-resistant, and grows to a monumental 2 metres (6½ feet). This creates shade, which discourages weeds and, in turn, removes the need for weed killers and pesticides. The downside is that khorasan isn't machine-friendly – it's difficult to harvest and thresh. As a result, it was gradually abandoned over the centuries in favour of more easily processed varieties of wheat. The good news is that it's enjoying a well-deserved renaissance, thanks to enthusiastic farmers, millers and chefs, and a prominent presence in food media.

The plant itself is striking, instantly recognizable by its dramatic super-long black awns, or whiskers, protruding from the seed head. The grains nestling at their base are colossal – about three times the size of wheat grains. With their bronze colour and a marked cleft, they remind me of mini hot dog rolls.

The flour is delightful – creamy yellow, slightly clumpy, with a clean buttery flavour that really shines through. During milling, the nutritious outer layer of bran is left intact, so the flour is naturally whole grain. It's high-protein, high-fibre, and a good source of resistant starch (see page 205), which generally improves gut health. Anecdotally, khorasan flour is tolerated by people who are sensitive to wheat. Though it contains gluten and is therefore off-limits for coeliac sufferers, the structure is weaker than the gluten in modern wheat, which may account for the reputed tolerance.

Khorasan flour works well in any recipe specifying wheat flour. In general, substitute about 50 per cent khorasan for wheat flour. You can bump it up to 100 per cent, but the texture is likely to be more dense and crumbly. This is fine for items that don't need to rise very much, such as biscuits and brownies, or the topping for the Pear, Cranberry and Cardamom Cobbler (see page 115), but not so good for items where the rise is important. For light, fluffy cakes and muffins you'll need help from a raising agent such as baking powder or bicarbonate of soda. Bear in mind, too, that the flour is hydroscopic, meaning it absorbs more liquid than wheat flours. To compensate, gradually add about 25 per cent more water or other liquid such as buttermilk, which usefully acts as a raising agent too. I like to use khorasan flour for trouble-free quick breads such as soda bread or banana bread. I have also used it successfully for a crackling crisp pizza crust (substitute it for emmer flour in the recipe on page 105), as well as immaculate scones and muffins.

Khorasan flour isn't always on supermarket shelves, but it's easy to find online and in good health food shops. To keep it at its best, empty it into an airtight container rather than leave it in an opened packet, and store in a cool, dry place.

flour

pear, cranberry and cardamom cobbler

khorasan flour 175g (6oz)
baking powder 1½ teaspoons
sea salt ½ teaspoon
cardamom pods seeds from
 4, ground to a powder
caster sugar 55g (2oz)
unsalted butter 55g (2oz)
 chilled, diced, plus extra for
 greasing
egg yolk 1, organic or free-
 range
buttermilk 75ml (2½fl oz)

for the filling
pears 6 firm, such as
 Conference
lemon juice of 1 large
unsalted butter 55g (2oz)
caster sugar 55g (2oz), plus
 extra for sprinkling (see
 Cook's note)
cardamom pods seeds from
 5, lightly crushed
cranberries 75g (2¾oz),
 pickled, fresh or defrosted
 frozen (see Cook's note)
flaked almonds 2 tablespoons

serves 5–6

A high-protein alternative to ordinary wheat flour, khorasan makes an easy-to-handle nutty-flavoured dough, which is lovely on top of the pears and cranberries. The cobbler is also good made with spelt flour (see page 208).

· · ·

To make the pastry, put the flour, baking powder, sea salt and ground cardamom into a sieve set over a bowl. Muddle with your fingers, then shake through the sieve. Sieve once more until well blended. Tip into the bowl of a food processor, add the sugar, then pulse briefly to mix. Add the butter and pulse briefly again until the mixture looks like coarse breadcrumbs. Be careful not to overwork.

Lightly beat the egg yolk with the buttermilk. Add to the dry ingredients, then pulse in two or three short bursts to form a soft dough. Tip on to the work surface and knead very briefly into a ball. Cover with a clean tea towel and set aside.

Preheat the oven to 190°C/Gas Mark 5. Lightly grease a 1.4-litre (2½-pint) baking dish, 6cm (2½in) deep.

To make the filling, quarter, core and peel the pears. Slice each quarter in half lengthways and put in a bowl with the lemon juice.

Melt the butter in a large frying pan over a medium-high heat. Stir in the sugar and crushed cardamom pods. Fry for a few seconds, then add the pears and their juices. Fry for 3–5 minutes, or until heated through.

Tip the pear mixture into the baking dish. Strew with the cranberries and a little sugar if necessary (see Cook's notes). Top with craggy dollops of the dough – there's no need to roll it out – leaving space in between so you can see the filling. Sprinkle with the flaked almonds then bake for 30–40 minutes, rotating halfway through, until the topping is cooked through and golden. Sprinkle with a little more sugar and serve warm or at room temperature.

cook's note
· I used pickled cranberries because they were to hand, and they added a contrasting tartness to the sweet pears. If using fresh or defrosted cranberries, sprinkle with a little extra sugar. Dried cranberries aren't juicy enough.

lupin *flour*

plant source pulse
aka lupine
latin name *Lupinus augustifolius* (Australian sweet lupin)
gluten none
protein 43%
goes with bananas, berries, citrus, dairy products, eggs
uses biscuits, bread, cakes, coating for fried foods, pancakes, smoothies, thickener for sauces, soups and stews

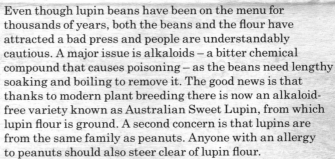

Even though lupin beans have been on the menu for thousands of years, both the beans and the flour have attracted a bad press and people are understandably cautious. A major issue is alkaloids – a bitter chemical compound that causes poisoning – as the beans need lengthy soaking and boiling to remove it. The good news is that thanks to modern plant breeding there is now an alkaloid-free variety known as Australian Sweet Lupin, from which lupin flour is ground. A second concern is that lupins are from the same family as peanuts. Anyone with an allergy to peanuts should also steer clear of lupin flour.

Putting alkaloids and allergies aside, this creamy yellow flour is high-protein, high-fibre and low-fat. It contains valuable antioxidants and it's gluten-free. Popular in Australia and Eastern Europe, it's added to wheat flour as a flavour-enhancer and to boost nutrients.

Writing about the lupin bean, Pliny the Roman naturalist commented: 'If taken commonly at meals, it will contribute a fresh colour and a cheerful countenance.' I'm not clear whether he was writing about the colour and countenance of people or food, but I was certainly won over by the flour and its nutritional credentials. Seeded Lupin Bread (see page 119) and Frosted Lime Biscuits (see page 118) are both a striking buttercup-yellow with a deliciously rich flavour.

Uncooked, the flour has a sweet, milky aroma with a very faint hint of pea. It's clumpy rather than free-flowing, so it needs sieving a couple of times with other dry ingredients before using. In baking, you can replace up to 50 per cent of wheat flour with lupin flour. For gluten-free bakes, blend it with flours such as tapioca, coconut or sorghum. You will also need eggs and/or xanthan gum to help bind the dough.

At the time of writing, the flour isn't on supermarket shelves but you'll find it in good health food shops and online (see Sources, page 280).

frosted lime biscuits

unsalted butter 100g (3½oz)
caster sugar 100g (3½oz)
lupin flour 85g (3oz)
tapioca starch 85g (3oz)
xanthan gum ¼ teaspoon
baking powder ½ teaspoon
egg ½ large, lightly beaten
lime juice 1 tablespoon
lime finely grated zest of ½, plus
   1 tablespoon to decorate

for the lime frosting
icing sugar 150g (5½oz), sifted
lime juice 3–4 teaspoons

makes 12

Eye-catchingly yellow, these protein-rich biscuits are beautiful to look at and easy to make. Lime juice and zest add bright flavour to the earthy notes of lupin flour. Tapioca starch (see Cassava Flour, page 44) and xanthan gum help bind the dough. The biscuits will keep for up to one week, stored in an airtight box.

. . .

Preheat the oven to 180°C/Gas Mark 4. Line a baking tray with a sheet of silicone.

Tip the butter and sugar into a large deep bowl. Using an electric whisk, cream for 4–5 minutes until pale and fluffy.

Put the lupin flour, tapioca starch, xanthan gum and baking powder into a sieve set over a bowl. Muddle with your fingers, then shake through the sieve. Sieve once more until well blended.

Gradually beat the flour mixture into the creamed butter mixture, alternating with the egg and the lime juice. Stir in the lime zest.

With well-floured hands, divide the mixture into 12 walnut-sized lumps and arrange them on the silicone-lined baking tray. Flatten into 6cm (2½in) discs, leaving about 5cm (2in) between them.

Bake for 15–20 minutes, rotating the tray halfway through, or until golden brown around the edge. Remove from the oven and put the tray on a wire rack. Leave for 5 minutes while the biscuits firm up. Remove the biscuits from the tray and arrange directly on the rack. Leave to cool completely.

To make the frosting, put the icing sugar in a bowl. Stir in the lime juice a little at a time – just enough to make a thick but pliable icing that will hold its shape once piped. Spoon into a piping bag and pipe over the cold biscuits. Sprinkle with lime zest.

seeded lupin bread

vegetable oil for greasing
lupin flour 140g (5oz)
coconut flour 2 tablespoons
sorghum flour 2 tablespoons
bicarbonate of soda
  1 teaspoon
baking powder ½ teaspoon
sea salt ½ teaspoon
dill seeds 1½ tablespoons
eggs 6 large, organic or free-
  range lightly beaten

makes 1 small loaf

Packed with protein and fibre, this dense buttercup-yellow gluten-free bread is delicious spread thickly with butter and cream cheese. A little goes a long way.

The recipe was inspired by one from chocolatechillimango.com, a blog that focuses on recipes for athletes and fitness enthusiasts.

• • •

Preheat the oven to 180°C/Gas Mark 4. Grease a 20x10x7cm (8x4x2¾in) loaf tin. Line with baking parchment and grease the paper too.

Put the flours, bicarbonate of soda, baking powder and sea salt into a sieve set over a bowl. Muddle with your fingers, then shake through the sieve. Sieve once more until well blended. Mix in the dill seeds.

Make a well in the middle of the dry ingredients and pour in the eggs. Stir with a fork, gradually drawing in the ingredients from around the edge. Once you have a smooth batter, spoon it into the prepared tin. Use a wet palette knife to push it into the corners and smooth the surface.

Bake for 25–30 minutes, rotating halfway through, or until a skewer inserted in the middle comes out clean. Be careful not to overbake.

Leave to settle in the tin for 10 minutes, then turn out on to a wire rack to cool completely. Wrap in foil and store in the fridge. The bread will keep for up to a week.

cook's notes
· The eggs make the batter fairly thin, but the coconut and sorghum flours help absorb the liquid as the bread cooks.
· The seeds provide all-important texture and flavour. You could also add some chopped green herbs such as chives or parsley.

flour

maida *flour*

plant source grain
aka n/a
latin name *Triticum aestivum*
protein/gluten 7.5–11.5%
goes with anything
uses batters, fritters, milk puddings, pancakes, pastry, soft flatbreads

Widely used in India, maida is a highly refined white flour milled from a soft variety of wheat. Though sometimes described as 'all-purpose flour', in reality it's more like soft cake flour (see Wheat flour: fine, page 232) because of its relatively low gluten content.

Indian cooks use it for soft flatbreads, milk breads, pastry, biscuits and desserts. It's a must for pillowy naan bread and crisp samosas (see page 124). It's also used for *jalebi*, a sweet, sticky snack made with deep-fried spirals of batter, bathed in syrup.

Uncooked maida flour is off-white and free-flowing, with a faint wheaty aroma.

It's easy to find online and in shops selling Indian and Asian groceries (see Sources, page 280). If you don't have any, it's fine to use plain white flour or cake flour instead.

carrot and cashew samosas with peas and mint

maida flour 250g (9oz), or
strong white flour
fine semolina 2 tablespoons
sea salt ¼ teaspoon
nigella seeds 1½ teaspoons
(optional)
vegetable oil 2 tablespoons
warm water 125–130ml
(4¼–4½fl oz)
plain flour 1½ tablespoons
oil for deep-frying
tangy chutney such as lime or
tamarind, to serve
thick plain yogurt to serve

for the filling
carrots 2–3 (about 175g/6oz in
total), quartered lengthways
vegetable oil 1 tablespoon
cumin seeds 1 teaspoon
onion 1 small, finely chopped
mild green chillies 1–2, such
as Jalapeño, deseeded and
finely chopped
ginger root 1 tablespoon,
finely grated
sea salt ¾ teaspoon
turmeric ½ teaspoon
garam masala ½ teaspoon
peas 70g (2½oz) shelled, fresh
or frozen
lemon juice of ½
cashew nuts 25g (1oz),
roughly chopped
mint leaves 1 tablespoon
chopped

makes 20 small samosas

Samosas make a deliciously spicy starter or pre-dinner snack with drinks. Here, I've replaced the usual potato filling with a colourful mix of carrots and peas, plus chillies and ginger for heat, chopped cashew nuts for crunch, and fresh mint to perk up the flavour. Don't be daunted by the length of this recipe – break it down into easy parts that can be done at a time to suit you. Make the filling and dough in advance, then get a production line going for rolling and assembling the pastry cones. Maida flour is perfect for samosa pastry. It's elastic and easy to roll thinly without tearing. If you don't have any use strong bread flour.

. . .

First make the filling. Steam the quartered carrots over boiling water for about 10 minutes, or until just tender. Chop into small dice and put in a bowl.

Heat the oil in a frying pan over a medium-high heat. Add the cumin seeds and sizzle for a few seconds. Once they start to crackle, add the onion, reduce the heat and fry for 4–5 minutes until soft but not starting to brown. Stir in the chillies, ginger, salt, turmeric and garam masala. Fry for 3 minutes then add the peas and the lemon juice. Fry for another minute or two or until the peas are heated through. Add the mixture to the diced carrots. Stir in the cashews and mint and leave to cool.

Meanwhile, make the pastry. Put the flour, semolina and sea salt into a sieve set over a bowl. Muddle with your fingers, then push through the sieve once or twice until well mixed. Add the nigella seeds, if using. Sprinkle the oil over the top and rub in with your fingertips until you have a slightly crumbly mixture. Stir in the warm water a little at a time – enough to make a firm, pliable dough.

Tip the dough on to a floured surface and knead really well – 10 minutes at least, or 5 minutes in a standing mixer – until the dough is beautifully smooth and elastic and not at all sticky. Wrap it in greaseproof paper and leave to rest for about 30 minutes.

To make the flour paste (which you'll need to glue the pastry round the filling), put the flour in a small bowl and add just enough cold water to make a smooth slurry.

Divide the dough into ten ping-pong-sized balls. Put them on a plate and cover with a damp cloth. Working with one ball at a time, roll out really thinly to a 15cm (6in) circle (see Cook's notes). Cut round an upturned saucer to neaten the edge. Cut the circle in half. Dab half of the rounded edge with the paste. Place the semi-circle in the palm of one hand. Using the thumb and index finger of the other hand, overlap the pasted edge with the non-pasted edge and press together to form a cone. Drop some of the filling into the cone – not quite to the top. Dab the pointed top edge with a little paste, then fold it over the filling to seal the opening, creating a plump triangular parcel. Place on a tray and gently pat with your finger to even out the filling. Repeat with the remaining balls of dough.

Meanwhile, pour enough oil into a medium-sized high-sided pan to come to a depth of 3cm (1¼in). Heat it to 160°C (325°F) on a thermometer, or until a small piece of the pastry bubbles and gently floats to the top. Very carefully, and without crowding the pan, slip three or four samosas into the hot oil. Cook for a few seconds, then as soon as the pastry begins to bubble, turn them over using tongs. Cook until golden brown – about 2½ minutes. Remove from the pan and drain on paper towels. Keep warm while you fry the rest.

Serve hot or warm with tangy chutney and cooling yogurt.

cook's notes
- Use a slim rolling pin when rolling out the pastry.
- It's easiest to use your index finger and thumb, rather than a teaspoon, to fill the pastry cones.

millet *flour*

plant source seed
aka bajri (Indian pearl millet), ragi (Indian finger millet)
latin name *Eleusine coracana* (finger millet), *Panicum miliaceum* (proso millet),
   Pennisetum glaucum (pearl millet)
gluten none
protein 11%
goes with bananas, berries, cardamom, cream, eggs, milk, nuts, sweet spices
uses biscuits, bread, cakes, desserts, Indian flatbreads, milk puddings, pastry,
   porridge, thickener for sauces, soups and stews

A leading staple in India, China and West Africa, millet is sadly under-rated in the West. Perusing my extensive collection of grain cookbooks, I found only one listing, while the Wikipedia flour entry doesn't even mention it. Maybe this is to do with the bird food connection, or simply because millet hasn't yet been accoladed 'super-food' status.

In Taiwan, however, millet is celebrated. Here, the indigenous Bunun people hold an important millet festival during which they chant a resonating prayer for a successful harvest. The Chinese respect millet too. They classify it as one of their five sacred crops, referring to it as 'little' or 'lesser rice'.

Cultivated in East Asia 10,000 years ago, millet is now the world's sixth most important grain. It's drought-resistant, matures quickly even in poor soil, and it's also one of the tastiest. With high protein, vitamin and mineral levels, it packs a nutritional punch.

There are, in fact, many millets. *Proso*, or common millet, is the variety generally sold in the West. The flour is a beautiful cream colour, rather like the top of Jersey milk. In contrast, pearl millet flour, or *bajri*, is the colour of cement – as is bread made with it. Finger millet flour, or *ragi*, is a pleasant reddish brown. I used it to make milky Sweet Millet Pudding (see page 131), which looks good and tastes delicious.

Millet is my go-to flour when I'm in gluten-free mode. I made the best ever gluten-free pastry with a combination of millet flour, rice flour and potato starch, plus xanthan gum to help bind the dough. It's miraculously easy to roll without cracking and produces a beautifully crisp crust. Try it in Spring Vegetable Pies (see page 129).

If you have no problems with gluten, begin by substituting up to a quarter of wheat flour with millet flour. Add even more if you're making batters or biscuits that don't need to rise very much.

Millet flour becomes rancid quite quickly, so buy a little at a time and store it in the fridge. If you become hooked, you can have fun grinding your own. It's easy to do with a milling attachment that fits on a standing mixer. You can also use a NutriBullet or blender, but you will need to sieve the flour to get rid of coarse bits and pieces.

You'll find Indian millets online (see Sources, page 280) or in shops selling Asian and African groceries. Good health food shops and some supermarkets sell ordinary millet.

flour

spring vegetable pies with herbs and lemon

chard 225g (8oz)
spinach 225g (8oz)
olive oil 1 tablespoon, plus
   extra for greasing
unsalted butter 35g (1¼oz)
shallots 4 small, finely chopped
baby broad beans 55g (2oz)
   shelled (fresh or defrosted
   frozen)
wild garlic 110g (4oz) (see
   Cook's notes)
nettle leaves 15g small (½oz)
   (see Cook's notes)
thyme leaves 2 teaspoons,
   chopped
lemon finely grated zest of 1
sea salt ¼ teaspoon, plus sea
   salt flakes for sprinkling
freshly ground black pepper
   ¼ teaspoon
ricotta cheese 3 tablespoons
Parmesan cheese
   4 tablespoons, freshly grated
eggs 2, organic or free-range,
   lightly beaten

for the pastry
millet flour 85g (3oz)
rice flour 70g (2½oz)
potato starch 85g (3oz)
xanthan gum ¾ teaspoon
sea salt ¼ teaspoon
unsalted butter 100g (3½oz)
   chilled, diced
egg 1 large, organic or free-
   range, beaten
lemon juice 2 teaspoons
chilled water 1–2 tablespoons

makes 4

you will need:
four round metal or
disposable pie dishes, 10cm
(4in) in diameter, 3cm
(1¼in) deep

These gorgeous little pies are a celebration of spring. The ingredients list is long but the pies are fun to make, especially combined with a forage for greenery (see Cook's notes). Backed up with rice flour and potato starch, millet flour makes lovely gluten-free pastry – easy to roll and beautifully crisp.

• • •

First make the pastry. Put the flours, potato starch, xanthan gum and salt into a sieve set over a bowl. Muddle with your fingers, then push through the sieve once or twice until well mixed. Work in the butter with your fingertips until the mixture looks like fine breadcrumbs. Mix in the beaten egg and lemon juice, then add a little water, half a tablespoonful at a time, until the dough comes together.

Tip the dough on to a floured work surface and form into a thick disc. Wrap in greaseproof paper and chill for 1 hour.

Separate the chard stalks from the leaves. Slice the stalks into bite-sized pieces and the leaves into ribbons. Place the stalks in the bottom of a steamer basket and top with the leaves and the spinach. Steam for 3 minutes, in batches if necessary, until only just tender. Remove the stalks and set aside. Put the chard and spinach leaves in a sieve and use the back of a wooden spoon to squeeze out as much moisture as possible. Squeeze with your hands as well, to extract every last drop.

Next, heat the oil and butter in a high-sided frying pan over a medium heat. Fry the shallots for 2 minutes until translucent, then add the chard stalks, broad beans, wild garlic, nettles, thyme and lemon zest. Season with the salt and pepper, and fry for another minute. Reduce the heat to medium-low, then stir in the squeezed-dry chard and spinach leaves. Fry for 2 minutes to heat through. Remove from the heat and leave to cool slightly.

Preheat the oven to 180°C/Gas Mark 4. Lightly grease the pie dishes.

Mix together the ricotta cheese, Parmesan and all but 1 tablespoon of the beaten egg in a bowl. Stir into the vegetables.

Divide the pastry into four equal-sized chunks. Pinch off about a quarter from each chunk for the lids. Roll out the larger pastry pieces to 17cm (6½in) circles. Lift carefully and

millet *flour*

place in the pie dishes, pushing into the corner with the edge of your index finger. Trim the edge with scissors, reserving the trimmings. Patch any cracks by pressing the dough together with your fingers.

Fill with the vegetable mixture, packing it in well. Paint the pastry edges with some of the saved beaten egg.

Combine the pastry trimmings from each dish with the smaller pieces of dough. Form into four small balls and roll out to 11cm (4½in) circles. Place on top of the pies and seal the edges by pressing with your fingers or the back of a fork. Brush with the beaten egg and sprinkle with a few sea salt flakes. Prick the surface in several places with a fork.

Put on a baking tray and bake for 20 minutes, or until golden. Serve hot or at room temperature.

cook's notes
- If you can't get hold of wild garlic or nettle leaves, use a little more chard and spinach.
- If using nettles, be sure to protect your hands with gloves. They lose their sting once cooked.

sweet millet pudding with nuts, saffron and cardamom

whole milk 450ml (16fl oz), preferably organic
ghee or unsalted butter
1½ tablespoons
red millet flour (ragi)
2 tablespoons
caster sugar 5 tablespoons
saffron strands pinch
cardamom pods seeds from
5, ground to a powder
mixed nuts 25g (1oz), such
as cashews, pistachios and
almonds, roughly chopped

to decorate
halved grapes
banana slices
chopped nuts

serves 3–4

Popular with children in India, this is perfect for when you're feeling in need of comfort. It's easy to make and slips down a treat. Red millet flour, or *ragi* (see page 127), is said to be particularly rich in calcium and iron. It makes the dessert an attractive pinkish brown – certainly more appetizing than desserts made with grey millet flour (*bajri*). It's easy to buy online (see Sources, page 280), or you can enjoy rummaging for it in Indian grocery shops.

• • •

Pour the milk into a thick-based non-stick pan and bring almost to the boil. Remove from the heat.

Melt the ghee or butter in another thick-based pan over a medium-low heat. Stir in the flour with a wooden spoon, then keep stirring for 2–3 minutes, just as you would when making a wheat flour-based roux.

Gradually stir in the hot milk, 2 tablespoons at a time. Keep stirring to prevent lumps forming. Once all the milk is in, add the sugar, saffron and cardamom. Stir over a medium-low heat for 3–4 minutes until thickened and smooth. Increase the heat slightly and continue to stir until the mixture starts to bubble and plop. Remove from the heat and add most of the nuts – keep a few for decoration.

Pour into serving bowls and leave to cool a little. Top with the fruit and nuts. Serve warm, cool or chilled, at any time of day.

mung bean *flour*

plant source pulse
aka moong bean, mung bean starch, green pea flour
latin name *Vigna radiata*
gluten none
protein 7–8%
goes with coconut, ginger, jaggery, salt
uses breads, dumplings, glass noodles, jelly, pancakes, porridge, steamed cakes, sweetmeats, thickener for soups

Hindu teaching classifies mung beans as a food that produces 'cheerfulness, serenity and mental clarity'. In *Beans: A History*, food historian Ken Albala writes that Buddha included mung beans in a list of foods that are 'devoid of faults'. There is even an Indian website which recommends the flour as a face pack 'guaranteed to bestow radiance'. With such impressive credentials, both the beans and the flour now have a place in my pantry.

Unusually, mung bean flour is made by pounding soaked beans rather than dried. The slurry is filtered and the resulting liquid dried and ground to a powder. Depending on processing, the colour and texture range from a fine pristine white starch to a clumpier cream flour flecked with what look like mites but are in fact microscopic pieces of husk. The aroma is extraordinary – floral and pea-like. Lick a flour-dipped finger and the pea flavour really comes across.

The flour is impressively versatile, as good in savoury dishes as in sweet. It becomes transparent when mixed with water and heated, so not surprisingly it's the one used commercially for glass noodles, aka cellophane noodles.

On the domestic front, mung bean flour is a must for Indian savoury pancakes known as pudlas (see page 136). I particularly like it in a popular Thai dessert, Rose-scented Coconut Custards (see page 135), a delicious combination of a sweet base with a slightly salty topping.

Nutrient-wise, mung bean flour is gluten-free. It provides valuable protein and dietary fibre, plus resistant starch (see page 205), which generally improves gut health. It's also quite filling, staving off hunger pangs, and easy to digest.

The flour is easy to find online (see Sources, page 280), or you can have fun rummaging in shops that sell Indian and Asian groceries. Look for 'washed' flour if you'd rather not have the dark flecks.

spicy onion and tomato pudlas with mint and cucumber relish

mung bean flour 125g (4½oz)
sea salt ½ teaspoon
ground turmeric ½ teaspoon
cumin seeds ½ teaspoon,
  lightly crushed
freshly ground black pepper
  ¼ teaspoon
water 200ml (7fl oz)
onion ¼ medium,
  finely chopped
tomato 1 large, peeled and
  finely chopped
ginger root small chunk,
  peeled and finely chopped
green or red chilli 2 teaspoons,
  finely chopped
mint leaves 3 tablespoons
  chopped
baking powder ¼ teaspoon
vegetable oil for frying

*for the mint and cucumber
relish*
cucumber ½ or 1 ridge
  cucumber
fresh mint large bunch, tough
  stalks removed, leaves
  roughly chopped
spring onions 2, some green
  included, roughly chopped
cherry tomatoes 125g (4½oz),
  quartered
fleshy green chillies 1–2,
  deseeded and roughly
  chopped
ginger root ½ teaspoon,
  finely chopped
cumin seeds 1 teaspoon,
  lightly crushed
freshly ground black pepper
  ¼ teaspoon
lime juice of ½
vegetable oil 2 tablespoons
sea salt

makes 6–8

Pudlas are savoury Indian pancakes – easy to make, gluten-free and utterly addictive. Serve with the relish, or a ready-made one from a jar, and eat hot, straight from the pan.

. . .

Combine the flour, salt, turmeric, cumin seeds and pepper in a bowl. Whisk in the water to make a lump-free batter. Stir in the onion, tomato, ginger, chilli and mint, then set aside for 30 minutes while you make the relish.

Peel the cucumber, leaving alternate stripes of green. Slice in half lengthways and scoop out the seeds. Slice each half lengthways into four strips, then crossways into small chunks. Tip into a sieve set over a bowl and toss with ¼ teaspoon of sea salt. Leave to drain briefly.

Once the cucumber has lost some of its liquid, put it in the bowl of a food processor. Add the rest of the relish ingredients plus another ¼ teaspoon of sea salt. Pulse very briefly to a chunky relish. Scoop into a serving bowl and set aside.

When you're ready to cook the pancakes (not before), stir in the baking powder. Place a non-stick pancake pan over a medium to medium-low heat. Heat 1 tablespoon of oil, then stir the batter once more to mix in the vegetables.

Pour a small ladleful of batter into the pan, swirling it to make a 13–14cm (5–5½in) circle. Use the back of your ladle to gently flatten and spread the batter. Fry for 1½ minutes or until the underside is lightly browned in patches. Flip the pancake and fry for another 1–1½ minutes or until browned. Slide on to a plate and keep warm while you cook the rest. Stir the batter each time before you pour it into the pan, adding more oil to the pan as necessary. Serve the pancakes with the relish.

cook's note
• It's important to cook the pancakes over a medium to medium-low heat, rather than a sizzling heat, otherwise the batter will burn. As with most pancakes, the first one should be looked on as a trial run.

rose-scented coconut custards

mung bean flour 3 tablespoons
concentrated rose water
    1 teaspoon
water 400ml (14fl oz)
caster sugar 75g (2¾oz)
beetroot powder ¼ teaspoon
    (or a drop of red food
    colouring, see Cook's notes)
sesame brittle (see page 194),
    toasted sesame seeds or
    dried rose petals to decorate

for the coconut topping
organic coconut milk 125ml
    (4fl oz) (without any additives)
rice flour 1½ tablespoons
sea salt ⅛ teaspoon

serves 6

You will need:
six 150ml (5fl oz) moulds,
such as small soufflé dishes
or espresso coffee cups; and
a piping bag fitted with a star
nozzle (see Cook's notes)

The most mildly flavoured of bean flours, mung bean flour is used as a thickener for this delicate Thai dessert. I am not a great fan of sweet desserts, so I love the typical Thai flavour combination of mildly sweet custard with a salty coconut topping. Rice flour (see page 164) is used to thicken the topping.

. . .

Tip the bean flour into a saucepan. Combine the rose water and water in a jug, then gradually whisk this into the flour. Whisk in the sugar and beetroot powder. Stir over a medium-low heat for 10–15 minutes, or until the mixture is smooth and thick. Pour it into the moulds, leave to cool, then chill in the fridge for 1–2 hours.

To make the topping, mix the coconut milk, rice flour and salt in a small saucepan. Stir over a medium heat for 8–10 minutes until thickened and the rice flour is cooked through. The spoon should leave a well-defined trail when you lift it from the mixture. Remove from the heat and leave to cool.

Pipe the cooled topping attractively over the chilled bases. Add your chosen decoration just before serving.

cook's notes
· I have used flavourless beetroot powder to tint the bean flour base a delicate pink. If you don't have any, use a drop of liquid food colouring instead.
· If the bean flour mixture looks lumpy when cooked, push it through a fine sieve.
· If you don't want to pipe the coconut topping, it's fine to simply spread a thin layer over the base.

mung bean *flour*

flour

mung bean *flour*

oat *flour*

plant source grain
aka n/a
latin name *Avena sativa*
gluten none (if uncontaminated)
protein 15–18%
goes with apples, bacon, berries, cheese, chocolate, cream, dried fruit, herrings, leeks, mushrooms, nuts, onions
uses bars, binder for burgers and meatballs, biscuits, coating for fried foods, crumble topping, flapjacks, oat cakes, pancakes, pastry, quick breads, scones, thickener for sauces and soups

The prolific eighteenth-century diarist Doctor Samuel Johnson dismissively defined oats as 'a grain which in England is generally given to horses but in Scotland supports the people'.

While it's true that they play a big part in Scottish cuisine, and English horses are undoubtedly partial to them, oats are worthy of greater accolades. For thousands of years oats were an important staple, not only in British Celtic regions but also in Scandinavia and central Europe. It's a uniquely rugged crop that can hold its own, more so than any other grain, in driving rain and Arctic temperatures.

Oats are particularly nutritious, and easy to include in your diet, thanks to the impressive range of oat-based products: groats, steel-cut, rolled, jumbo, pinhead, instant, bran, meal and flour.

Most of us are familiar with oatmeal but a relative newcomer is oat flour. Milled from oat groats (the whole kernel), the flour differs from oatmeal in the same way that wheat flour differs from semolina, as food writer Jenni Muir points out in *A Cook's Guide to Grains*. It's soft and delicate with a pleasing aroma – a faint hint of porridge perhaps – and an unexpected whiff of lemon and toffee. It's mellow and comforting and makes you want to cook with it.

Like barley flour (see page 28), oat flour is particularly valued for its soluble dietary fibre called beta-glucan, known to lower blood cholesterol and reduce the risk of heart disease. It's also a source of resistant starch (see page 205), which generally improves gut health. Oat flour is gluten-free, provided it hasn't been cross-contaminated by grains that aren't gluten-

free – wheat or rye, for example. If you're a coeliac or following a gluten-free diet, check the label to make sure.

If you're using oat flour for bread and cakes, you'll need to combine it with wheat flour to give the dough the necessary structure and stretch. Substitute about a quarter to one-third of the wheat flour with oat flour. It absorbs more water than other flours so add a little extra to compensate. For yeasted items, increase the yeast slightly to encourage the dough to rise. If gluten is off-limits, combine oat flour with another gluten-free flour such as rice or tapioca instead of wheat. You'll also need an extra egg or two to help bind the dough.

For dense items that don't need to rise very much – biscuits and flapjacks, for example – you can use oat flour by itself; it adds great depth of flavour and a pleasing chewy texture. Try Black Pepper and Potato Oatcakes (see page 140). It's also good mixed with rolled oats in a homely crumble. For pastry, add an egg and extra water to make a pliable dough, plus a binding agent such as xanthan gum to make it easier to roll.

You'll find oat flour online and in good health food shops. I particularly like Bob's Red Mill brand (see Sources, page 280), which is guaranteed gluten-free. Oat flour goes rancid quite quickly because of its fat content, so store it in an airtight container in the fridge.

An alternative option is to mill your own flour as and when you need it. It's easy to do in a food processor or in a milling attachment to a standing mixer. You'll need to sieve scrupulously and re-mill the coarse residue, but your flour will be super-fresh and extra tasty.

black pepper and potato oatcakes

floury potatoes 2 (weighing
   about 250g/9oz in total),
   preferably organic, cut into
   chunks (see Cook's notes)
unsalted butter 25g (1oz),
   diced, plus extra for greasing
sea salt ¼ teaspoon
freshly ground black pepper
   ½ teaspoon (see
   Cook's notes)
oat flour 50g (1¾oz) (see
   Cook's notes)
porridge oats 25g (1oz)
plain flour for dusting

makes 9

A combination of oatmeal flour, porridge oats, homely mashed potato and a generous grinding of black pepper makes particularly nutritious oatcakes with a subtle comforting flavour. Pleasantly chewy but crisp at the edges, they're equally delicious slathered with butter or left unadorned. Enjoy them at their best soon after cooking.

· · ·

Put the potato chunks into a large saucepan of salted water. Bring to a boil, then simmer briskly for 10 minutes, or until tender. Drain the potatoes, then put them back in the pan and cover with a clean tea towel. Leave for 5 minutes to absorb excess moisture.

Preheat the oven to 200°C/Gas Mark 6. Line a baking tray with a silicone sheet or well-greased baking parchment.

Mash the potatoes until smooth, then stir in the butter, salt, pepper, oat flour and porridge oats. Pack the dough together well and put on a well-floured board. Using a well-floured rolling pin, roll it out to a thickness of 5mm (¼in). Cut into rounds with a 7cm (2¾in) cutter. Lift carefully on to the baking tray using a spatula. Re-roll any leftover dough until it's all used up.

Bake for 20 minutes, turning the tray halfway through, until golden at the edges. Remove from the oven and leave on the tray to firm up. Carefully transfer to a wire rack to cool completely.

cook's notes
· Mashed potato may seem mundane, but it's well worth using good-quality organic potatoes for a good flavour.
· For the best flavour it is well worth looking for good-quality black peppercorns such as Wynad or Tellicherry. Don't be tempted to use pre-ground pepper – it simply doesn't have the appetizing aroma and flavour of freshly ground.
· If you can't get hold of oat flour, it's fine to use pinhead oatmeal.

pea *flour*

plant source pulse
aka peasemeal
latin name *Pisum sativum*
gluten none
protein 18–24%
goes with almonds, bacon, cream, eggs, lemon, mint, parsley, soft cheese
uses batters, binding, bread, flatbreads, fritters, pakoras, pancakes, pastry, popovers, scones, thickener for sauces and soups

There is something so satisfying about peas – the way they pop out of their pods, some into the bowl, some into the mouth. They reassuringly show up in directors' dining rooms and school canteens across the world, eaten by many and spurned by few. The flour, however, is a different matter. Though peas themselves are an ancient crop, the flour is relatively new to the culinary map. It's milled from smooth-skinned varieties of green or yellow field peas, which, unlike garden peas, are left on the vine until fully mature and dry. Once dry, they're harvested, split and skinned, then milled to a very fine flour.

I find pea flour one of the most versatile and pleasing flours to work with. With a silky smooth texture and soft pastel colours, it must be the prettiest of all flours. It comes in pale pistachio green and creamy primrose yellow, with an aroma and flavour faintly redolent of freshly picked peas. If gender could be ascribed to flour, pea flour would be feminine. If a season could be ascribed, it would be early summer.

In contrast, and not to be overlooked, is a sturdy pea flour known as peasemeal, The flour, or meal, has a long history in Scotland but went off-radar in the 1970s. It's now back on the market thanks to popular demand. Made from roasted yellow field peas, it has a texture similar to cornmeal. It's typically used for brose, an uncooked porridge served with butter and raisins, and bannocks, a substantial flat, round griddle cake.

Digging deeper into the world of pea flour, there is also *hoen kwe* from Singapore. Unlike most flours, it's not packaged in wholesome paper but comes instead in a scientific-looking white plastic tube. The label describes it as 'green pea flour' though the contents are pure white. Singaporean cooks mix it with coconut milk and sugar to make a popular blancmange-like dessert that's wrapped in banana leaves and chilled before eating.

Regardless of provenance, pea flour ticks all the right nutritional boxes. It's high-protein, high-fibre, well endowed with vitamins and minerals, and a good source of resistant starch (see page 205), which generally improves gut health. It's also gluten-free.

As far as the cook is concerned, the green pea flour has slightly stronger flavour than the yellow; both are equally at home in sweet and savoury dishes. It can be used in anything from flatbreads and fritters to pastry and pancakes. Unlike many gluten-free flours, it doesn't necessarily need combining with other flours to make it workable. I used it alone in exquisitely crisp pastry in Plum and Frangipane Tart (see page 146) and in Sweet Green Pea Pancakes (see page 144). For bread dough and other baked items where rise is important, you'll need to combine it with about 50 per cent wheat flour to give it the structure and stretch normally supplied by gluten (see page 60). If gluten is off-limits, use a raising agent such as baking powder, plus buttermilk and/or an egg or two to help bind the dough.

For an extra hit of nutrients, use pea flour instead of wheat flour as a thickener for sauces and soups. A couple of tablespoons stirred into ham stock and milk make a vibrant parsley sauce for anointing a succulent gammon chop. Another option is to add a little to a smooth green soup of garden peas, sweetcorn kernels and diced courgettes whizzed in a blender with a handful of mint leaves.

Pea flour hasn't yet hit many supermarket shelves, but you can buy it in farm shops, health food shops or online. I get mine from Hodmedods, a pioneering company committed to growing and marketing British-grown pulses and grains (see Sources, page 280).

To keep the flour at its best, empty it into an airtight container rather than leave it in an opened packet, and store in a cool place.

sweet green pea pancakes with ricotta, honey and apricots

green pea flour 100g (3½oz)
water 180ml (6½fl oz)
olive oil 2 tablespoons, plus
   extra for frying
sea salt pinch

to garnish
ricotta cheese 150g (5½oz),
   drained if wet
clear mild honey such
   as acacia
coarsely ground black pepper
mint leaves a few small
ripe apricots or peaches
   thin slices

**makes about 30 small
   pancakes**

Contributed by queen of pulses Jenny Chandler, these gorgeous little pancakes will open your eyes to the culinary possibilities of green pea flour. They are a striking green and look beautiful topped with a sliver of apricot – an impressive snack to serve at a drinks party. Allow plenty of time for resting the batter. You can buy pea flour online from Hodmedods (see Sources, page 280), health food and farm shops.

. . .

Tip the pea flour into a jug, add about half the water, then stir to a thick, smooth paste. Whisk in the remaining water, the olive oil and salt. Leave to rest for at least 1 hour, or up to 24 hours in the fridge, to allow the starch grains to swell.

Pour a thin film of olive oil into a roomy non-stick frying pan over a medium-high heat. Once searing hot, drop in 2 teaspoonfuls of the batter, letting it spread to form 6cm (2½in) circles. Fry for 30–40 seconds until set underneath but still uncooked on top. Flip and fry for another 20–30 seconds. Drain on paper towels and keep warm while you fry the rest of the batter, adding more oil as necessary.

Arrange the pancakes on warm serving platters and top with a spoonful of the ricotta. Drizzle with honey, sprinkle with black pepper, then add a mint leaf and a slice of apricot.

banana, walnut and raspberry cake

vegetable oil for greasing
bananas 4 small, ripe
lemon juice of 1
yellow pea flour 110g (4oz)
wholemeal flour 60g (2¼oz)
baking powder 2 teaspoons
mixed spice 2 teaspoons
sea salt good pinch
unsalted butter 85g (3oz),
    at room temperature
golden caster sugar
    100g (3½oz)
eggs 2, organic or free-range,
    lightly beaten
raspberries 150g (5½oz)
shelled walnuts 50g (1¾oz),
    preferably new season,
    roughly chopped
clear honey to glaze

makes 1 loaf

This loaf-shaped banana cake is an intriguing partnership of pea flour, wholemeal flour, walnuts and raspberries – but it works. It's also particularly nutritious – the combination of pulse and grain flours creates the kind of 'complete' protein found in meat and fish (see Protein, page 59), so it's a useful cake for vegetarians. It's best left to firm up for 24 hours before slicing. This recipe was inspired by Jenni Sherington's recipe on Hodmedod's website (see Sources, page 280).

• • •

Preheat the oven to 160°C/Gas Mark 3. Grease the base and sides of a 20x13x8cm (8x5x3¼in) loaf tin, then line with baking parchment and grease the paper too.

Slice the bananas into a bowl and mash with the lemon juice to a very smooth pulp.

Put the flours, baking powder, mixed spice and salt in a sieve set over a bowl. Muddle with your fingers, then push through the sieve. Sieve once more until well blended. Mix the bran left in the sieve into the bowl.

Using an electric whisk, cream the butter and sugar together in a bowl for 3–4 minutes until fluffy. Gradually whisk in the eggs, alternating with the flour mixture. Next, fold in the banana mixture, raspberries and chopped walnuts. Spoon into the tin, levelling the surface with a wet palette knife.

Bake on the second shelf of the oven for 65–75 minutes, rotating the tin every 15 minutes, until a skewer inserted in the centre comes out clean. Remove from the oven and leave to settle in the tin for 10 minutes. Turn out on to a wire rack and leave to cool before brushing with clear honey. Ideally, leave for 24 hours before slicing.

plum and frangipane tart

vegetable oil for greasing
red plums 6 ripe
caster sugar for sprinkling
melted quince, redcurrant or
    apricot jelly 4 tablespoons,
    to glaze

for the pastry
yellow pea flour 160g (5¾oz)
icing sugar 2 tablespoons
cold unsalted butter 100g
    (3½oz), roughly chopped
thick plain yogurt
    1½ tablespoons
beaten egg 1½ tablespoons

for the frangipane
unsalted butter 75g (2¾oz),
    melted and cooled slightly
caster sugar 125g (4½oz)
egg 1 large, organic or free-
    range
egg yolk 1 large, organic
    or free-range
brandy or amaretto liqueur
    1 tablespoon (optional)
ground almonds 125g (4½oz)

serves 6–8

Yellow pea flour makes the most beautiful melt-in-the-mouth pastry. It's gluten-free and wonderful to work with. Crimson plums set off the rich yellow colour. The idea for the filling came from my food writer friend Lesley Mackley, who does a lovely version with pears instead of plums.

· · ·

First make the pastry. Sift the pea flour and icing sugar then tip into the bowl of a food processor. Add the butter and pulse briefly until the mixture looks like breadcrumbs. Add the yogurt and egg, then pulse in short bursts until the mixture begins to clump. Be careful not to overwork the dough.

Tip the dough on to a well-floured surface. Roll into a ball, then flatten into a 12cm (4½in) disc, ready for rolling out. Wrap in greaseproof paper and chill for 30 minutes.

For the frangipane, beat the butter and sugar in a large bowl with an electric whisk for a few minutes until light and fluffy. Gradually beat in the whole egg, followed by the yolk. Finally add the brandy, if you're using it, and the ground almonds. Mix well to combine, then set aside.

Preheat the oven to 180°C/Gas Mark 4. Put a baking tray in to heat. Grease the base and sides of a 24.5x2.5cm (9¾x1in) fluted metal tart tin, making sure the sides are well lubricated. Line the base with a circle of baking parchment and grease the paper too.

Once the dough is chilled, remove from the fridge. Dust your work surface and rolling pin with flour. Roll out the pastry to a thin 30cm (12in) circle. Carefully drape it over your rolling pin and lower it into the tin. Press the side of your index finger into the edge to even out the thickness. Trim the top with a small sharp knife. Spoon the frangipane into the pastry case, smoothing the surface with a spatula.

Slice the plums in half lengthways and remove the stone. Slice each half lengthways into four segments. Starting from the outer edge of the tart, arrange a double row of overlapping segments in four north-south-east-west 'spokes', leaving a quadrant of uncovered frangipane between each spoke. Make an attractive rosette of slices where the spokes meet. Sprinkle the plums with caster sugar.

Bake for 35–40 minutes, rotating the tin halfway through. Cover the edges with foil if they brown too much. Remove from the oven and leave to settle in the tin for 20 minutes.

flour

Carefully ease the tart out of the tin and slide on to a serving plate. Brush with the melted jelly and serve warm or at room temperature.

peanut *flour*

plant source nut
aka groundnut, monkey nut
latin name *Arachis hypogaea*
gluten none
protein 34%
goes with bananas, carrots, celery, chicken, chocolate, coriander, duck, lime, prawns
uses biscuits, cakes, pancakes, smoothies, thickener for sauces, soups and stews

According to Diane Spivey, author of *The Peppers, Cracklings, and Knots of Wool Cookbook*, the Mandingo people in Mali, West Africa, used peanuts as early as the 1300s. They ground the nuts and added the resulting flour to bread and cake dough.

Spivey goes on to point out that in spite of Africa's early use of the peanut, some writers suggest erroneously that there is confusion about its origins, implying that America was the birthplace, and that Americans created peanut butter. Be that as it may, my stash of authentic African cookbooks reveals recipe after recipe for pastes and sauces made with groundnuts (aka peanuts), plus breads, cakes, vegetable dishes and stews. As a high-protein flour, it's obviously a valuable indigenous crop in countries where animal protein foods are lacking.

The flour is made by grinding roasted peanuts to a paste, pressing out the oil, then drying and milling the remaining mass. Though gluten-free, it's a versatile flour, adding a typical nutty flavour to anything from sweet doughs and batters to savoury sauces and stews. I like it pounded with kaffir lime leaves, garlic and lime juice in a dressing for Asian-style Duck and Noodle Salad (see page 151).

Peanut flour is also a natural thickener. Try adding a couple of tablespoons to a spicy root vegetable stew, or stir it into soups and smoothies. For a simple protein boost, just sprinkle some over yogurt, fruit or breakfast cereal.

You'll find peanut flour online (see Sources, page 280), in health food shops and in good supermarkets.

asian-style duck and noodle salad with peanut dressing

duck breasts 2 boneless
sea salt flakes
freshly ground black pepper
medium egg noodles 125g
(4½oz)

for the dressing
lime leaves 4–5 large/double-
lobed (fresh or frozen but
not dried)
**palm sugar or muscovado
sugar** 2 teaspoons
garlic clove 1 large,
lightly crushed
rapeseed oil 1½ tablespoons
lime juice of 1
soy sauce 2 teaspoons
rice vinegar 2 teaspoons
roasted peanut flour 50g
(1¾oz)
water 3–4 tablespoons, or more

for the salad
red cabbage ½ small, outer
leaves discarded
baby leaf greens small bunch
(about 100g/3½oz)
carrots 3–4 small, preferably
organic, trimmed and peeled
red onion ½, thinly sliced
crossways into crescents
fleshy red chilli ½ –1, deseeded
and thinly sliced
sea salt ½ teaspoon

to garnish
Thai basil leaves
coriander leaves
dry-roasted peanuts

serves 4 as a light meal

Protein-rich roasted peanut flour makes a punchy dressing for a salad of crisp duck breasts, crunchy vegetables and noodles. If you don't have any peanut flour, grind dry-roasted peanuts to a coarse powder using a NutriBullet or blender.

• • •

Preheat the oven to 220°C/Gas Mark 7. Slash the duck breast skin diagonally in three or four places. Rub with sea salt flakes and freshly ground black pepper.

Heat a small ovenproof frying pan over a medium-high heat. Add the duck breasts skin-side down and sizzle for 3–4 minutes until the skin is lightly browned. Put the pan in the oven and roast the breasts for 5 minutes, then turn them over and roast for 5 minutes more. Leave to rest in a warm place while you make the dressing and salad.

To make the dressing, cut away the central vein from the lime leaves and roughly shred the leaves. Using a mortar and pestle, crush the shreds to a paste with the sugar and garlic. Mix in the oil, lime juice, soy sauce and vinegar. Put the peanut flour in a bowl and mix with the lime leaf mixture. Gradually whisk in the water – enough to make a smooth, slightly thick dressing – and set aside.

To make the salad, slice the cabbage half in two and cut out the core. Slice the leaves crossways into thin ribbons. Remove any tough stems from the greens, stack the leaves and slice crossways into ribbons. Using a swivel peeler, shave away wafer-thin slivers of flesh from the carrots, rotating the carrot as you work. Put the cabbage, greens and carrots in a bowl with the onion and chilli. Toss with the salt and leave to wilt slightly while you cook the noodles.

Prepare the noodles according to the packet instructions and drain well. Don't let them cool too much, otherwise they'll stick together. Divide the noodles between serving plates, along with the salad. Slice the duck breasts thinly at an angle, then arrange them attractively on top. Pour over the dressing, then strew with Thai basil leaves, coriander leaves and dry-roasted peanuts.

variation
· For a vegetarian version, leave out the duck breasts. The salad is pretty substantial without them.

potato *starch*

plant source tuber
aka fecola (Italian), fécule (French), potato flour, potato starch flour
latin name *Solanum tuberosum*
gluten none
protein >0.1%
goes with anything
uses binder, bread, brioche, cakes, muffins, pancakes, pastry, thickener for fruit pie
fillings, sauces, soups and stews

Potato starch and potato flour are the most confusing products I have ever come across. There are bloggers, recipe writers and online suppliers who insist the two are different, and there are others who claim they're the same. And then there are suppliers selling what appear to be two products, misleadingly labelled potato starch and potato flour, which are in fact both potato starch. There are also recipe writers who specify potato flour when they mean starch, or insist you use one and not the other.

Regardless of misleading facts and labelling, you can tell the difference between the starch and the flour just by looking, feeling and sniffing. Potato starch, even when labelled flour, is 100 per cent starch. It's dazzling white like an Arctic landscape, it drifts silkily through the fingers, settling like fallout, and squeaks when you rub it. It's the fine residue left at the bottom of the bowl when you soak sliced potatoes in water. It's made from a watery slurry of raw, peeled, chopped potatoes, which is filtered and dehydrated to form starch. It's odourless and flavourless, and suitable for both sweet and savoury baked items and other dishes.

Potato flour, on the other hand, is creamy yellow and coarser – it looks and feels more like wheat flour. It's ground from dehydrated cooked potatoes, as opposed to raw, and may or may not include the skin. It has a definite potato flavour and aroma, it's dense and heavy, and best used sparingly – to thicken a soup perhaps. That said, I did read about someone who uses 100 per cent potato flour to make dog biscuits, which seems an excellent idea as long as you're after something dense and chewy.

Potato starch is versatile and amenable. Italian cooks seem more at home with it than those in the UK and US. In *La Scienza in Cucina e l'Arte di Mangiar Bene* (*Science in the Kitchen and the Art of Eating Well*), nineteenth-century businessman and food writer Pellegrino Artusi gives a recipe for an iconic feather-light cake, Pasta Margherita, made with *fecola de patate* (the Italian name for potato starch), icing sugar and eggs. Esteemed food writer Anna Del Conte's recipe for a very light Madeira-style cake (Paradise Cake from Pavia, see page 157) is made almost entirely with what she calls potato flour but is in fact starch.

The late Carol Field, American Italophile and food writer, uses one part potato starch and sugar to two parts plain flour and butter in a recipe for crisp, fine-textured pasta *frolla* (sweet shortcrust pastry) – ambrosial with a creamy custard filling topped with apricots. Meanwhile, in the UK, expert baker and teacher Emmanuel Hadjiandreou combines the starch with brown rice flour and buckwheat flour to lighten the texture of a gluten-free loaf.

Potato starch also works its magic in pancakes, adding unmistakable fluffiness to the cooked batter. Try it in Korean-style Kimchi Pancakes (see page 154).

The starch comes into its own as a natural thickener for soups, stews and sauces. I much prefer it to cornflour, particularly in a stir-fry sauce. It's less gloopy, sets to a clear gel and doesn't taste floury. Scientist and writer Harold McGee enthuses that it is 'especially useful for last minute corrections' to a sauce since it thickens at a lower temperature than cornflour, and therefore more quickly, and only a teaspoon or so does the trick.

The best places to find potato starch are health food shops and shops specializing in Asian groceries. It's also easy to find online (see Sources, page 280). Be aware it might be called potato flour, so check that it looks white and starchy and read the small print to make sure it's been ground from raw potatoes. It can be stored for months in a sealed container in a cool place.

kimchi pancakes with ginger dipping sauce

plain flour 120g (4¼oz)
potato starch 70g (2½oz) (see
   Cook's notes)
sea salt ½ teaspoon
egg 1, organic or free-range,
   lightly beaten
water 350ml (12fl oz)
cabbage kimchi 175g (6oz),
   roughly chopped (see
   Cook's notes)
vegetable oil for frying

for the ginger dipping sauce
ginger root 5cm (2in) piece,
   peeled and roughly chopped
soy sauce 3 tablespoons
rice wine vinegar 1 tablespoon
dried chilli flakes ¼ teaspoon
   (Korean, if you have them)

makes 3 pancakes
serves 6–10 as a canapé

A popular snack with drinks in Korea, these thick tortilla-style pancakes are made with a mixture of potato starch and wheat flour. Some recipes specify wheat flour only, others add rice flour for crispness, but I find potato starch works really well. Sliced into bite-sized segments and served with the zesty dipping sauce, the pancakes certainly pack punch – chewy, crisp, sour and hot all at the same time. They will disappear quickly so it's worth making plenty.

• • •

Put the flour, potato starch and salt into a sieve set over a bowl. Muddle with your fingers, then push through the sieve once or twice until well mixed. Pour in the egg and water, and whisk to a smooth batter. Stir in the chopped kimchi and leave to rest while you make the dipping sauce.

Squeeze the ginger chunks in a garlic press to extract the juice. You should have about 1½ teaspoonfuls. Mix with the other ingredients, then pour into small serving bowls.

Heat 2 tablespoons of vegetable oil in a 24cm (9½in) non-stick pancake pan over a high heat. Give the batter a good stir to distribute the chopped kimchi. Pour in 2 ladlefuls (about 250ml/9fl oz), using the back of a spoon to help spread the batter to the edges of the pan. Fry for 20 seconds then reduce the heat to low and cook, uncovered (see Cook's notes), for 10–12 minutes. Once the underside is cooked, gently turn it over and cook the other side for 10–12 minutes. Slide from the pan on to a plate and keep warm in a low oven (120°C/Gas Mark ½) while you cook the rest of the pancakes.

Slice the pancakes into 10–12 segments, roll up starting from the outer edge, then spear with cocktail sticks. Serve with the ginger dipping sauce.

cook's notes
- Confusingly, potato starch is sometimes labelled potato flour. They are not the same thing; see page 153 for clarification.
- Shop-bought kimchi varies in quality. It's well worth buying a good one for these pancakes. My favourite is from mrkimchi.co.uk.
- Don't be tempted to put a lid on the pan, otherwise condensation will drip from the underside and make the batter too wet to set.

potato *starch*

flour

paradise cake from pavia
(la torta paradiso)

unsalted butter 325g (11½oz), at room temperature, plus extra for greasing

caster sugar 325g (11½oz)

eggs 3 very fresh large, organic or free-range

potato starch 325g (11½oz) (see Cook's notes)

cream of tartar generous ½ teaspoon

bicarbonate of soda generous ½ teaspoon

sea salt generous ½ teaspoon

unwaxed lemon finely grated zest of 1

icing sugar for dusting

serves 10–12

This deliciously light cake is a speciality of Pavia, south of Milan, where it's traditionally enjoyed with sparkling wine at the end of a meal. Made with potato starch only, it's perfect for people who avoid wheat flour. Make sure you use genuine potato starch rather than the heavier potato flour (see Potato Starch, page 152). The recipe is based on one kindly given to me by Italian food writer Anna del Conte who, in turn, received it from the owner of a local pasta shop. As Anna herself was advised, success depends entirely on the quality of the ingredients – the very best potato starch, very fresh eggs from happy chickens and top-notch unsalted butter.

• • •

Preheat the oven to 160°C/Gas Mark 3. Put a baking tray in to heat. Grease the base and sides of a 24–25cm (9½–10in) springform cake tin. Line the tin with baking parchment and grease the paper too.

Cut the butter into small pieces and put in a bowl. Add the sugar and beat with an electric whisk for about 5 minutes until fluffy and completely blended. Add 1 egg at a time to the creamed mixture, beating constantly. Do not add a second egg until the previous one is totally incorporated.

Sift the potato starch into a bowl with the cream of tartar, bicarbonate of soda and salt. Sprinkle large spoonfuls over the surface of the creamed mixture. Mix in each spoonful with a large metal spoon, lifting it high above the bowl to incorporate some air as well. Sprinkle in the lemon zest and mix well.

Spoon the cake mixture into the tin, then give the tin a shake or two to settle the mixture. Bake on the pre-heated tray for 45–55 minutes, rotating halfway through, until the cake is dry inside and has shrunk from the edge. Leave to settle in the tin for 10 minutes, then turn out the cake (take care – it's very fragile) on to a wire rack and leave to cool. Dust thickly with icing sugar before serving.

cook's notes
- Confusingly, potato starch is sometimes labelled potato flour. They are not the same thing; see page 152 for clarification.
- The cake can be wrapped in foil and kept for a week or so, but, as Anna says, it will lose its fragrance.
- Credit: Anna Del Conte, *The Classic Food of Northern Italy* (2017). Reproduced with kind permission of Pavilion Books Company Ltd.

quinoa *flour*

plant source seed
aka n/a
latin name *Chenopodium quinoa*
gluten none
protein 18%
goes with cheese, chocolate, coffee, stone fruit, sweet spices such as cinnamon, cardamom and vanilla, tomatoes
uses binder for burgers and meatballs, biscuits, bread, cakes, coating for fried foods, pancakes, pastry, thickener for sauces, soups and stews

Quinoa trumps the nutritional credentials of most other plant foods. It contains a complete set of essential amino acids that make up protein (see page 59), putting it on a par with foods from animal sources. It's also a rich source of resistant starch (see page 205), which generally improves gut health.

Native to the Andes and domesticated thousands of years ago, quinoa was known as the 'golden rain' of the Incas and respected as a vital and sacred food. In recognition of this and its superior nutritional value, the United Nations declared 2013 the International Year of Quinoa. The result was a seemingly unstoppable stream of quinoa dishes on restaurant menus and in the food media. Though well intentioned, the upturn increased production costs. The knock-on effect was that the indigenous population could no longer afford to buy their sacred grain, and understandably turned to cheaper junk food. The good news is that quinoa is now grown in the US, mainland Europe and even the UK, taking the pressure off Andean farmers.

Quinoa comes from the same family as beets and spinach, so botanically speaking it's not actually a grain – it's usually called a 'pseudo-grain'. With towering stalks and wonderfully shaggy heads of brightly coloured seeds, it's one of the most striking plants imaginable. I have been known to stop the car to marvel at fields of it in France.

Though seeds range from buttercup yellow to sunset pink and orange, the flour is usually ground from the white variety. It's a non-descript chalky beige with a slightly clumpy texture, faint grassy aroma and mildly bitter aftertaste. It's gluten-free and can be used in any recipe that calls for wheat. You can substitute up to 30 per cent, but you'll need a raising agent such as baking powder or bicarbonate of soda for bread and cakes.

The flour goes well with strong flavours that mask its slight bitterness – chocolate, coffee and cheese, for example. It certainly hits the spot in Roasted Tomato and Gruyère Cheese Tart (see page 160) and in a biscuity Greengage and Cobnut Crumble (see page 163). It's especially good in pancakes and fritters, too.

roasted tomato and gruyère cheese tart

quinoa flour 150g (5½oz)
rice flour 90g (3½oz)
xanthan gum 1½ teaspoons
sea salt pinch
unsalted butter 150g (5½oz)
  chilled, diced
egg yolks 4, organic and free-
  range, lightly beaten
water 1½ –2 tablespoons
vegetable oil for greasing

for the filling
plum tomatoes 12–14, halved
  crossways
extra-virgin olive oil
sea salt flakes
freshly ground black pepper
muscovado sugar
Gruyère cheese 150g (5½oz),
  coarsely grated
eggs 4, organic or free-range
organic double
cream 125ml (4fl oz)
oregano or marjoram leaves
  2 tablespoons chopped

**serves 8–10 as a snack
or 6 as a light meal**

Gluten-free pastry is rarely as crisp as wheat flour pastry. That said, this quinoa flour pastry is a good solution when a tart is a must-have – for a picnic or buffet lunch, for example. With added rice flour and xanthan gum to help bind the dough, the pastry is lovely to work with, tastes good and looks great when baked. Topped with juicy roasted tomatoes and nutty Gruyère cheese, the tart is packed with flavour. Make the roasted tomatoes in advance and keep in the fridge until ready to use.

. . .

Preheat the oven to 150°C/Gas Mark 2.

To make the filling, arrange a single layer of halved tomatoes on a roasting tray. Sprinkle with olive oil, sea salt flakes, freshly ground black pepper and a good few pinches of muscovado sugar. Roast for 1½ –2 hours, rotating the tray every 30 minutes, until the tomatoes are shrivelled but still slightly moist. Set aside to cool.

For the pastry, put the two flours, xanthan gum and sea salt into a sieve set over a bowl. Muddle with your fingers, then push through the sieve once or twice until well blended. Get your fingertips nice and cold then lightly rub in the butter. Hold your hands well above the bowl so that the flour drifts gently down, incorporating air as it does so, and you can see any fragments of butter that still need rubbing in. Mix in the egg yolks with a fork, followed by enough of the water to make a dough.

Tip the dough on to a floured work surface and knead briefly until smooth. Gather the dough into a ball, then flatten it into a thick disc about 12cm (4½in) in diameter, ready for rolling out. Wrap in greaseproof paper and chill for 30 minutes.

Preheat the oven to 160°C/Gas Mark 3. Lightly grease a 28cm (11in) loose-based tart tin.

Using a well-floured rolling pin, roll out the pastry on a large piece of baking parchment to a rough-and-ready circle measuring about 33cm (13in) in diameter. Place your tart tin upside down over the circle. Lift up the four corners of the parchment and fold them towards the middle of the underside of the tin. Using both hands, hold the corners

flour

in place and quickly turn the tin over, allowing the dough
to flop into the base of the tin. There will be inevitable cracks
– just press the dough together.

Pass a rolling pin over the top of the tin to trim surplus
dough; save the trimmed dough to patch any cracks. Using
the side of your index finger, press the dough into the edge of
the tin to raise it slightly above the rim. Line the base with
foil and weigh down with baking beans, making sure they
fill the base and go all the way to the edge. Bake blind for 15
minutes, rotating the tin halfway through.

Remove the foil and beans and check that the pastry
hasn't cracked; if there are cracks, patch with the reserved
dough trimmings. Bake for 5–7 minutes more, until the
pastry is pale golden. Remove from the oven and raise the
temperature to 180°C/Gas Mark 4. Put a baking tray in
to heat.

Arrange the tomato halves in the pastry case in concentric
circles. Sprinkle the cheese evenly over the top. Beat the
eggs lightly then stir in the cream, herbs and salt and
pepper to taste. Mix well, then pour into the pastry case and
immediately put in the oven (see Cook's note). Bake for 20
minutes or until puffy and golden. Serve hot or warm.

cook's note
• Once you've filled the pastry case, immediately put it in the
oven on the heated baking sheet. This will quickly set the
filling and stop it seeping through any cracks in the pastry.

greengage and cobnut crumble

greengages 600g (1lb 5oz)
granulated sugar 85g (3oz)
water 150ml (5fl oz)
orange peel 3–4 thinly
  pared strips
thick cream to serve

for the topping
rolled oats 40g (1½oz)
quinoa flour 40g (1½oz)
tapioca starch 25g (1oz)
unsalted butter 60g (2¼oz),
  diced
granulated sugar 60g (2¼oz)
vanilla extract 1 teaspoon
salt pinch
shelled cobnuts 25g (1oz),
  roughly chopped (see
  Cook's note)

serves 4

Enjoying a brief season together, greengages and cobnuts make a lovely late summer crumble. Unlike most crumbles, I've pre-cooked the topping like a giant biscuit that's then broken into crunchy chunks and scattered over the fruit fruit.

· · ·

Preheat the oven to 190°C/Gas Mark 5. Line a baking tray with a silicone sheet.

Combine all the topping ingredients, except the chopped nuts, in the bowl of a food processor. Pulse a few times in 8-second bursts until the mixture starts to clump together. Alternatively, mix by hand, rubbing the butter into the flours first then adding the rest of the ingredients.

Tip on to the lined baking tray and gather the dough together. Flatten with the palm of your hand, then sprinkle the nuts evenly over the surface, squidging the dough with your fingers to disperse the nuts. Flatten the dough again, this time spreading it more thinly – it should be about 5mm (¼in) thick. Bake for 20 minutes, rotating the tray halfway through, or until golden at the edges. Remove from the oven, leaving the oven on, and set aside to cool – it will become crisp as it does so.

Meanwhile, slice the greengages in half along the indentation. Twist the two halves to separate. Remove the stone with a pointed teaspoon and slice each section in half again. Arrange in a single layer in a 1.4-litre (2½-pint), 5cm (2in) deep baking dish.

Put the sugar, water and orange peel in a small saucepan over a medium heat. Heat without stirring until the sugar has dissolved, then increase the heat and boil rapidly for 5 minutes or until the bubbles start to look large and syrupy. Pour the syrup over the greengages.

Once the topping is cool enough to handle, break it into bite-sized chunks and scatter over the fruit. Bake for about 15 minutes, or until the juices are bubbling. Remove from the oven and leave to settle for about 30 minutes to allow the juices to flow from the fruit and into the base of the topping.

variations
· Use skinless hazelnuts if you can't get hold of cobnuts.
· Use crimson-fleshed plums if you can't find greengages (but make sure they're sweet and luscious).

rice *flour*

plant source grain
aka ground rice, rice powder
latin name *Oryza sativa*
gluten none
protein 6–11%
goes with bananas, chicken, citrus, coconut, dairy products, eggs, fish, nuts, seafood, sesame, spices
uses batter, binder, biscuits, bread, brownies, cakes, coating for fried foods, crumble topping, desserts, dumplings, ice cream, muffins, noodles, pancakes and waffles, pastry, pizza, rice cakes (mochi), rice balls, shortbread, soufflés, thickener for soups and sauces

My appreciation of rice flour began on a memorable press trip to the Ferron mill near Verona, northern Italy, where sought-after Vialone Nano and Carnaroli rice are produced. We were treated to a cooking lesson hosted by chef Gabriele Ferron, who demonstrated recipes for rice flour pastry and an incredible rice flour ice cream. I tried them at home later and could immediately see why rice flour is a cook's best friend. I love its quiet supportiveness, its comforting neutral flavour, and the way it absorbs and harmonizes other ingredients. It's these understated qualities that make rice flour one of the most widely used gluten-free flours and a key ingredient in an eye-opening number of recipes.

Since there are reputedly more than 100,000 varieties of rice, it stands to reason there is a choice of rice flours, albeit not numbering into the thousands. Probably the most familiar, certainly in Europe and the US, is plain white rice flour, milled from short- or long-grain polished white rice. Since the bran and germ have been removed, it's a high-starch flour, rich in carbohydrates but containing very little dietary fibre. It's the colour of parchment and has a fine, sandy, free-flowing texture. It contributes an appetizing crunch to baked items – it helps 'shorten' shortbread, for example – and makes superb brownies and blondies. There is also ground rice, a similar product but with a slightly grittier texture. The two are combined in White Chocolate Blondies (see page 170).

Brown rice flour contains the bran and the germ so it's well endowed with nutrients. It's a mousy beige colour, with a faintly caramel flavour and a similar texture to white rice flour. It can be used in much the same way, though it needs more time to absorb liquids. Try it with muscovado sugar and butter in a richly flavoured crumble topping for autumn fruit, or with dark chocolate for superb brownies.

Similar to brown rice flour is roasted red rice flour, popular in Indian and Sri Lankan cuisine. The bran has been removed, but the flour still contains the nutritious germ. It's an unusual pinkish grey, with a very slightly gritty texture and a complex toasty flavour. It's used all over south India for a seemingly unending number of specialities. My favourites are lacy fermented pancakes such as *dosas* and *appams*, and fluffy steamed cakes known as *idlis* and *puttu*.

Though red rice flour is fairly easy to find in the UK and US, I first came across it at a cookery school in Kerala, southwest India. Our patient teacher showed us how to make *vatti pathiri*, puffy rice flour flatbread. The trick was to add exactly the right amount of liquid to create a dryish but pliable dough that could be rolled super-thin. It was easier said than done.

From eastern Asia comes another type of white rice flour, or rice powder, as it's sometimes called. Ground from long-grain polished white rice, it's snow-white, looks and feels like talcum powder, and squeaks when pressed. It behaves very differently to ordinary white rice flour, so be careful not to confuse the two. It's a key ingredient in a classic Singaporean street food speciality, Singapore Oyster Omelette (see page 169). This is a different take on an omelette, starting with a startlingly pristine white batter that's allowed to set before the eggs are added.

David Thompson, Thai food supremo, also puts the flour to good use in authentic desserts and sweet snacks. He lists at least nine in his book *Thai Food*. Though I'm unlikely to attempt it, I'm intrigued by his recipe for an exotic concoction of roasted smoked rice flour mixed with beaten duck egg yolks. The resulting batter is dropped into boiling syrup to form golden teardrops which must be exactly the right shape, size and density. As David warns, 'patience and skill are required'.

Not to be confused with Asian rice flour is glutinous rice flour, aka sweet rice flour, or sticky rice flour. Despite the name, it contains no gluten. It's finely milled from short-grain Japanese rice, it's super-starchy and incredibly sticky when mixed to a dough. The flour is rumoured to have been one of the components in the mortar holding the Great Wall of China together. Widely used in Japan, there are two types: mochiko and shiratamako. Shiratamako is a kind of 'instant' mochiko flour – smoother, with a more elastic texture that's easier to work with. It was unavailable at the time of writing, so I used mochiko flour for *dango* – Japanese Rice Dumplings (see page 167).

They were fun to make but had a somewhat challenging texture. The flour can also be used sparingly in cakes and bread, and even to make ice lollies.

It's easy to find glutinous rice flour and Asian rice flour online (see Sources, page 280) or in shops specializing in Oriental groceries. If you're after Asian rice flour, check that the label says 'rice flour' or 'farina' rather than 'sweet rice flour', which is the glutinous type. Both have a long shelf life and can be stored in a sealed container at room temperature for a year or more.

You'll find roasted red rice online and in large supermarkets, usually in urban areas. Plain white rice flour is also easy to find in supermarkets. Health food shops and online suppliers are better bets for brown rice flour. It goes rancid more quickly than white so it's best kept in an airtight container, ideally in the fridge for no more than six months.

Rice flour is really easy to mill at home with a NutriBullet or a milling attachment for a standing mixer. Not only will you have super-fresh flour, but you'll also have an opportunity to experiment with rare gems such as Nanjing Black or Emperor's Green or Imperial Red rice. They're grown in limited quantities but fairly easy to find online. My favourite is Nanjing Black, or 'forbidden rice' as it's sometimes called in China. It makes an ashy-grey-purple flour which I've used as dramatic dredging for fried fish. Also good is freshly milled jasmine rice flour – delicious for Oriental desserts.

japanese rice dumplings with roasted soybean topping

glutinous rice flour 100g (3½ oz), plus extra for rolling
water 100ml (3½fl oz), plus extra for boiling and cooling
roasted soybean flour (*kinako*) 4 tablespoons
golden caster sugar 1–2 tablespoons
sea salt ¼ teaspoon, or to taste

serves 2–3 as a snack

A Japanese friend once made these for me as part of a special New Year's Day brunch. The glutinous texture of the rice flour dumplings may be a little challenging for Western palates, but as my friend explained, it's important to include contrasting textures and flavours in a meal. I loved the warm biscuit flavour of the roasted soybean flour topping, known as *kinako* and quite different from regular soya bean flour (see Soya Flour, page 202). In Japan, *kinako* is commonly sprinkled over ice cream, desserts, dumplings, or rice, adding flavour, colour, a touch of sweetness and extra nutrients.

· · ·

Bring a large pot of water to the boil. Set aside a bowl of cold water for cooling the dumplings.

Sieve the rice flour into a bowl. Stir in the water and mix to a smooth paste. Set aside for 5 minutes until the water is completely absorbed.

Pinch off small chunks of the dough – about the size of a small chestnut – and roll into balls on a plate of rice flour to stop them sticking. Drop them into the boiling water. Boil for a few minutes until they rise to the top, then let them simmer on the surface for 2 minutes until cooked through. Remove with a slotted spoon and put in the bowl of cold water. Leave to cool for 5 minutes, then drain.

Meanwhile, sift the roasted soybean flour with the sugar and salt into a bowl. Tip half of it into a shallow serving dish. Arrange the drained rice dumplings on top, then sprinkle over the rest of the soybean mixture.

flour

singapore oyster omelette

eggs 4, organic or free-range
sea salt pinch
Chinese rice flour
    2 tablespoons
tapioca starch 1 tablespoon
water 100ml (3½fl oz)
fish sauce 1 tablespoon
vegetable oil 1½ tablespoons
garlic clove 1, finely chopped
spring onion 1 large, cut into
    short lengths, separated into
    white and green
raw shucked oysters
    200g (7oz)
fresh coriander sprigs
    to garnish
chilli sauce mixed with rice
    vinegar to serve

**serves 2 as a main course or
4 with other dishes**

Deftly fried to order, oyster omelette is a classic Singaporean speciality, freshly cooked at the hawker stalls. Despite the name, this is more of a broken-up pancake than an omelette. Part of the appeal is the characteristic soft yielding texture of the rice flour pancake that forms the base of the dish. If oysters are hard to come by, thick slices of portabello mushrooms are a good substitute. The recipe was given to me by my food writer friend Jenny Linford, whose mother is Singaporean. Jenny lived there as a child and has vivid memories of the remarkable food scene.

· · ·

Beat the eggs in a jug and season with a pinch of salt.

In a second jug, whisk together the rice flour, tapioca starch and water to form a very thin batter. Whisk in the fish sauce.

Heat 1 tablespoon of the oil in a large non-stick frying pan over a high heat. Pour in the rice flour batter, spreading it evenly in a thin layer in the pan. Fry for 2–3 minutes until set. Use your spatula to slice the pancake a few times to break it up a little.

Pour the beaten egg into the pan, spreading the egg evenly and thinly so that it forms a layer over the pancake. Fry briefly until the egg begins to set, then fry for 1–2 minutes more, using the spatula to break the omelette-pancake into pieces (see Cook's note), turning them so that they brown and become crisp at the edges.

Make a space in the corner of the pan and pour in the remaining ½ tablespoon of oil. Once hot, add the garlic and fry briefly until just starting to colour. Add the white spring onion and the oysters, mixing well with the garlic. Fry for 2–3 minutes, gently stirring the oysters into the omelette-pancake. Sprinkle over the green spring onion and coriander sprigs and serve at once with the chilli-vinegar sauce.

cook's note
· To avoid a scrambled egg appearance, leave big chunks of the omelette-pancake intact without stirring too much.

rice flour

white chocolate blondies with hazelnuts and cranberries

good-quality white chocolate
85g (3oz)
unsalted butter 85g (3oz), plus
extra for greasing
eggs 2, organic or free-range
caster sugar 150g (5½oz)
vanilla extract 1 teaspoon
rice flour 75g (2¾oz)
ground rice 75g (2¾oz)
cornflour 1 tablespoon
baking powder ½ teaspoon
sea salt pinch
shelled hazelnuts 55g (2oz),
roughly chopped
dried cranberries
55g (2oz)

makes 16

Contributed by France-based food writer Sarah Beattie, this recipe uses a mixture of rice flour and ground rice. Ground rice is slightly coarser than rice flour and adds a pleasant graininess to the otherwise squidgy texture. Sarah advises storing the blondies in a tin for a day or two before serving.

• • •

Preheat the oven to 150°C/Gas Mark 3. Grease an 18cm (7in) square tin, line with baking parchment and grease the paper too.

Combine the chocolate and butter in a bowl set over simmering water. Stir until melted then leave to cool slightly (see Cook's note).

Using an electric whisk, beat together the eggs and sugar for 3–4 minutes until light and thick, and the beaters leave a firm trail when lifted out of the mixture. Add the vanilla extract, then gradually beat in the cooled chocolate mixture.

Put the rice flour, ground rice, cornflour, baking powder and sea salt into a sieve set over a bowl. Muddle with your fingers, then push through the sieve once or twice until well blended. Beat into the chocolate mixture, then stir in the nuts and cranberries.

Spoon the mixture into the prepared tin. Bake for 40–50 minutes until a skewer inserted in the centre comes out clean. Leave in the tin until completely cold before slicing into 16 pieces.

cook's note
• The chocolate and butter can be melted in the microwave on Low for 2–3 minutes, stirring every 30 seconds.

rye *flour*

plant source grain
aka pumpernickel, rye meal
latin name *Secale cereale*
protein/gluten 8–14%
goes with bacon, bay leaves, buttermilk, caraway, chocolate, cheese, dill, ginger, honey, molasses, nuts, onion, pastrami, pickles, plums, smoked salmon
uses bagels, biscuits, bread, brownies, buns, cakes, crispbreads, pastry, porridge

My first taste of rye was as a young teenager on a visit to my German penfriend. Like most of the food on the trip, it was unfamiliar and served at unusual times of day. Plates of challenging rye bread sandwiches with herring and sweet-sour cucumber salad would appear mid-evening, not long after a filling supper. Strange though these customs were, the sour flavour and dense texture of the bread appealed; it was pleasantly chewy and left me feeling satisfied. Since then, rye has been my bread of choice – the darker the better.

Though rye is now grown in many parts of the world, with Germany the leading producer, it was not always a sought-after grain. Roman naturalist Pliny the Elder dismissed it as 'a very poor food and only serves to avert starvation', while Galen, the Greek physician, complained that the black bread baked from rye 'does not smell nice'. In 1943 The Wine and Food Society of London in *A Concise Encyclopaedia of Gastronomy* rather snootily described rye as 'more northern in its requirements than wheat', and then went on to state, 'In Sweden, rye cakes are to the peasantry what oat cakes are to the Scotch.'

While it's true that rye was thought of as poor man's flour, it was an important staple, and still is in parts of Central and Eastern Europe and Scandinavia. The Vikings were in fact what marketing people call 'early adopters', no doubt because rye is an excellent source of energy-rich carbohydrate and protein. The so-called 'northern requirements' mean that, unlike wheat, rye is sturdy enough to survive poor soil and a harsh climate.

Even the flour itself has a sturdy look. It's a wholesome beige, coarse-textured and flecked with sizeable fragments of husk – it reminds me of the knitting wool used for Shetland jumpers. It also has an inviting aroma that's somehow reassuring and timeless.

Rye has interesting nutritional credentials. Unusually for a grain, it has a high level of dietary fibre in the actual endosperm – the starchy inner part of a grain – whereas fibre is normally located in the outer layer of bran. This particular fibre is called beta-glucan, known to lower blood cholesterol and reduce the risk of heart disease. Rye flour is also a good source of iron, B-vitamins and resistant starch (see page 205), which generally improves gut health.

Depending on processing, rye flour is high in certain types of protein (see page 59), though not in the two proteins that make up gluten: glutenin and gliadin (see Gluten, page 60). It's low in glutenin, which gives strength and structure to dough, but high in gliadin (aka 'secalin' in rye), which is responsible for stretchiness. As far as the baker is concerned, this means that the bread dough will be elastic but won't have the necessary strength to hold its shape.

At the risk of being overly scientific, it's worth mentioning that rye flour contains substances known as pentosans, which to some extent compensate for the lack of strength. Pentosans are a type of carbohydrate that suck up water, and then swell during proving and baking, trapping gases and creating a firm structure once adequately heated. The inherent moisture is the reason rye dough can be a challenge to work with, but it's also why a loaf will last for a week or more without drying out.

Moving from lab to kitchen, the cook has a choice of light, medium and dark flours; the more bran left in after processing, the darker the flour. Light rye flour has had all the bran removed and, some would say, most of the flavour. Pumpernickel flour, aka rye meal or whole rye, is the darkest. It's coarsely ground and sometimes contains cracked rye grains.

Bread made purely with dark rye flour will be incredibly dense and dark. As well-known UK food writer Nigel Slater says, 'it can often be a step away from a house brick'. Less challenging is a lighter and easier loaf made with a 2:1 mix of strong wholemeal bread flour and dark rye flour, as in Seeded Rye Bread (see page 175). Buttermilk and dried yeast increase the rise, while plenty of cracked rye grains and mixed seeds provide texture. A generous amount of time allowed for proving will reward with satisfying flavour.

Chocolate and rye flour make good culinary partners in tangy pastry for Chocolate Tartlets with Ganache and Ginger Cream (see page 178) and in crisp Chocolate-Dipped Spiced Biscuits (see page 177). The flour goes well with savoury ingredients, too. Gherkins and pastrami, and smoked salmon and cream cheese are classic sandwich fillings, especially in the US. Scandinavia is well known for its superb tangy rye-based crispbreads, while in the Karelian district of Finland an iconic open-faced pasty is made with thin rye dough filled with mashed potatoes or rice. There is also *kalakukko*, a rye pastry pie filled with fish meat or vegetables.

A leftover rye loaf can be put to work in a surprisingly cloudlike dessert that I enjoyed on a trip to Denmark. Slices of dense dark rye bread were gently torn and crumbled with sugar and cocoa, left to amalgamate to a rich chocolatey pap, and then layered with whipped cream. Composed in a deep glass bowl, the alternating sepia and cream strata looked stunning and tasted even more so.

Thanks to an increasingly health-conscious public with a passion for baking, there is now a very good choice of rye flours in supermarkets, health food shops and online. Medium and dark rye flours contain the oily germ and will therefore become rancid more quickly than light rye flour. Keep them for up to six months in a sealed container in the fridge, or even in the freezer if you don't use it regularly. Light rye flour can be stored in a cool room for up to a year.

seeded rye bread

dark rye flour 150g (5½oz)
strong wholemeal bread flour
    250g (9oz)
easy-bake dried yeast
    2 teaspoons
sea salt 1½ teaspoons
caster sugar 1½ teaspoons
chopped rye grain 125g (4½oz)
    (see Cook's note)
mixed seeds, such as pumpkin,
    caroway and linseed 75g
    (2¾oz), plus extra
    for sprinkling
vegetable oil 1 tablespoon,
    plus extra for greasing
buttermilk 100ml (3½fl oz)
tepid water 225–275ml
    (8–9½fl oz)

makes 1 loaf

This is craggy hard-core rye bread. Danish and Eastern European friends have told me how grandmothers would tuck a loaf like this under their upper arm while deftly slicing it with the bread knife. Given the nature of the crust I can well imagine the scene. The dough is a mix of rye flour and strong wholemeal bread flour that helps it rise. Allow at least 12–18 hours for the first rising, 4–8 hours for the second.

· · ·

Put the flours, dried yeast, salt and sugar into a sieve set over a large bowl. Muddle with your fingers, then push twice through the sieve. Stir in the chopped rye grain and the seeds. Make a well in the centre and pour in the oil, buttermilk and tepid water. Stir to mix, drawing in the dry ingredients from around the edge. The dough will be sticky, so flour your hands well before gathering it together.

Tip the dough on to a floured work surface and form into a ball. Ideally, put the dough in the bowl of a standing mixer fitted with a dough hook. Knead on speed 2 for 15 minutes, or until the dough clumps around the hook. Alternatively, give your arms a workout and knead by hand, pulling and stretching the dough until elastic and springy. Tip the dough into an oiled bowl, cover with a clean damp tea towel and leave in a cool place for at least 12–18 hours.

Grease the base and sides of a bread tin measuring about 17x10x9cm (6½x4x3½in). Line with baking parchment and grease the paper too.

Turn the dough on to a floured work surface, and knead for 5 minutes. Push it into the bread tin, lightly cover with cling film and leave to rise at room temperature for 4–8 hours.

Preheat the oven to 220°C/Gas Mark 7. Slash the dough in a criss-cross pattern and sprinkle with water. Bake for 15 minutes, then reduce the temperature to 180°C/Gas Mark 4 and bake for a further 45–50 minutes, rotating the tin every 15 minutes. The bread is cooked when the base of the tin sounds hollow when you rap it. If it doesn't seem quite cooked, turn the loaf out of the tin and bake for 5 minutes more. Put on a wire rack to cool completely before slicing.

cook's note
· You can buy pre-chopped rye grain, or you can use a NutriBullet or a flour grinder attached to a standing mixer.

flour

chocolate-dipped spiced biscuits with walnuts and black pepper

medium or light rye flour 150g
(5½oz)

plain flour 100g (3½oz), plus
extra for dusting

bicarbonate of soda
½ teaspoon

unsalted butter 150g (5½oz)

granulated sugar 75g (2¾ oz)

clear mild honey
2 tablespoons, such as acacia

egg yolks 2, organic or free-
range

sea salt pinch

ground cinnamon 1 teaspoon

cloves 3, finely crushed

freshly ground black pepper
2 teaspoons

lemon finely grated zest of 1

shelled walnuts 150g (5½oz),
ground finely

whole peppercorns to decorate

plain chocolate 200g (7oz)
(85% cocoa solids)

makes about 24

These Eastern European biscuits have a beautiful spicy fragrance that reminds me of Christmas. Traditionally they were cut into heart shapes and given as love tokens – the mixture of honey and pepper was thought to be an aphrodisiac. This is based on a recipe from *The Melting Pot: Balkan Food and Cookery* by Maria Kaneva-Johnson.

• • •

Preheat the oven to 150°C/Gas Mark 2. Line a couple of baking sheets with silicone or baking parchment.

Put the flours and bicarbonate of soda into a sieve set over a large bowl. Muddle with your fingers, then push through the sieve once or twice until well blended.

Using an electric whisk, cream the butter, sugar and honey in a bowl for about 4 minutes until pale and fluffy. Beat in the egg yolks, followed by the salt, cinnamon, cloves, black pepper and lemon zest. Next, stir in the walnuts and the flour mixture and mix to a soft pliable dough.

Lightly flour the work surface and your rolling pin. Tip the dough on to the work surface and knead briefly until smooth. Roll out to a thickness of 5mm (¼in). Cut into circles with a 6cm (2½in) cutter. Re-roll the trimmings and cut out more circles. Arrange on the baking sheets, allowing room for the biscuits to spread. Decorate the lower half of each biscuit with peppercorns to represent eyes and a mouth. Leave the top half empty for dipping in chocolate once the biscuits are cooked.

Bake for 20–25 minutes, rotating the trays halfway through, until starting to turn golden brown at the edges. Remove from the oven and leave on the baking trays to firm up. Carefully move to wire racks and leave to cool completely.

Break the chocolate into small chunks and put in a shallow microwave-proof bowl. Microwave on medium for several 30-second bursts, swirling the bowl each time. Alternatively, melt in a bowl set over simmering water. Be careful not to let any moisture get into the bowl, otherwise the chocolate will 'seize' or thicken to a lump that's difficult to work with.

Once melted, tilt the bowl so the chocolate goes to one side. Dip the half of each biscuit without the peppercorns in the chocolate so the chocolate will look like a hat. Allow each biscuit to drip over the bowl, before placing it on a rack set over a tray. Repeat with the rest of the biscuits. Leave in a cool place for 30–40 minutes to set. Store in an airtight tin.

chocolate tartlets with ganache and ginger cream

medium or light rye flour 70g
  (2½oz)
plain flour 50g (1¾oz)
caster sugar 3 tablespoons
unsweetened cocoa powder
  2½ tablespoons
unsalted butter 85g (3oz)
  chilled and diced
thick double cream
  3 tablespoons
chilled water ½ tablespoon
vegetable oil for greasing
preserved stem ginger
  2 nuggets, sliced into thin
  matchsticks, to decorate

for the ganache
plain chocolate 100g (3½oz)
  (85% cocoa solids)
thick double cream 225ml
  (8fl oz)

for the ginger cream
double cream 150ml (5fl oz)
syrup from a jar of preserved
  stem ginger 2 tablespoons

makes 6

you will need:
six fluted metal tart tins, 10cm
(4in) in diameter

Mixed with chocolate and cream, rye flour loses its rather wholesome image. Decadent and deadly, these tarts will dazzle. One is enough.

. . .

Put the flours, sugar and cocoa powder into a sieve set over a bowl. Muddle with your fingers, then push through the sieve once or twice until well blended. Tip into the bowl of a food processor with the chilled butter and cream. Pulse briefly until the dough starts to clump together, dribbling in the chilled water if it seems too dry. Wrap in greaseproof paper and chill for 30 minutes.

To make the ganache, break the chocolate into pea-sized pieces and put in a bowl. Heat the cream until almost boiling, pour over the chocolate and beat until melted. Leave to cool, then chill while you make the pastry cases.

Meanwhile, preheat the oven to 180°C/Gas Mark 4. Put a baking sheet in to heat. Lightly grease the tart tins.

Lightly flour the work surface and your rolling pin. Divide the dough into six equal pieces and form into balls. Roll out into 12cm (4½in) circles, then carefully lower each one into the tins, pressing the dough well into the edges with the side of your index finger. Pass a rolling pin over the top to trim off surplus dough, then press the dough into the edge again, to raise it very slightly above the rim (see Cook's notes).

Line the bases with foil and weigh down with baking beans. Bake blind for 10 minutes, then remove the foil and beans, and bake for another 7–8 minutes, or until the pastry is firm. Remove from the oven, put on a wire rack and leave to cool for 10 minutes. Turn out by inverting the tins and tapping gently on the base.

Using an electric whisk, whip the chilled ganache for about 3 minutes until thickened and the beaters leave a trail when lifted (see Cook's notes). Divide the ganache between the pastry cases. If necessary, chill for 30 minutes to firm up.

To make the ginger cream, use an electric whisk to whip the double cream with the ginger syrup for 4–5 minutes, or until the beaters leave a definite trail when lifted. Pipe or spoon the cream over the ganache, leaving a visible border of chocolate. Sprinkle with the preserved ginger matchsticks and serve.

flour

- Make sure the pastry doesn't spill over on to the outside of the tin, otherwise the tartlets will be difficult to remove when baked.
- Take care not to overwhip the ganache. It shouldn't become grainy.

semolina

plant source grain
aka semola (Italian), sémola (Spanish), semoule (French)
latin name *Triticum durum*
protein/gluten 10–12%
goes with anything
uses biscuits, bread, cakes, coating for fried food, croquettes, dumplings, flatbreads, gnocchi, pasta, porridge, puddings

Creamy yellow with a faint wheaty aroma, semolina is one of the world's most widely used products, yet it's one of the trickiest to describe and understand. The word comes from the Latin *simila* meaning 'finest wheat flour', yet as the late Alan Davidson rightly points out in *The Oxford Companion to Food*, this is at odds with the English use of the word, which usually means the coarse residue from milled wheat grains. Those of a certain age may shudder at memories of the claggy semolina pudding which, as Davidson states, 'does not show off the product to advantage'.

The Wine and Food Society, London, in the Cereals section of *A Concise Encyclopaedia of Gastronomy*, describes semolina as a 'pappy food for infants', then finger-waggingly states: 'The name *Semolina*, and even more the French culinary form *Semoule*, are used wrongly, but not infrequently, for fine forms of different flours.' So this leaves us with a product that can be anything from a milky pudding or baby food to a fine flour or a coarse meal milled from a particular type of wheat.

Let's go back to basics. Semolina is typically milled from hard wheat (*Triticum durum*), though it can also be milled from other varieties of wheat, and even from barley, rice or maize. During the milling process the grain is separated into its constituent parts: bran, germ and the starchy endosperm. Depending on hardness, the endosperm is milled into fine flour or a coarser one, i.e. semolina.

Confusingly, semolina itself isn't necessarily coarse; it comes in fine and medium grinds, too. The fine grind can be justifiably called flour and is used as one. Medium and coarse grinds are used as a crisp coating for fried foods, or mixed with ordinary flour to add texture to baked items or to prevent dough from sticking to surfaces – to help a pizza base glide smoothly from the peel and into the oven, for example. The coarse grind is also used for couscous, meaning the grain itself rather than the dish of the same name.

Semolina is perhaps best known as a flour for making a particular type of pasta. In Italy it's called *semola* (bran) *di grano duro* (from hard wheat). There is also *semola rimacinata* (re-milled), which is finer and easier to work with (see Sources, page 280). It makes a tasty but challengingly stiff pasta dough, as in Orecchiette with Leafy Greens (see page 184), a popular dish from southern Italy. With a pleasing rough-and-ready texture, it's quite different from egg-based pasta. Also popular in Italy is *pane di Altamura*, a special semolina bread from the region just above Italy's heel. Made with *semola rimacinata*, it's a rich golden yellow with a contrasting dark crust that, by law, must be more than 3mm (1⁄10in) thick. It's one of the most enticing breads imaginable.

Heading west to Spain, semolina is used in much the same way as elsewhere – in bread, cakes and other baked items. The Spanish also have a special coating flour for deep-frying (see Sources, page 280), which perhaps reflects the importance to them of immaculate deep-fried foods. Described on the packet as *para fritos y rebozados* (for frying and batters), the flour is a mixture of soft wheat semolina and durum wheat semolina. It makes perfect creamy batter for Deep-Fried Squid with Paprika Mayonnaise (see page 186).

Continuing round the Mediterranean, durum wheat semolina certainly holds pride of place in Morocco. The coarsest grind is used for couscous granules, laboriously rolled by hand in ordinary wheat flour to keep them separate. Writing about couscous in the late 1950s, Madame Guinaudeau, author of the classic *Traditional Moroccan*

Cooking, memorably waxes lyrical: '... each grain separated from the other, so light, so smooth and scented, and digested with incredible ease'.

Medium-grade semolina is equally important. It's used for pasta, delicious little biscuits and satisfying flatbreads – essential with any Moroccan meal. The finest grade is used for *warqa* – a filo-like pastry – and for deliciously crisp sweet or savoury pastries, and several kinds of pancakes. I particularly like *beghrir*, Thousand-Hole Pancakes (see page 183), which I learned to make at a homely rhiad in Marrakech. Delectably light and spongy, rather like a thin English crumpet, they do indeed have many holes.

Jumping to Eastern Europe, you'll find all kinds of dumplings, porridges and sweetmeats made with fine semolina.

I'm not a great lover of desserts but am curiously addicted to *túrógombóc*, Hungary's ambrosial cream cheese dumplings sprinkled with crisp buttery breadcrumbs (see page 191).

Another favourite is *sheera*, a celebratory dessert from India made with fine semolina. This is really a super-exotic and colourful version of British semolina pudding. Try the recipe on page 188.

It's easy to find all grades of semolina in supermarkets and online (see Sources, page 280), but do check the packet and make sure it's milled from hard durum wheat. Soft wheat semolina is lower in gluten and behaves very differently. I've also found that brands vary in how much liquid needs adding. Again, check the packet instructions before you begin.

moroccan thousand-hole pancakes (beghrir)

dry active yeast ½ tablespoon
tepid water 350ml (12fl oz)
fine semolina 110g (4oz)
pasta flour or fine cake flour
    55g (2oz)
sea salt ½ teaspoon
sugar ½ teaspoon
baking powder 1 teaspoon
unsalted butter to serve
honey, jam or cream cheese
    to serve

makes 8–10

Beghrir are thick pancakes made from a yeasted batter, which is a mix of semolina and fine plain flour. The yeast causes hundreds of bubbles to break on the surface as the pancake cooks. I love the way the bubbling surface gradually changes from a pale yellow liquid to cooked dough, and the very last smidgen of uncooked dough just fades away. The charming cook at the Marrakech rhiad where I was staying taught me to make them. As she explained, the batter must be exactly the right consistency – fairly thin. If it is too thick the bubbles can't form. Enjoy them for breakfast slathered with butter and honey or jam, or cream cheese.

• • •

Whisk the yeast into the lukewarm water. Put the semolina, cake flour, sea salt, sugar and baking powder into a sieve set over a bowl. Muddle with your fingers, then push through the sieve. Sieve once or twice more until well mixed.

Using a stick blender or electric whisk, whisk the yeast mixture into the flour mixture. Keep beating for about 1 minute until bubbly and creamy. The batter should be thin like crêpe batter. Cover and leave to stand for 30 minutes to 1 hour, or until the top is foamy.

Heat a shallow non-stick frying pan over a medium heat. Stir the batter then carefully and slowly pour a small ladleful into the centre of the pan. Allow the batter to naturally spread into a circle – don't swirl the pan. Cook for about 3 minutes or until bubbles appear on the surface and the batter no longer looks wet or sticky. Cook on one side only. Slide on to a clean tea towel and repeat with the remaining batter. Arrange the beghrir in a single layer to cool.

Serve right away with butter and honey, jam or cream cheese. Alternatively, spray a little vegetable oil over the bubbly side and store them in pairs, bubbly sides facing, like a sandwich. They can be wrapped in foil and kept in the fridge for 2–3 days.

orecchiette with leafy greens

Made with a simple flour and water dough, orecchiette (little ears) are popular in southern Italy. They are easy to buy dried, but so much better fresh – they're simple and satisfying to make once you get the hang of it. The flour used is *semola di grano duro* (Italian semolina made with hard wheat). It makes the dough a little bit rough, which, in turn, encourages the oil or sauce to cling to it. Orecchiette are good served simply with olive oil, garlic and pepper, but wilted leafy greens, particularly *cime di rapa* (turnip tops), are a traditional accompaniment. This recipe is based on one from *The Geometry of Pasta* by Caz Hildebrand and Jacob Kennedy.

flour

Italian semolina flour 300g
(10½oz) (see Cook's notes)
water 150ml (5fl oz)
leafy greens 450g (1lb) such
as turnip tops (*cime di rapa*),
chard, cavolo nero
extra-virgin olive oil
dried chilli flakes ¼ teaspoon
sea salt 2 teaspoons, plus an
extra pinch for seasoning the
greens
freshly ground black pepper
freshly grated Parmesan
cheese to serve

serves 4–6

Sift the flour into a large bowl. Make a well in the middle
and pour in the water. Whisk with a fork, gradually drawing
in the flour from around the edge. Once the dough starts to
come together, tip on to a clean work surface and knead to
incorporate all the flour. Keep kneading for 7–10 minutes
or until the dough feels pliable (see Cook's notes). Wrap in
greaseproof paper and leave to rest for at least an hour.

Meanwhile, trim any tough stalks from your chosen greens.
Slice the leaves crossways into ribbons. Have ready a
steamer set over boiling water.

Divide the dough into six, then roll into thin sausages about
1cm (½in) in diameter. With the sausage facing away from
you, hold a round-tipped knife (a butter knife is ideal) with
two hands, horizontally across the dough sausage, one hand
just short of the tip and the other close to the handle. Tilting
the knife blade back towards you, slice or scrape the dough
into little discs, pushing away from you as you do so.

Gently hold the sides of each disc between the finger and
thumb of one hand. Press the tip of the knife into the dough
about halfway along the disc. Coax the knife down and
forwards towards your fingertips, pressing into the disc, then
quickly pull it out. You should be left with a piece of dough
that looks like a tiny ear. Repeat with the rest of the dough –
you'll soon get the hang of it.

Meanwhile, bring a very large pot of water to the boil. While
you're waiting for this to boil, steam the greens for 5–7
minutes, or until just tender. Tip into a warm serving dish
and toss with a dribble of olive oil, chilli flakes, and a little
salt and pepper. Keep warm while you cook the pasta.
Once the pasta water is boiling, add the 2 teaspoons of salt
and the orecchiette. Bring back to the boil, then cook for
about 3 minutes, or until just al dente. Drain and add to the
dish of greens. Toss well, sprinkle with Parmesan and serve.

cook's notes
- It's well worth getting hold of Italian semolina flour – *semola
di grano duro* (see Sources, page 280). It's ground from hard
wheat and high in gluten. *Semola rimacinata* is the same
flour but ground more finely. I find this easier to work with
than the medium-ground version.
- As Caz Hildebrand and Jacob Kennedy specify, the texture
of the dough should be soft enough to work (like a stress ball)
but dry enough not to stick to itself.

deep-fried squid with paprika mayonnaise

squid 6 small, cut into rings,
   plus tentacles if you have
   them (about 275g/9½oz in
   total)
vegetable oil for deep-frying
Spanish flour 6 tablespoons for
   frying (*para fritos y rebozados*)
sea salt flakes
freshly ground black pepper
sage leaves or oregano leaves
   handful to garnish
lemon wedges to garnish

for the paprika mayonnaise
good-quality mayonnaise
   6 tablespoons
Greek yogurt 4 tablespoons
garlic cloves 2, crushed
smoked paprika ½ teaspoon,
   plus extra for sprinkling
lemon juice 1 teaspoon
sea salt 2 pinches

serves 2–3

This is adapted from a recipe by food writer Kay Plunkett-Hogge, from *A Sherry & A Little Plate of Tapas* – such an enjoyable book. As Kay points out, in Spain there is a special coating flour for deep-frying (*para fritos y rebozados*), particularly useful for seafood. You can buy it online (see Sources, page 280) or in speciality shops. If you can't get hold of it, use a 50/50 combination of plain wheat flour and fine breadcrumbs or cornmeal.

• • •

First make the mayonnaise. Put all the ingredients in a serving bowl, give them a good stir and set aside.

Wash and thoroughly dry the squid. Snip off any thread-like trailing bits and remove any cartilage from the tentacles.

Pour enough oil into a deep pan (see Cook's notes) to come to a depth of about 5cm (2in). Heat over a medium-high heat until very hot but not smoking – 180°C (350°F) on a thermometer, or until a cube of bread browns in 1 minute.

While the oil is heating, tip the flour into a shallow dish and season with salt and pepper. Coat the squid with the flour (see Cook's notes), shaking off any excess.

Lower the squid into the oil and fry for 3–4 minutes, or until crisp. Remove and drain on crumpled paper towels. Tip into a warm serving dish.

Reheat the oil if necessary. Throw in the sage leaves and fry for 2–3 minutes, or until crisp. Drain on paper towels and strew over the squid. Serve with lemon wedges on the side and the mayonnaise for dipping.

cook's notes
• I use a relatively small deep pan (20x8cm/8x3¼in) that doesn't need vast quantities of oil for deep-frying.
• Coat the squid with the flour just before you're about to fry. Don't be tempted to get ahead by doing it earlier – you'll end up with a soggy coating.

flour

the miller's tale

To find out more about traditional flour production I visited Cann Mills, a working watermill near Shaftsbury, Dorset. Here, fifth-generation miller Michael Stoate produces stone-ground flours, both organic and non-organic, for the domestic and bakery trade. The Stoate family have been milling flour since 1832, first at Watchet in Somerset and then in Bristol, before finally settling at Cann Mills in 1947. The mill's history goes back to the Domesday Book, and it is the remaining working watermill of the five once located on the River Sturkel.

The ancient buildings make a bucolic sight set deep in a green wooded valley a few miles from the river's source. A large and limpid millpond is home to slumbering swans, drifting ducks and glistening dragonflies, while in an adjacent meadow chickens contentedly scratch and lambs gambol.

In contrast to the external peace and quiet, the mill machine room is a truly awesome and noisy place. At the heart of the operation is a massive iron waterwheel that harnesses the power of the rushing river. The wheel is connected to a Heath Robinson-style arrangement of overhead belt-driven wheels and spindles which, in turn, drive two huge horizontal millstones that grind the grain into flour.

Shouting over the thump and clatter of the machinery, Michael explains that the majority of his wheat for bread-making is sourced locally but always blended with a proportion of high-gluten wheat (see Gluten, page 60) from elsewhere. Like a wine producer, he must continually taste and adjust this symbiotic mix to create flour with consistent baking and eating qualities.

Though the actual term 'stone ground' is a familiar one, I hadn't previously seen the process in action. Flour is funnelled through a wooden hopper into a 'shoe' in which a rotating metal device called a 'damsel' (apparently on account of its continual chatter) dribbles the flour on to the grinding stones below. The lower or 'bed' stone remains stationary while the upper or 'runner' stone rotates. The stones do not actually touch – it is the carved furrows on the surface that shear the grain and shunt the ground flour into a sack below. It is fascinating to watch this ancient process, and also to learn how the slow grinding generates a gentle warmth that ensures that the wheat germ oil in the grain is distributed evenly through the flour, maximizing nutrients as well as flavour.

Once ground, the flour is sieved, which, depending on the grade, removes a proportion of the bran. The flour is then weighed and sealed in Cann Mills distinctive white paper sacks before distribution to local delis and farm shops. There is also an on-line shop from which customers can buy direct.

The milling revolution Michael Stoate is not alone in milling with care. A strong but quiet revolution is taking place that has resulted in a growing number of artisan mills producing quality flour. Another aspect is a welcome and steady increase in bakers, both professional and amateur, who are milling their own flour in-house. As a regular user of the KitchenAid milling attachment, I can vouch for a difference in freshness and flavour, plus significantly improved baked items.

Roller milling This high-speed system was developed in the late nineteenth century when refined white flour became fashionable and stone-ground flour was considered rather too rustic. A series of steel rollers and sieves separate the bran and germ from the endosperm (see Wheat and heritage flours, page 262). The downside is that the force of the mechanism fractures and partially damages the grains, and also generates heat that destroys some of the nutrients. However, as Tess Lister of UK-based Shipton Mill points out, milling technology is continually evolving, and attempts are being made to prevent the damage and nutrient loss by reducing the temperature and pressure between the rollers.

diwali dessert with cardamom, nuts and sultanas (sheera)

whole almonds 1½ tablespoons
unsalted shelled pistachios
  1 tablespoon
whole milk 600ml (1 pint)
saffron strands ¼ teaspoon
ghee, clarified butter or
  unsalted butter 55g (2oz)
fine semolina 175g (6oz)
sugar 85g (3oz)
green or golden raisins
  1 tablespoon
ground cardamom 1 teaspoon

*to serve (optional, but
recommended)*
diced mixed fresh fruit
  such as banana, apple,
  orange, mango, pineapple,
  pomegranate seeds and
  halved green grapes

serves 6

Sheera is India's most ubiquitous and best-loved sweet, made during festivals and on auspicious occasions, including Diwali, birthdays and whenever anyone passes an exam or driving test. Observant Hindus offer a small portion to deities in temples or home shrines before distributing the rest to family and friends. The recipe was contributed by food writer Sejal Sukhadwala. Though she likes to eat *sheera* as a dessert, Sejal explains that it's more like a sweet snack eaten at breakfast or as part of a special occasion meal. It's at its best hot, but room temperature is fine too.

• • •

Put the nuts in a bowl and cover with boiling water. Leave to soak for 20–30 minutes, then slip off the skins.

Heat the milk to just under boiling point. Crush the saffron strands in a mortar, add to the warm milk and set aside.

Heat the ghee or butter in a wide non-stick pan. Tip in the semolina and cook, uncovered, over a medium heat for 10 minutes, stirring often. When cooked through, the semolina should become a couple of shades darker and give off a nutty aroma; you don't want it to taste raw.

Turn down the heat to low. Pour in the saffron-flavoured milk a little at a time, stirring continuously. Cook for 3–4 minutes until the milk is absorbed and the mixture resembles porridge. Make sure there are no lumps.

Add the sugar and raisins, stirring until all the sugar is incorporated. The mixture should just begin to look like light flaky dough – that's how it's supposed to be. Add the cardamom powder and half the nuts, then remove from the heat and stir well (see Cook's notes).

Serve hot or warm, decorated with the rest of the nuts and a couple of tablespoonfuls of diced fruit on the side.

cook's notes
• The finished consistency should be not too dry or too moist – somewhere between a freshly baked sponge and fine oatmeal porridge.
• Any leftovers can be reheated in a steamer set over boiling water.
• Though not traditional, a scoop of good-quality vanilla ice cream goes well with hot sheera.

semolina

flour

hungarian cream cheese and orange dumplings (túrógombóc)

full fat soft cheese 500g (1lb 2oz), preferably organic
sea salt pinch
eggs 2, organic or free-range, lightly beaten
fine semolina or Italian semolina rimicinata (see Sources, page 280) 100g (3½oz), plus extra for dusting
caster sugar 2 tablespoons
orange finely grated zest of 1
unsalted butter 50g (1¾oz)
fresh breadcrumbs 60g (2¼oz)
soured cream 200ml (7fl oz)
icing sugar 4 tablespoons
orange segments to decorate

makes 15–16

Trawling through Eastern European cookbooks, I found an enormous number of recipes for sweet cheese dumplings. I particularly like the introduction to one in Lesley Chamberlain's *The Food and Cooking of Eastern Europe*. She quotes the late writer and gourmet Joseph Wechsberg describing the pleasure such dumplings bring: 'You … perform the ritual of sprinkling them with brown butter, cottage cheese and sugar, and the same ingredients again, with the sugar last. You may add more layers … ad infinitum, until the dumplings have disappeared like a northern landscape under the snow.'

My recipe evolved through trial and error, but it was well worth experimenting for such a delightful dessert. You will need to allow 1–6 hours for the dough to rest.

• • •

Whisk together the soft cheese, sea salt, eggs, semolina, caster sugar and orange zest in a bowl. Cover and leave to rest in the fridge for at least an hour, or up to 6 hours.

Bring a very large saucepan of salted water to the boil. Sprinkle some semolina over the base of a shallow dish. Shape the dough into 15–16 dumplings, about 5cm (2in) in diameter, gently rolling them in the semolina. Simmer in batches for 15 minutes or until they float to the top and are cooked through (see Cook's notes). Use a slotted spoon to move them to a warm dish. They will be quite soft so handle them with care.

While the dumplings are cooking, heat the butter in a frying pan over a medium-high heat. Add the breadcrumbs and sizzle for about 5 minutes until golden and crisp. Sprinkle over the dumplings.

Gently warm the soured cream with the icing sugar. Trickle some of it over the breadcrumbs and dumplings, and pour the rest into a small jug. Decorate with the orange segments and serve right away.

cook's notes
- Boil the dumplings in batches. They will expand and won't cook evenly if they're overcrowded.
- To check if the dumplings are cooked, lift one from the pan and slice it in half. The dough should be evenly cooked all the way through.

sesame *flour*

plant source seed
aka sesame meal
latin name *Sesamum indicum*
gluten none
protein 46%
goes with bananas, chocolate, dried fruit, lime leaves, milk, nuts, pears, poultry, seafood
uses binding, coating for fried foods; dips, pancakes, smoothies, thickener for sauces, soups and stews

Milled from sesame seeds, this understated and underused flour certainly delivers on the nutritional front. It contains an impressive amount of essential amino acids that make up protein (see page 59), plus iron, dietary fibre and important B-vitamins – and no gluten whatsoever. Since the oil has been extracted from the seeds before milling, it's also low in fat. All in all, it's the flour to use if you're vegan or following a gluten-free diet, or simply want to make sure you're getting nutrients that might otherwise be missing from your diet.

As far as the cook is concerned, sesame flour also delivers on versatility. Its mild tahini flavour co-exists happily with a range of other ingredients. It makes excellent pancake batter and is a nutritious thickener for sauces and milky puddings – try Lime Leaf-scented Blancmange with Sesame Brittle (see page 194). You can add it to cakes and biscuits, or use it for binding bars and flapjacks. Try it instead of breadcrumbs in stuffings, or for coating egg-dipped fish fillets and vegetables before frying. Otherwise, keep things simple and just add a spoonful to a smoothie, sprinkle over yogurt, fruit or breakfast cereal, or stir it into a spicy vegetable stew or curry towards the end of cooking.

Unlike most flours, sesame flour has a clumpy texture, rather like damp sand on a tropical beach. It's a good idea to sieve it, and then to stir meticulously to prevent lumps when mixing with liquids.

You'll find sesame flour online (see Sources, page 280), in health food shops and good supermarkets.

lime leaf-scented blancmange
with sesame brittle

double-lobed lime leaves
  3 large, fresh or frozen but
  not dried
whole milk 600ml (1 pint),
  preferably organic
cornflour 4 tablespoons
sesame flour 4 tablespoons
caster sugar 3 tablespoons,
  or to taste

for the sesame brittle
caster sugar 200g (7oz)
toasted sesame seeds
  4 tablespoons

serves 4–6

You will need:
  up to six 150ml (5fl oz) metal
  heart-shaped moulds or
  ramekin dishes

One of my favourite desserts, this is an irresistible combination of soft, scented milky blancmange and gleaming shards of crunchy brittle. Sesame flour adds subtle flavour and helps thicken the blancmange. You can buy it in good supermarkets, health food shops and online (see Sources, page 280).

. . .

Remove the tough stalk from the lime leaves and roughly shred the leaves. Save a few shreds as a garnish and put the rest in a saucepan with all but 4 tablespoons of the milk. Slowly bring to a simmer over a medium heat. Remove from the heat and leave to infuse for about 20 minutes.

In a second saucepan, blend the cornflour and the reserved 4 tablespoons of milk to a smooth slurry. Stir in the sesame flour and caster sugar. Strain the infused milk on to the slurry, stirring to mix. Bring to the boil, whisking constantly until thickened – about 3 minutes. Simmer gently for another 3 minutes, continuing to whisk. Pour into the moulds, leave until cool, then chill for 2 hours, or until set.

Meanwhile, make the sesame brittle. Line a baking sheet with a sheet of silicone. Pour the sugar into a heavy-based saucepan over a medium heat. Let the sugar melt without stirring, shaking the pan occasionally until all the sugar has dissolved. Increase the heat slightly and bring to the boil. Let it bubble away for a few minutes until evenly golden. Stir in the sesame seeds and boil for a few more seconds. Pour on to the silicone-lined baking sheet, tilting it so that the brittle spreads in a very thin layer. Once it's set solid, break into shards or small fragments.

When ready to serve, turn the blancmange out on to serving plates. Decorate with two or three sesame shards and a sliver of lime leaf.

cook's notes
- When making the sesame brittle, watch the bubbling sugar like a hawk. It can burn very quickly.
- The brittle will keep for a week or more as long as it's stored in an airtight container.
- If the blancmange is reluctant to leave the moulds, invert the moulds over serving plates and cover with a tea towel soaked in hot water and wrung out. Give the plate and mould a shake to release the blancmange.

sesame *flour*

sorghum *flour*

plant source seed
aka great millet, juwar, milo
latin name *Sorghum bicolor*
gluten none
protein 9%
goes with almonds, bananas, fennel, nuts, oranges, warm spices
uses biscuits, bread, cakes, Indian flatbreads, muffins, pancakes, porridge

Sorghum flour is what I think of as an accommodating flour. It's sweet and gentle, easy to use, and doesn't overpower other ingredients. The plant itself is robust, surviving arid soils and long-term droughts by becoming dormant until conditions improve. As such, it's a vital subsistence crop for impoverished populations in rural Africa, India and Central America.

Though sorghum is the world's fifth largest crop with a history dating back thousands of years, in the US it isn't particularly well known as a cooking ingredient. There, it's mainly used in animal fodder, syrup and biofuel. In the UK, though, sorghum has enthusiastic followers. It's been tipped as the new quinoa, and as a result is increasingly featured in food media and on menus in health-food-orientated cafés and restaurants.

Ground from pendulous seed heads, the flour has a sweetish aroma, a mild flavour and feels beautifully silky when rubbed between the fingers. The colour ranges from brownish red to an understated creamy beige. The nutritious outer layers of the seeds are left intact during milling so the flour is naturally whole grain. It's high-protein, high-fibre and gluten-free, and a good source of resistant starch (see page 205), which generally improves gut health.

According to gluten-free baking diva Emma Goss-Custard, sorghum flour is a must-have. Like all gluten-free flours, it needs to be combined with other flours to give it structure and stretch. Emma likes to pair it with oil-rich almond flour, as in Clementine Gateau with Whipped Ricotta Frosting (see page 198). Almond flour has a soft texture and more moisture than other gluten-free flours, so your cake will potentially last longer – if it doesn't get eaten right away. Where softness and fluffiness aren't an issue, in biscuits and shortbread for example, you can add sorghum flour to a shop-bought gluten-free mix, as in Orange, Fennel and Black Pepper Biscotti (see page 199). Even though the mix might already include sorghum flour, adding more will help lighten the texture and improve the flavour.

For a tart crust, use a half-and-half mix of sorghum flour and cornflour or tapioca starch. Though crisp once cooked, the dough will be very soft and need dexterous pressing into the tin rather than rolling. A useful trick is to place a circle of baking parchment over the base of the dough once it's in the tin, then press with a flat-bottomed implement to thin and ease it up the sides (see Piña Colada Tart method, page 72).

If gluten isn't off-limits, sorghum flour can be combined with wheat flour – up to one-third sorghum to two-thirds wheat. A slight drawback is that sorghum flour is slightly dry and tends to produce a coarser crumb. Adding an egg or two, extra oil or fat, and perhaps a raising agent such as baking powder or bicarbonate of soda, will help compensate.

Sorghum flour isn't always found on supermarket shelves, but it's easy to find online (see Sources, page 280) and in good health food shops. It's sometimes labelled 'Sweet White Sorghum Flour'.

Since sorghum is a whole grain flour it becomes rancid relatively quickly. Buy it in small quantities and check that it's well within the use-by date. Store it in a tightly sealed container in the fridge or a cool, dry place.

clementine gateau with whipped ricotta frosting

vegetable oil for greasing
sweet sorghum flour
    150g (5½oz)
almond flour 125g (4½oz)
baking powder 2 teaspoons
unsalted butter 125g (4½oz)
caster sugar 125g (4½oz)
eggs 4, organic or free-range,
    yolks and whites separated
clementines finely grated zest
    and juice of 2

for the syrup
caster sugar 100g (3½oz)
clementines juice of 4, strained

for the ricotta frosting
ricotta cheese 250g (9oz)
caster sugar 2 tablespoons
extra-thick double cream
    2 tablespoons, preferably
    organic

serves 8–10

This gluten-free cake is beautifully light-textured, thanks to a mixture of sorghum flour, almond flour and beaten egg whites. With clementine syrup drizzled over and a creamy ricotta topping, the cake is lovely for a special occasion.

. . .

Preheat the oven to 180°C/Gas Mark 4. Grease the base and sides of a 23cm (9in) springform tin. Line the base and sides with baking parchment, then grease the paper too.

Put the flours and baking powder into a sieve set over a bowl. Muddle with your fingers, then push through the sieve. Sieve once more until well mixed.

Using an electric whisk, beat the butter and sugar in a bowl for 3 minutes until fluffy. Gradually beat in the egg yolks, alternating with the flour mixture. Stir in the clementine juice, reserving the grated zest.

Tip the egg whites into a scrupulously clean bowl and whisk until stiff but not dry. Using a large metal spoon, gently fold about one-third into the cake mixture to slacken it, then fold in the rest. Gently spoon into the prepared tin and level the surface with a wet palette knife.

Bake for 30–40 minutes, rotating the tin halfway through, until a skewer inserted in the centre comes out clean. Leave to settle in the tin while you make the syrup.

Put the sugar and clementine juice in a saucepan over a medium heat. Melt the sugar without stirring, then raise the heat and boil for about 5 minutes, or until the bubbles look large and syrupy. Make holes all over the surface of the cake with a skewer, then pour over the hot syrup. Once it has trickled into the holes, remove the cake from the tin and cool on a wire rack. It's a good idea to put a tray underneath the rack to catch any syrupy drips.

To make the topping, beat together the ricotta cheese, sugar and cream. Spread over the cooled cake, and sprinkle with the reserved grated clementine zest.

orange, fennel and black pepper biscotti

eggs 2, organic or free-range
egg yolk 1
caster sugar 200g (7oz)
vanilla extract ½ teaspoon
orange 1 tablespoon finely
  grated zest (from 2 oranges)
all-purpose gluten-free baking
  flour 200g (7oz), plus extra for
  kneading
sweet sorghum flour 100g
  (3½oz)
baking powder 1 teaspoon
xanthan gum ¼ teaspoon
fennel seeds 2 teaspoons,
  crushed
freshly ground black pepper
  1 teaspoon
whole almonds with skin 100g,
  roughly chopped

makes about 24

Adding sweet sorghum flour to a standard gluten-free flour mix adds extra flavour and improves the texture. These biscuits are deliciously crunchy – just right for dunking in coffee or, even better, a glass of sweet *vin santo*. They will keep for at least a week in an airtight container.

· · ·

Preheat the oven to 180°C/Gas Mark 4. Line a large baking tray with a silicone sheet.

Using an electric whisk, whisk the eggs, egg yolk, sugar, vanilla extract and orange zest in a large bowl for about 3 minutes until pale and creamy.

Tip the flours, baking powder and xanthan gum into a sieve set over a bowl. Muddle with your fingers, then push through the sieve once or twice until well blended. Gradually beat into the egg mixture, followed by the fennel seeds and black pepper.

Tip the dough out on to a very well-floured work surface. Flatten with the palm of your hand into a rough circle. If the dough is still too sticky, add a little more flour. Sprinkle over the almonds and press them into the dough.

Form the dough into two balls, then roll out into logs about 4cm (1½in) wide and 24cm (9½in) long. Place the rolled logs on to the prepared tray. Flatten slightly using the palm of your hand. Lightly score the dough diagonally with a blade or sharp knife at 2cm (¾in) intervals.

Bake in the middle of the oven for 15–20 minutes, or until pale golden and firm to touch. Remove from the oven and reduce the oven temperature to 150°C/Gas Mark 2.

Cut all the way through the score lines. Place the slices cut side down on the baking sheet. Return to the oven for 15 minutes, and bake until golden and no longer sticky.

cook's notes
· If the biscotti start to brown too quickly during the first baking, cover them with a loose piece of baking parchment.

flour

soya *flour*

plant source pulse
aka soybean flour, kinako (Japanese)
latin name *Glycine max.*
gluten none
protein 35—45%
goes with bananas, carrots, cheese, eggs, honey, milk, peanuts, pumpkin, rice
uses biscuits, bread, cakes, coating for desserts and sweetmeats, flatbreads, fritters, pancakes, thickener for sauces, soups and stews

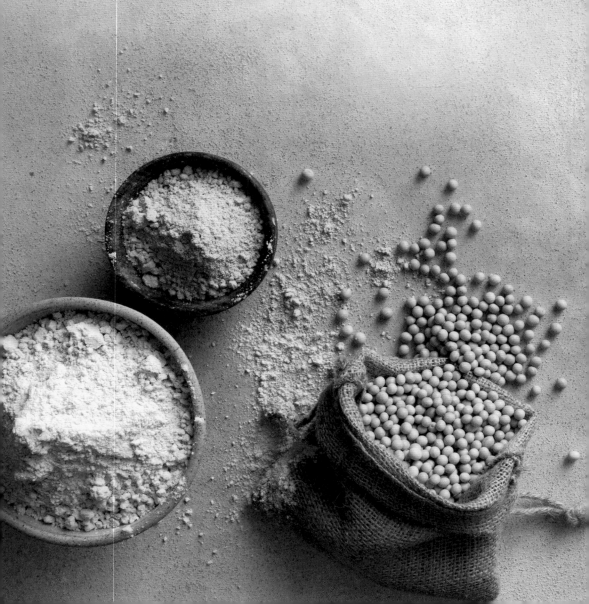

Years ago, as an impoverished student in London, I relied on soya flour as a cheap source of protein since I couldn't afford to eat meat very often. Soya flour pancakes were a regular feature on the menu, as were soya flour cakes, bread and biscuits. I also used it as a thickener, and a nutrient boost, for vegetarian soups and stews.

Unlike most plant-derived foods, soya beans and the flour milled from them are one of the richest sources of 'complete' protein (see page 59). They're also an important source of B-vitamins, iron and calcium. These nutritional credentials put soya on a par with animal-derived foods such as meat and cheese – hence my avid use of the flour.

Milled from roasted yellow soya beans, the flour is attractive to look at. The colour ranges from rich cream – good vanilla ice cream comes to mind – to deep gold. The aroma is toasty and faintly sweet, and the flavour somewhere between peanuts and sesame seeds.

Soya flour is easy to use. It's a good-natured mixer, and can be added to doughs and batters without any problems. I particularly like Griddled Soya Chapatis with Garlic Chives and Turmeric (see page 204). Somewhat surprisingly, Tibetan-style Syrup-soaked Soya Balls with Sultanas and Cardamom (see page 207) are also good.

If you're combining it with other flours, a useful rule of thumb is to replace up to a quarter of the total amount of flour with soya flour. Use less if the item contains yeast – no more than 15 per cent – otherwise the dough will be too dense. Since soya flour is gluten-free, partner it with wheat flour if gluten isn't a problem, or other gluten-free flours (see Gluten, page 60) plus a binding agent, such as xanthan gum, to hold it together.

Be aware that soya flour browns more quickly than other types. You'll need to keep an eagle eye on fried items such as pancakes and fritters, and preferably use a non-stick pan. If you're adding soya flour to a baking recipe, it's a good idea to either shorten the cooking time or lower the oven temperature.

A slightly different and unusual soya flour is Japanese *kinako* (meaning 'yellow flour'). In Japan it's typically sprinkled over ice cream and other desserts, or even used to coat chocolate truffles. Also popular is a challengingly textured dessert of *dango* (glutinous rice dumplings), liberally dusted with a mixture of *kinako*, sugar and a pinch of salt (see Rice Flour, page 164).

Ordinary soya flour is easy to find in health food shops and online (see Sources, page 280). You'll also find *kinako* online, or you can have fun rummaging in shops that specialize in Japanese groceries. If you want to avoid GM foods, check the label and buy an organic brand.

The flour becomes rancid quite quickly, so store it in an airtight container in the fridge.

griddled soya chapatis with garlic chives and turmeric

soya flour 50g (1¾oz)
wholemeal chapati flour
    150g (5½oz) (see Atta Flour,
    page 20)
ground turmeric 1½ teaspoons
xanthan gum 1 teaspoon
sea salt ½ teaspoon
**garlic chives or thin spring
    onion tops** 3 tablespoons,
    snipped
black onion seeds 2 teaspoons
    (aka *kalonji* or nigella seeds)
red chilli flakes 1 teaspoon
    (optional)
vegetable oil 1 tablespoon
tepid water 125–150ml
    (4–5fl oz)

makes 4

Soya flour bumps up the nutritional value of these wheat-based flat breads. Serve as a snack with a pickle and some yogurt sauce, or use to scoop up dips and curries.

. . .

Put the flours, turmeric, xanthan gum and sea salt into a sieve set over a bowl. Muddle with your fingers, then shake through the sieve. Sieve once or twice more until well blended. Mix in the garlic chives, onion seeds, and chilli flakes if you are using them.

Make a well in the centre of the flour mixture. Pour in the oil and most of the water. Mix with a fork, stirring from the centre and gradually drawing in the dry ingredients from around the edge. If the dough seems too dry, gradually add a little more water. If it's too wet, sprinkle in more flour.

Once the dough feels nice and pliable, tip it on to a floured work surface and roll into a ball. Put in a bowl, cover with a clean damp cloth and leave to rest for 30 minutes at room temperature.

Divide the dough into four chunks and roll into golf-ball-sized balls. Place on a well-floured surface and roll out very thinly to 15cm (6in) circles. You will get better results using a slender chapati rolling pin if you have one.

Heat a non-stick pancake pan over a medium heat (see Cook's note). Have ready a bowl of water and a brush. Place a chapati in the pan and cook for about 30 seconds, or until speckled with brown spots on the underside. Brush the upper surface with water, then turn the chapati over and cook for another 30 seconds, or until the underside is developing brown spots and bubbles are starting to form on top. Gently press the top to encourage the chapati to puff up, then flip once more and press the top gently. Move to a plate and keep warm while you cook the rest of the chapatis.

cook's note
· The pan needs to be at just the right temperature. If it's too hot, the chapati will burn. If it's too cool, the chapati will stick. The cooking time also depends on the thickness of the dough and how moist it is. It's best to treat the first chapati as a trial run.

resistant starch

As the name may suggest, resistant starch resists digestion. The formal definition is 'The total amount of starch and the products of starch degradation that resist digestion in the small intestine of healthy people.' In simpler terms, this means that once swallowed in food the starch passes through the gut to the colon (aka large intestine), unscathed by the digestive enzymes and stomach acid that would normally get to work on it higher up in the small intestine. This is different from other types of starch that are digested earlier on in the process.

Once it reaches the colon, resistant starch becomes a food source for the resident beneficial bacteria, which multiply and in doing so improve gut health. It is this perceived benefit, plus others, that have generated a significant amount of scientific research plus trumpeting from nutritionists and health bloggers.

After decades of defamatory comment from low-carb fanatics, I'm a little surprised by the about-turn on starchy foods. That said, there are apparently as many as forty clinical trials that have examined the effects of resistant starch, and the perceived benefits do seem compelling. These include:

- Improved digestive health
- Increase in satiety i.e. the sense of fullness, which could help with weight loss
- Stabilization of energy peaks and troughs
- Reduction in risk of chronic diseases such as obesity, type 2 diabetes, heart disease and colon cancer

Bear in mind that not all starches are resistant, and not all resistant starches are the same. Here's how they are classified:

- RS1: starch found in whole grains, pulses and some seeds with an indigestible protective coating e.g. barley flour, cornmeal, emmer flour, fava bean flour, oat flour, pea flour, rye flour, quinoa flour, teff flour

- RS2: indigestible raw starch molecules that resist attack from digestive enzymes and stomach acids e.g. banana flour, cornflour, potato starch
- RS3: gelatinized starch produced by heating and then cooling starch granules e.g. mung bean flour, tapioca starch
- RS4: chemically modified starch mainly used in food processing

Some of the research studies indicate that when foods containing resistant starch are heated, the starch is partially destroyed. Other suggest that undercooked foods, or cooked and cooled foods, contain more resistant starch than fully cooked or hot foods. To add to the debate, a study reported by agris.fao.org (Food and Agricultural Organisation of the United Nations) suggested that heating did not significantly destroy the starch. It seems that it depends somewhat on the amount of starch present to begin with; those high in amylose are apparently fairly foolproof.

Bear in mind that resistant starch is a relatively new topic with constantly developing research, and conclusions are not cast in stone.

For more information check out the following websites:

- digestivehealthinstitute.org
- marksdailyapple.com
- agris.fao.org (Food and Agricultural Organisation of the United Nations)
- indiegogo.com

If you have a health problem that you feel might benefit from resistant starch, check with your doctor, a dietician or a qualified nutritionist before embarking on changes to your diet.

flour

syrup-soaked soya balls with sultanas and cardamom

soya flour 85g (3oz) (see Cook's note)
plain flour 1 tablespoon
cardamom pods seeds from 3 crushed
sultanas 1 tablespoon
vegetable oil 5 tablespoons
unsalted butter 50g (1¾oz)

for the syrup
granulated sugar 200g (7oz)
water 450ml (16fl oz)

makes about 10 balls

This recipe is based on one in a very old stapled-together Tibetan cookery booklet that I enjoy using now and again; the balls come from a chapter called 'Treats'.

Soya flour contains what's known as 'complete' protein (see Protein, page 59) and plenty of other valuable nutrients. If you happen to have a nearly empty bag of the flour, this is a pleasing way of using it up. Even better, kids will enjoy making the balls, as long as you do the frying and make the syrup. It's really important to leave the balls in the syrup for at least an hour before eating them. The cardamom flavour will develop and the syrup will soak into the dough.

. . .

Put the soya flour and plain flour into a sieve set over a bowl. Muddle with your fingers, then shake through the sieve. Sieve again until well blended. Mix in the cardamom seeds.

Sprinkle 2–3 tablespoons of water over the flour mixture, and stir in using a fork. Gradually add more water, a tablespoonful at a time, until the mixture starts to clump. Once it clumps enough to make a ball, stir in the sultanas. Roll the dough into a ball, put in a bowl, cover with a damp cloth and leave for 30 minutes.

Meanwhile, make the syrup. Put the sugar and water in a wide heavy-based saucepan over a medium-high heat. Bring to the boil, then simmer briskly for 10–12 minutes until the bubbles look big and syrupy. Remove the pan from the heat and set aside.

Pinch off small chunks of dough and roll into walnut-sized balls. Heat the oil and butter in a smallish high-sided frying pan – just big enough to take the balls in a single layer. Once the butter is foaming, add the balls. Fry for 7–8 minutes over a medium-high heat, turning with tongs until golden. Remove from the pan and drain on paper towels.

Put in a shallow dish and pour the warm syrup over the balls. Leave to soak up the syrup for at least 1 hour before serving.

cook's note
- Make sure you use ordinary soya flour, rather than Japanese soybean flour (kinako), which has been defatted and roasted. This has its uses but will not work for these Tibetan-style balls.

spelt *flour*

plant source grain
aka Dinkel (German), grand épautre (French), farro grande (Italian)
latin name *Triticum spelta*
protein/gluten 11–14%
goes with anything
uses batters, biscuits, bread, cakes, crackers, flatbreads, pancakes, pastry, scones, thickener for sauces, soups and stews

An ancestor of modern wheat and a popular 'ancient grain', spelt is a hybrid of emmer (see page 102) and wild goat grass. Experts differ as to the origins, but it was probably cultivated in Europe, the Middle East and southwest Asia at least 9,000 years ago.

Spelt gets a mention in early Greek and Roman texts, and even the Old Testament. It's listed as one of six grains and pulses that God instructed the prophet Ezekiel to use for bread during a prolonged sojourn in the desert. Whether by accident or design, the combination of grains and pulses provided him with 'complete' protein (see page 59) and other valuable nutrients, which no doubt explains why 'Ezekiel' bread, or bible bread, is enjoying an unexpected renaissance today.

As British spelt farmer Roger Saul explains, modern wheat has been bred to a machine-friendly waist height, whereas spelt is about 1.5 metres (5 feet) tall and more difficult to harvest. In the Cereals section of *A Concise Encyclopaedia of Gastronomy*, London's Wine and Food Society describes spelt rather disparagingly as 'a chaffy wheat grown on poor ground'. As far as profit-seeking farmers were concerned, an inconveniently tall plant and chaffy grains meant harvesting and milling problems, and consequential low yields. As a result, spelt gradually fell out of use in favour of modern wheat.

The good news is that spelt has had a meteoric rebirth in recent decades, thanks to its nutritional credentials, an increasingly health-conscious public, and dedicated farmers and millers. Spelt is now grown in Britain, the US, Russia and many parts of Europe. Both the grain and the flour are easy to find in the shops and online.

Spelt flour really is a cook's best friend. It behaves in much the same way as wheat flour; the mild nutty flavour doesn't overwhelm other ingredients, and unlike gluten-free flours it can be used without a backup team of other flours. High-protein and high-fibre, spelt flour trumps wheat in terms of nutrients, and it's said to be easier to digest. This may be because the gluten in spelt flour (see Gluten, page 60) has a weaker structure and breaks down more easily.

Because of the weaker gluten, it's critical not to over-knead bread dough, otherwise it will start to break up. It's best to do it by hand, rather than in a mixer, so you have more control over the texture. Knead it just enough to make the dough soft and pliable, rather than super-stretchy. It's also best to bake your loaf in a tin rather than freeform on a baking sheet.

As well as nutritious tasty bread, spelt flour makes fluffy cakes, scones, crisp golden pastry and crunchy crackers. Try Leek, Cheese and Peppercorn Tart (see page 215), and the Seeded Spelt and Beetroot Crackers (see page 210). It's also excellent for batter-based dishes such as Yorkshire pudding, toad-in-the-hole and pancakes.

For most recipes you can substitute 100 per cent spelt flour for wheat without any problem. It's hydroscopic, which means you might need to add a little more liquid than for other flours; buttermilk or egg are good options. Depending on the amount of rise needed, you might also need to add a raising agent such as baking powder or bicarbonate of soda.

Whole grain spelt flour is also available. It has a heavier texture and is best used for yeasted breads or shortcrust pastry, either alone or combined with white spelt flour. It contains fat and therefore has a shorter shelf life. To keep it fresh, store it in an airtight container in the fridge or another cool place.

seeded spelt and beetroot crackers with smoked salmon pâté

white spelt flour 190g (6½oz)

beetroot powder 2 teaspoons
  (see Cook's notes)

sea salt 1 teaspoon

freshly ground black pepper
  1¼ teaspoons

iced water 100ml (3½fl oz)

extra-virgin olive oil
  2 tablespoons

egg white 1, lightly whisked

black onion seeds 1½
  teaspoons (aka kalonji or
  nigella seeds) (see Variation)

sea salt flakes for sprinkling

for the smoked salmon pâté

ready-to-eat hot-smoked
  salmon fillets 225g (8oz)
  skinned

quark or curd cheese 110g
  (4oz)

lemon juice 2 teaspoons

hot horseradish sauce
  1 teaspoon

freshly ground black pepper
  ½ teaspoon

sea salt pinch

smoked salmon 85g (3oz),
  chopped

makes 24

Tinted with beetroot powder, these crackers look so lovely sprinkled with black onion seeds and served with the pretty pink salmon pâté. They're really good eaten on their own too, or with another type of dip. And they certainly live up to their name – run away now if you don't like noisy crunching.

• • •

First make the salmon pâté. Whizz all the ingredients, except the chopped smoked salmon, in the bowl of a food processor. Scrape into a serving bowl, stir in the chopped smoked salmon, and chill.

Preheat the oven to 200°C/Gas Mark 6. Put the flour, beetroot powder, salt and pepper into a large sieve set over a bowl. Muddle with your fingers, then shake through the sieve. Sieve once or twice more until well blended.

Whisk together the iced water and olive oil. Make a well in the centre of the flour mixture and pour in all the liquid. Mix with a small whisk, stirring from the centre and gradually drawing in the dry ingredients from around the edge. Gather the dough into a ball, then flatten into a thick rectangle. Wrap in greaseproof paper and chill for at least 30 minutes.

Roll out the dough on a large sheet of silicone to a rectangle measuring 30x36cm (12x14in). The rolled dough will be very thin, but the thinner you can make it, the crisper your crackers will be. Using the tip of a small knife, and without cutting into your silicone sheet, deeply score the dough into 24 rectangles measuring 5x9cm (2x3½in) (six along the shorter side and four along the longer side). Prick the dough all over with a fork. Brush with the egg white, then sprinkle with the onion seeds and a smattering of sea salt flakes.

Carefully lift the silicone sheet on to a baking sheet. Bake for 15–20 minutes, rotating the tray halfway through, until beginning to look crisp. Check them often and take care that they don't burn. Remove from the oven and leave to cool on the baking sheet.

Break into crackers once cool and serve with the salmon pâté. If you're not eating the crackers right away, store them in an airtight container but make sure they're completely dry and crisp before you do so.

- Black onion seeds give the crackers a specific flavour, redolent of Turkish bread. Dill, caraway or sesame seeds would be good alternatives.

cook's notes
- You can buy sachets of beetroot powder in good supermarkets and health food shops.
- The uncooked dough is too thin to handle and lift on to the baking sheet as individual crackers. The way round this is to bake it as one large sheet, scored where you intend to break it, and then break into separate crackers once cooked.

spelt *flour*

flour

celery and cheddar scones

celery stalks 5 tender, trimmed
   (about 125g/4½oz)
mature Cheddar cheese 150g
   (5½oz)
white spelt flour 400g (14oz)
baking powder 2 tablespoons
caster sugar 1 tablespoon
freshly ground black pepper
   1½ teaspoons
sea-salt 1½ teaspoons, plus a
   pinch for the glaze
unsalted butter 75g (2¾oz)
   chilled, diced
flat-leaf parsley leaves
   3 tablespoons chopped
tender celery leaves
   3 tablespoons chopped
eggs 3, organic or free-range
buttermilk 165ml (5½fl oz) (see
   Cook's note)
ajwain seeds or celery seeds
   a few (optional) for sprinkling
   (see Cook's notes)

makes 14–15

White spelt flour replaces ordinary wheat flour here, providing a subtle nutty flavour and softish texture. Nuggets of celery create a contrasting crunch, while chopped celery leaves emphasize the vegetable flavour. Serve the scones warm and thickly buttered, or fill with more Cheddar, pickles or some good country ham if you like.

This is loosely based on a recipe by Beca Lyne-Pirkis, a former *Great British Bake-Off* contestant.

• • •

Remove the strings from the celery, slice the stalks lengthways into two or three strips, then crossways into very small dice. Dice the cheese into very small nuggets.

Put the flour, baking powder, sugar, black pepper and sea salt into a large sieve set over a bowl. Muddle with your fingers, then shake through the sieve. Sieve once or twice more until well blended.

Tip the diced butter into the flour mixture. Rub the butter into the flour between the tips of your fingers and thumbs using a flicking movement – imagine you are playing castanets. Hold your hands well above the bowl so that the flour drifts down, incorporating air as it does so, and you can see any fragments of butter that still need rubbing in.

Once you have a mixture that looks like large breadcrumbs, add the celery, cheese, parsley and celery leaves, mixing well so they are evenly spread.

Lightly beat 2 of the eggs. Stir into the mixture along with the buttermilk. Gently knead until the mixture clumps enough to form a ball (see Cook's notes).

Tip the dough on to a floured work surface. Dust your rolling pin with flour, then lightly press (don't roll) the dough into a rectangle about 15x30cm (6x12in) (the long edge should be twice as long as the short edge). Fold the dough in half and give it a quarter turn. Shape it into a rectangle, then fold and turn as before. Repeat the process twice more. Cover with a clean tea towel and leave to rest for 20 minutes.

Lightly flour your work surface and rolling pin again. Roll the dough (it's OK to roll rather than press this time) to a thickness of 2.5cm (1in). Use a 6cm (2½in) cutter to cut out the scones. Re-roll the trimmings and cut out more scones.

Line a baking tray with a silicone sheet or non-stick parchment paper. Arrange the scones on the tray, cover with the tea towel and leave to rest for another 15 minutes. Meanwhile, preheat the oven to 200°C/Gas Mark 6.

Whisk the remaining egg with a pinch of salt. Paint the top of the scones – take care to not let the egg drip down the sides (it will stop the scones from rising properly). Sprinkle with a few ajwain or celery seeds, if you're using them. Bake for 12–18 minutes, rotating the tray halfway through, until the scones are risen and golden on top.

cook's notes
· If you don't have any buttermilk, mix 2 teaspoons of lemon juice with 165ml (5½fl oz) of ordinary milk.
· Ajwain seeds are optional but their intense celery-like flavour does add a nice touch. You'll find them in shops selling Asian groceries, and they're easy to buy online.
· Don't worry about the dough being wet. This gives a better rise and keeps the scones nicely moist.

flour

leek, cheese and peppercorn tart

white spelt flour 280g (10oz)
sea salt ¼ teaspoon
unsalted butter 140g (5oz)
   chilled, diced
egg yolk 1, beaten
iced water 2–3 tablespoons

for the filling
leeks 2 medium, trimmed
mature Cheddar cheese 160g
   (5¾oz), coarsely grated
mozzarella cheese 160g (5¾oz)
   (see Cook's note), shredded
   or coarsely grated
dried green peppercorns
   1½ teaspoons, lightly crushed
sea salt
diced pancetta 150g (5½oz)
fresh thyme leaves
   1 tablespoon
egg yolk 1, beaten to glaze

makes one 30cm (12in)
   square tart, serves 6–8
   as a snack

Pastry made with spelt flour is extra crisp and crumbly – a good contrast to the soft-textured leek and cheese filling. I've used green peppercorns as I love their piquant and slightly grassy flavour with the leeks. They aren't obligatory – use black peppercorns if you prefer.

• • •

Sift the flour and salt into a large bowl. Add the diced butter and rub into the flour between the tips of your fingers and thumbs using a flicking movement – imagine you are playing castanets. Hold your hands well above the bowl so that the flour drifts down, incorporating air as it does so, and revealing any fragments of butter that still need rubbing in.

Using a fork, stir in the beaten egg yolk. Sprinkle 2 tablespoons of the water over the surface, and stir until the mixture begins to clump. Add more water if it seems dry. Gather the dough together, then lightly knead for a few seconds. Form it into a thick square, then wrap in greaseproof paper and chill for 30 minutes.

Meanwhile, slice the leeks in half lengthways, then crossways into 1cm (½in) slices. In a bowl, combine the Cheddar and about half the mozzarella, mixing well.

Preheat the oven to 230°C/Gas Mark 8. Line a baking sheet with silicone. Dust your work surface and rolling pin with flour. Roll out the pastry thinly to form a 32cm (12¾in) square. Trim the edges neatly. Carefully drape over a rolling pin and place on the lined baking sheet. Leaving a 2cm (¾in) border all round, scatter the combined cheeses evenly over the pastry. Sprinkle with the peppercorns and a little sea salt, bearing in mind the saltiness of the pancetta. Scatter the leeks, pancetta and thyme leaves over the cheese mixture. Sprinkle the rest of the mozzarella evenly over the top. Fold the pastry edges over the topping and brush with beaten egg yolk, especially at the corners to stick the overlapping edges together.

Bake for 15–20 minutes, rotating the tray halfway through, until the pastry is golden and the leeks look slightly charred. Remove from the oven and leave for 10 minutes before serving to allow the juices to settle.

cook's note
• Use mozzarella cheese specifically for baking.

teff *flour*

plant source seed
aka lovegrass, tef, teffa
latin name *Eragrostis tef*
gluten none
protein 12%
goes with bananas, chillies, chocolate, ginger, mushrooms, nuts, onions, warm and pungent spices
uses biscuits, bread, brownies, cakes, flatbreads, gingerbread, injeera, muffins, pancakes, pastry

Native to Ethiopia and neighbouring Eritrea, teff is an important crop dating back to prehistoric times. It's a variety of the charmingly named lovegrass, derived from the Greek *eros* meaning 'love', and *agrostis* meaning 'grass'. Ethiopians call it *teffa*, meaning 'lost', which possibly relates to the microscopic size of the seeds; individually they're almost invisible to the naked eye.

Though teff is the smallest of cereals, it's nutritionally superior. It supplies Ethiopians with an estimated two-thirds of their protein, plus dietary fibre, B-vitamins and minerals. It's also a good source of resistant starch (see page 205), which generally improves gut health. Like other nutritionally rich plants – quinoa, millet and oats, for example – teff holds its own in poor soils, droughts and floods.

Thanks to these nutritional credentials, teff has become an on-trend ingredient in the West. Though well intentioned, the knock-on effect has been that teff sells at vastly inflated prices – far more than Ethiopian farmers are paid, and so much that some can't even afford to buy it for themselves.

Moving on from political debate to culinary matters, teff flour is naturally whole grain since the bran can't be separated from the microscopic seeds. That said, it's fine and free-flowing, and comes in a warming palette of earthy colours: speckled ivory, light brown and reddish brown, reminiscent of the Ethiopian landscape itself. The flavour is slightly sweet and nutty, with an appealing aroma, faintly redolent of old-fashioned malty bedtime drinks.

In Ethiopia, teff flour is vital for injeera (see page 219), a fermented spongy flatbread with a somewhat addictive sour flavour. Making injeera is a time-consuming ritual that many Ethiopians repeat every few days. A recipe in an old cookbook instructs the cook to first remove the dirt by sifting teff thoroughly, and then take it to a mill for grinding. The next step is to sift the flour yet again, mix it with half an oil tin of water and a cup of batter saved from an earlier baking, and then leave to ferment for three days. As the late Alan Davidson writes in *The Oxford Companion to Food*, the bread is central to Ethiopian consciousness, the standard greeting being, 'Have you eaten injeera today?'

Ethiopian cooks wouldn't dream of using teff flour for anything but injeera. That said, I find it pleasingly versatile and easy to incorporate in baked items. It adds a rich molasses flavour to biscuits, muffins and brownies. It's good in gingerbread and fruited tea breads, too. Chocolate and nuts are natural culinary partners, as are savoury ingredients such as cheese, mushrooms and chillies.

Teff flour is gluten-free and needs to be combined with other flours to give it structure. If gluten isn't a problem, substitute wheat flour with about one-third teff flour for bread, and about a quarter for scones, muffins and fluffy pancakes. You can increase the amount for a more pronounced teff flavour, but the texture is likely to be dense and crumbly.

If gluten is off-limits, combine teff with other gluten-free flours, such as buckwheat and tapioca, plus a little xanthan or guar gum to help bind the dough. I've made excellent pastry with a combination of teff flour, rice flour and cornflour. Admittedly rather rustic-looking, it makes a lovely crust for a thyme-scented mushroom tart.

Teff flour is easy to find online (see Sources, page 280), in good health food shops, and shops selling African groceries. It goes rancid quite quickly so buy a little at a time and make sure it's well within the use-by date. Store it in a tightly sealed container in the fridge or a cool, dry place.

spiced onion bread

granulated sugar 2 teaspoons
tepid water 225ml (8fl oz)
active dried yeast 1 tablespoon
teff flour 125g (4½oz)
strong white bread flour 375g
(13oz)
sea salt 1½ teaspoons
unsalted butter 85g (3oz)
onion 1 small, finely chopped
garlic clove 1, finely chopped
melted butter for brushing

for the spice mix
cumin seeds 2 teaspoons
coriander seeds 2 teaspoons
sesame seeds 1 teaspoon
ground fenugreek 1 teaspoon
freshly ground black pepper
¾ teaspoon
cayenne pepper ¼ teaspoon
freshly grated ginger root
1 teaspoon

makes 1 loaf

If you enjoy spicy flavours, this is the bread for you. You need to allow plenty of time for the dough to rise, but the bread is much quicker to make than fermented injeera (see page 219). It still gives you a taste of Ethiopia. A slice is almost a meal in itself – delicious still warm from the oven and thickly slathered with unsalted butter.

• • •

First make the spice mix. Dry-fry the cumin, coriander and sesame seeds for a minute or two, without any oil, until they smell toasty. Immediately tip on to a plate to stop them cooking, then grind to a powder using a mortar and pestle. Mix with the ground fenugreek, black pepper and cayenne pepper, then stir in the grated ginger root and set aside.

Dissolve the sugar in the tepid water and stir in the yeast. Leave in a warm place for about 15 minutes until frothy.

Meanwhile, put the flours and sea salt into a sieve set over a bowl. Muddle with your fingers, then push through the sieve twice until well blended.

Heat one-third of the butter in a frying pan over a medium-high heat. Add the onion and fry for 5–7 minutes until translucent. Add the garlic and fry for another minute. Tip into a bowl and set aside.

Melt the rest of the butter in the same pan. Stir in the spice mix, then gradually sift in 110g (4oz) of the flour mixture, stirring to prevent lumps. Whisk in the yeast liquid, then stir in the fried onion mixture, mixing well. Pour into a bowl, cover and leave to rise in a warm place for 1 hour.

Stir in the rest of the flour. Put on a floured work surface and knead for 10–15 minutes until smooth and springy. Place the dough in an oiled bowl, cover and leave in a warm place for 1–2 hours, or until doubled in size.

Tip the dough out of the bowl, knock it back and form into a round loaf shape. Put on a silicone-lined baking sheet and cut a cross in the centre. Leave to rise for 20 minutes.

Preheat the oven to 180°C/Gas Mark 4. Bake in the middle of the oven for 50–60 minutes, rotating the tray every 20 minutes, until the bottom of the loaf sounds hollow when tapped. Brush with melted butter while still warm.

flour

ethiopian injeera

for the starter
teff flour 175g (6oz)
water 420ml (14fl oz) at room
  temperature
dried active yeast ⅛ teaspoon

for the bread
teff flour 250g (9oz)
water 435ml (15½fl oz) at room
  temperature
starter 4 tablespoons (see
  Cook's note)
sea salt ¼ teaspoon
vegetable oil for frying

makes 6

A traditional Ethiopian flat bread, injeera is made with fermented teff flour that gives it a distinctive sour flavour. This may be a little palate-provoking at first but the sourness can become addictive. The breads look like lacy pancakes – marvellous for mopping up spicy stews and soups. The starter takes five days to ferment so you will need to plan ahead. The recipe was adapted from the blog www.chefinyou.com.

• • •

To make the starter, mix 75g (2¾oz) of the teff flour in a bowl with 190ml (6½fl oz) of the room temperature water until smooth. Whisk in the yeast, cover with cling film and leave in a warm place for two days.

On the third day, give the starter a stir, then whisk in 50g (1¾oz) of the teff flour and 115ml (3¾fl oz) of the room temperature water. Cover and leave in a warm place for another two days.

On the fifth day, mix in another 50g (1¾oz) teff flour and 115ml (3¾fl oz) of room temperature water. Stir and leave for 24 hours.

Now you can get the bread going. Mix the 250g (9oz) teff flour with the 435ml (15½fl oz) room temperature water and 4 tablespoons of the starter. Stir, cover and leave in a warm place for 5–6 hours.

Stir in the salt just before you start to cook. Pour a thin layer of vegetable oil into a 24cm (9½in) non-stick frying pan with a lid, set over a medium heat. Swirl in a ladleful of batter, spiralling it from the centre to the edge of the pan. Fry for about 2 minutes, or until bubbles start to appear. Cover with the lid and cook for 3–4 minutes more, until there are no pools of uncooked batter and the bread is firm at the edges and spongy-looking. (There's no need to flip.) Give the pan a good shake now and again to stop the batter sticking.

Slide the bread on to a clean tea towel and keep warm while you cook the rest. Spray the pan with oil each time. Serve with a spicy stew or soup, or use as a wrap with the filling of your choice.

cook's note
· You will not need all of the starter but it's hardly worth making in smaller quantities. Keep the rest for another batch or make more than six and freeze the rest.

flour

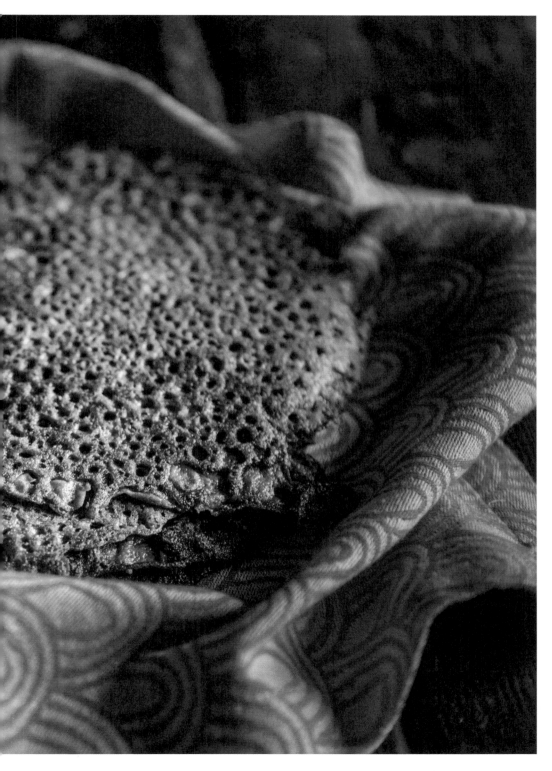

tiger nut *flour*

plant source tuber
aka chufa, earth almond, rush nut
latin name *Cyperus esculentus*
gluten none
protein 4–5%
goes with almonds, chocolate, coconut, coffee, ginger
uses binding for burgers and meatballs, biscuits, brownies, cakes, fritters, pancakes, pastry, smoothies, thickener for soups

Despite the name, tiger nuts are not actually nuts and have nothing to do with tigers – though their striped brown skin is a possible connection. Botanically speaking, tiger nuts are very small tubers that grow underground around the root of a variety of sedge. In most countries, the plant is a rampant weed that farmers and gardeners do their best to eradicate. Not so, however, in parts of Africa, Turkey and Spain. Here, the tubers have been an important food crop for centuries. They're typically eaten as a snack, or ground into flour, but are probably best known in *horchata*, a sweet milky beverage popular in Valencia, Spain – the region in which tiger nuts are grown.

As flours go, tiger nut flour is not particularly attractive. It's a dull fawn with dark flecks and a clumpy texture. That said, it's one of the very few flours that taste good raw. A dab on a wet finger is enticingly sweet – rather like macadamia nuts. It makes you want a second dab and probably a third.

The flour is certainly nutrient-rich. It contains as much iron and zinc as red meat and more than twice the potassium of bananas. Another plus factor is a high level of resistant starch (see page 205), which is generally good for gut health. The flour is also gluten-free and, since it's not actually ground from nuts, doesn't cause problems for people with nut allergies.

In baking, the flour not only provides valuable nutrients, but its natural sweetness means you can reduce the amount of sugar. If gluten and nut allergies aren't a concern, try substituting some of the wheat flour with tiger nut flour. For items that don't need to rise very much – biscuits and bars, for example – you can use tiger nut flour to replace all the wheat flour. If using the flour in pastry, remember that it's gluten-free and not very stretchy. You'll need to mix it with another gluten-free flour, such as tapioca flour, and a dash of xanthan gum or guar gum to compensate.

The flour works well as a binder and thickener. Add a spoonful or so to fishcakes and bean burgers, or stir it into a soup for extra richness and body. The fortifying Moroccan Chicken, Chickpea and Tomato Soup, aka *harire*, on page 224 is particularly good. Given the flour's natural sweetness, it also makes a superb smoothie, especially when sprinkled with chocolate, as in the recipe on page 225. When adding the flour to liquids be sure to stir well to get rid of lumps.

At the time of writing, tiger nut flour hasn't yet reached the majority of supermarkets, but you'll find it online (see Sources, page 280), in health food shops and in good supermarkets.

moroccan chicken, chickpea and tomato soup *(harire)*

boneless chicken thighs
6, weighing about 600g (1lb 5oz) in total (see Variation)
sea salt
olive oil 2 tablespoons
onion 1 large, roughly chopped
cumin seeds 2 teaspoons,
lightly crushed
turmeric powder ½ teaspoon
ground ginger ½ teaspoon
cinnamon powder ½ teaspoon
freshly ground black pepper
½ teaspoon
saffron threads ¼ teaspoon,
ground with 1 teaspoon
sea salt
good-quality chicken stock
1.7 litres (3 pints), heated
peeled tomatoes 400g (14oz)
can
chickpeas 400g (14oz)
can, drained
long-grain rice 100g (3½oz),
rinsed
tiger nut flour 5 tablespoons
lemon juice of ½, or to taste
flat-leaf parsley leaves
3 tablespoons chopped
coriander leaves 3 tablespoons
chopped
lemon wedges to garnish
harissa sauce to serve
(optional)

serves 6 as a main meal

This fortifying soup is traditionally served to break the fast every evening during the month of Ramadan. With a flavour reminiscent of almonds or macadamia nuts, tiger nut flour makes the soup even richer, as well as adding energy-giving nutrients – fat, protein and carbohydrates, for example.

• • •

Slice the chicken thighs into bite-sized chunks and sprinkle with a little sea salt. Heat the oil in a large frying pan over a medium-high heat. Fry the chicken for 5–7 minutes until no longer pink, then move the pieces to a large saucepan using a slotted spoon.

Fry the onion for 7–10 minutes over a medium heat in the pan used for the chicken; there should still be enough oil. Once the onion is lightly browned and soft, stir in all the spices. Cook for a few seconds, then moisten with a couple of ladlefuls of the stock. Scrape up the residue at the bottom of the pan, then pour the mixture over the chicken in the saucepan.

Chop the canned tomatoes into big pieces, and add to the saucepan along with their juice. Stir in the drained chickpeas, rice, and all but 200ml (7fl oz) of the remaining hot stock. Bring to the boil, then lower the heat and gently simmer with the lid askew for 15–20 minutes, or until the rice is cooked.

Mix the tigernut flour with the reserved stock to make a smooth slurry. Stir this into the soup, making sure there are no lumps. Simmer for a few minutes over a medium heat. Stir in the lemon juice and parsley, then simmer for another minute or two.

Ladle into large bowls, sprinkle with the coriander and garnish with a wedge of lemon. Serve with harissa sauce if you want a bit more heat.

variation
• The soup can be made with diced lamb instead of chicken. It will be a bit fattier but the tigernut flour will absorb it.

flour

warm ginger and nutmeg smoothie

tiger nut flour 3 tablespoons
organic whole milk 450ml
   (16fl oz)
freshly grated nutmeg
   ½ teaspoon
ginger juice 2 teaspoons (see
   Cook's note)
grated chocolate for sprinkling
   (optional)

serves 2

Ground tiger nuts are traditionally used in Spain to make a popular ice-cold drink called *horchata*. Here, I've used the flour, which is finer than ground nuts, to make a warming bedtime smoothie.

• • •

Mix the tiger nut flour to a smooth slurry with a little of the milk. Pour into a saucepan with the rest of the milk, the nutmeg and ginger juice. Heat gently, stirring all the time, for 5–7 minutes until thickened. Strain into mugs and sprinkle with grated chocolate, if you like.

cook's note
• Peel and roughly chop a fat piece of fresh ginger root. Put it in a clean garlic press and squeeze out the juice.

tiger nut *flour*

water chestnut *flour*

Chinese

plant source tuber, corm
aka water chestnut starch, water
  chestnut powder
latin name *Eleocharis dulcis*
gluten none
protein 2–3%
goes with coriander, ginger, palm sugar,
  sesame
uses coating for fried foods, dumplings,
  steamed cake, thickener for soup

Indian

plant source fruit
aka singoda, singhara atta
latin name *Trapa bispinosa*
gluten none
protein 3%
goes with starchy roots and tubers, e.g.
  colocasia, potatoes, yams
uses batter for deep-frying, coating,
  desserts, fritters, Indian flatbreads,
  pancakes, samosas, thickener for
  curries

There are two very different types of water chestnut flour: Chinese and Indian. I learned this from a failed attempt to make Chinese Water Chestnut Cake (see page 229) with Indian flour – the equivalent of making Turkish Delight with wholemeal flour, say. It simply did not work, and the reason now seems obvious. Chinese water chestnut flour is a starch similar to cornflour, whereas the Indian version is more like ordinary plain flour. Both come from completely different plants.

Chinese flour is ground from the corms or bulbs of an aquatic plant, *Eleocharis dulcis*. The corms are about the same size as ordinary chestnuts, with dark brown skin and lighter brown scales around the top. They're the ones you'll find in cans of water chestnuts.

Indian flour is ground from fruit, rather than a corm, from a different aquatic plant, *Trapa bispinosa*. The fruits are strange, almost sinister-looking, with dark skin and two distinctive horns or wings that make them resemble a flying bat or a bull's head. Between the horns is a large, very starchy, bulbous kernel or nut from which the flour is ground.

Chinese water chestnut flour is greyish white and granular. When rubbed between the fingers it crumbles to a very fine, odourless, tasteless powder. In contrast, the Indian flour is putty-coloured, with a texture rather like elephant's skin or a parched riverbed. The aroma is clean and fresh, with a pleasing hint of chestnuts.

The Chinese flour is used as a thickener for delicate soup, and as a particularly crispy coating for fried foods. Its gelatinous nature is essential for the steamed Chinese Water Chestnut Cake (see page 229), served to celebrate the Chinese New Year. Like cornflour, it becomes translucent when mixed with water and heated. It needs stirring well to get rid of any lumps.

The Indian flour is more versatile. Mixed with potato and grated paneer cheese, it makes the most addictive fritters (see page 228). It's also great for pancakes and flatbreads, and is a nutritious thickener for curries. Like the Chinese flour, it tends to form lumps so needs mixing with water before adding to hot liquid. Though it isn't an everyday flour even in India, it comes into its own during periods of fasting when the usual grain flours are forbidden for religious reasons. It has what nutritionists call high satiety value – in other words, it keeps you feeling full for longer.

Both flours are easy to find online (see Sources, page 280) and in shops selling Indian or Chinese groceries.

potato and paneer fritters

raw potato 200g (7oz) coarsely
   grated (see Cook's notes)
paneer cheese 100g (3½oz)
   coarsely grated
fresh green chilli 1, deseeded
   and finely chopped
onion ½ small, grated
Indian water chestnut flour
   (*singhara atta*) 4 tablespoons
baking powder ½ teaspoon
sea salt 1 teaspoon
freshly ground black pepper
   ¼ teaspoon
vegetable oil for for frying

makes 10–12

These raggle-taggle fritters are made with *singhara atta*, a flour ground from the Indian water chestnut rather than the Chinese variety. Make sure you use the correct type of flour (see page 227). Here, *singhara atta* makes a nutritious binder for grated potato and paneer cheese. Serve hot or warm with your favourite Indian pickle.

• • •

Rinse the grated potato in several changes of water to get rid of the starch. Drain, spread out on a clean tea towel and pat dry. Gather up the four corners of the tea towel, then twist and squeeze to get rid of any remaining liquid.

Put the potato in a bowl with the cheese, chilli and onion. Mix well, then sprinkle in the flour, baking powder, sea salt and pepper. Mix again, making sure the flour is evenly distributed.

Pour enough oil into a non-stick frying pan to come to a depth of 5mm (¼in). Heat over a medium-high heat until very hot but not smoking – 180°C (350°F) on a thermometer, or until a cube of bread browns in 1 minute.

Drop large spoonfuls of the mixture into the pan, pressing gently with the back of a spoon to flatten slightly. Fry for 1–1½ minutes each side until golden brown and the edges are crisp. Drain on paper towels and keep warm while you cook the rest.

cook's notes
- Use an all-purpose variety of potato, such as Desirée or King Edward, rather than a floury variety or a waxy salad potato.
- For pleasingly crisp fritters, make sure the oil is really hot before adding the potato mixture.

chinese water chestnut cake

vegetable oil for greasing
Chinese water chestnut flour
    125g (4½oz)
cold water 700ml (1¼ pints)
jaggery, palm sugar or caster
    sugar 200g (7oz)
drained water chestnuts 140g
    (5oz) (from a 250g/9oz can),
    chopped
edible glitter for sprinkling
    (optional)

**makes one 17cm (6½in)
    square cake**

Traditionally made to celebrate the Chinese New Year, this jelly-like cake/dessert/snack is made with starchy Chinese water chestnut flour, rather than the Indian flour that comes from another type of water chestnut (see page 227). The Chinese flour is similar to cornflour in that it thickens a mixture and then becomes translucent. It makes a fresh-tasting, satisfying dessert that I find surprisingly addictive. The recipe is based on one from the blog www.chinasichuanfood.com.

· · ·

Grease the base and sides of a 17cm (6¾in) square cake tin. Line the base of the tin with baking parchment, then grease the paper too. Have ready a large wok or deep frying pan with a trivet or small can set in the base to support the cake tin. Pour in enough hot water to come almost to the top of the trivet or can.

Tip the flour into a bowl and add 150ml (5fl oz) of the water, stirring until the flour granules have dissolved.

Pour the remaining 550ml (19fl oz) of water into a wide high-sided pan set over a medium heat. Add the sugar and heat until dissolved. Bring to the boil, then stir in the chopped water chestnuts.

Stir the flour mixture really well, especially on the bottom where there will be a floury sludge. Once the flour is evenly mixed, stir it into the water chestnut pan. Immediately turn the heat to low and stir, in one direction only, for 5–7 minutes. The mixture will thicken at first, then gradually become a little looser and easier to stir.

Tip the mixture into the prepared tin. It will be gelatinous, rather like slime balls that kids like to throw, and needs gentle coaxing to spread it evenly and into the corners of the tin. Put the tin in the wok, balanced on the trivet or can, and steam over a medium heat, uncovered, for 25–30 minutes, or until a skewer inserted in the centre comes out clean.

Leave the cake in the tin to cool – you can speed this up by placing the tin in a large bowl of cold water – then chill for an hour or more until set.

Turn out on to a board and cut into cubes or thick slices. Sprinkle with edible glitter if you like. The cake can be wrapped in foil and stored in the fridge for a few days.

water chestnut *flour*

flour

water chestnut *flour*

fine wheat *flour*

plant source grain
aka cake flour, pastry flour, Asian dumpling flour
latin name *Triticum aestivum*
protein/gluten 7–9.5%
goes with anything
uses cakes, muffins, pancakes, pastry, quick breads, steamed Asian-style bread and
buns, thickener for sauces and stews

Fine flour is a general term for light-textured flours that are relatively low in gluten (see page 60). The major players are cake flour and pastry flour, both milled from soft varieties of wheat. Cake flour is the finest, containing 7–8 per cent gluten, while pastry flour is slightly coarser and contains 8–9.5 per cent gluten.

Cake flour is very finely milled and then sifted, so it feels super-soft and silky. Cornflour (see page 78) is sometimes added during processing to make it even finer. It's typically used for high-rise fluffy cakes, particularly those containing a larger proportion of sugar and liquid to flour – angel food cake, for example. It's also a boon if you're making Asian-style scallion pancakes. Substitute 50 per cent of the plain flour with cake flour and you'll have a soft but pleasantly pliable dough that's easier to roll into the requisite paper-thin circles.

Pastry flour lies somewhere between cake flour and plain flour (see page 224) in terms of strength. Use it when you're after pastry with a feather-light and crumbly texture, rather than crisp and firm. Combined with a raising agent, the flour also comes in handy for muffins and quick breads such as banana bread or soda bread. There is also a whole grain version that's used in much the same way.

Also classified as fine-textured is Asian dumpling flour. Interestingly, the flour is usually trumpeted as high gluten, but this may well be the baker's equivalent of an urban myth since it contains only about 9 per cent. It's silky smooth and starchy, and the one to use for Steamed Gua Bao Buns (see page 234), folded pillowy circles of soft milk bread, sandwiching deliciously sticky red-cooked pork and crunchy condiments. The flour needs to be soft, i.e. low-gluten, but sufficiently stretchy to create thin circles of dough that are able to rise a little. If you can't get dumpling flour, it's fine to use cake flour instead.

If you're a baking enthusiast and like to use the right flour for the job, it's worth stocking up on cake and pastry flour. They're easy to find and come in smaller packets than plain flour, so you don't have to invest in a huge amount.

You'll find dumpling flour online and in shops specializing in Asian groceries. It has a reasonably long shelf life as long as it's stored in a cool, dark place. There are several brands and results tend to vary. I've had the most success with Honour (see Sources, page 280).

steamed gua bao buns with sticky pork and smashed cucumber

Asian dumpling flour or cake
   flour 300g (10½oz)
caster sugar 1½ tablespoons
sea salt ½ teaspoon
baking powder 1½ teaspoons
easy-bake dried yeast
   1 teaspoon
vegetable oil 1 tablespoon,
   plus extra for brushing
tepid water 75ml (2½fl oz) plus
   1 teaspoon
tepid milk 75ml (2½fl oz) plus
   1 teaspoon

for the sticky pork
star anise pod 1
cinnamon stick 2.5cm (1in)
fennel seeds ½ teaspoon
black peppercorns ¼ teaspoon
rice wine or dry sherry
   6 tablespoons
granulated sugar
   3 tablespoons
sea salt ½ teaspoon
dark soy sauce 1½ tablespoons
boneless pork belly 600g (1lb
   5oz) in one piece
groundnut oil 2 tablespoons
ginger root thumb-sized chunk,
   sliced into matchsticks
fresh red chilli 1, deseeded and
   sliced
salad onion 1 large, white part
   only, thickly sliced
garlic cloves 3, thinly sliced
hot chicken stock 400–500ml
   (14–18fl oz)

for the cucumber
ridge cucumber 1 or ½ large
   cucumber
garlic clove 1 large, thinly sliced
   lengthways
granulated sugar 1 tablespoon
sea salt ½ teaspoon
soy sauce 1½ teaspoons
rice vinegar 1 tablespoon

Stuffed with sweet, sticky pork and sharp cucumber pickle, these puffy milk buns are the equivalent of an Asian-style burger. Don't be daunted by the length of the recipe. Make the pork and pickle a day ahead, then get a production line going for the buns. They're as fun to make as they are to eat. Most recipes specify strong plain flour for the dough, but I find this a bit too chewy. The buns need the delicacy of a relatively low-gluten flour (see Gluten, page 60), such as Asian dumpling flour or cake flour.

. . .

For the pork, lightly crush the star anise, cinnamon stick, fennel seeds and peppercorns using a mortar and pestle. Add the rice wine, sugar, salt and soy sauce, stirring to dissolve the sugar.

Discard the tough rind of the pork but not the outer layer of fat. Cut the meat into 1cm (½in) slices, then cut each slice into 4cm (1¾in) chunks.

Heat the oil in a wide high-sided frying pan, large enough to take the pork chunks in a single layer. Add the ginger, chilli and onion, and fry over a medium-high heat for 30 seconds until fragrant. Add the pork, fry for 3–4 minutes or until starting to brown, then add the garlic and fry for a few seconds. Stir in the rice wine mixture and bubble for 2–3 minutes, then add just enough hot stock to barely cover the meat. Cover, bring to the boil then simmer over a very low heat for 30 minutes, or until the meat is just about tender.

Remove the lid from the pan and increase the heat to medium. Bubble down for 15–25 minutes, stirring all the time once the mixture starts to look sticky. Watch it like a hawk – it can burn very easily – turning the heat down if necessary. Remove from the heat once the liquid has almost evaporated and is clinging to the meat. Tip into a bowl and set aside.

To make the pickle, peel the cucumber, leaving alternate stripes of green, and trim the ends. Smash with a rolling pin to split, scrape out the seeds, then cut the flesh into small bite-sized pieces. Combine the rest of the ingredients in a bowl, add the cucumber and set aside.

Now for the buns. Put all the dry ingredients in a sieve set over a bowl. Muddle with your fingers, then shake through the sieve once or twice until well blended. Combine the oil, tepid water and milk, and whisk this into the flour mixture.

to garnish
chopped coriander leaves
shredded spring onions
sriracha sauce

makes 12

Once you have a flaky dough, finish mixing with your hands.

Tip the dough on to a floured work surface and knead for about 10 minutes until smooth and springy. Divide into 12 smooth balls, then roll into ovals measuring 12x8cm (4½x3¼in) (see Cook's note). Lightly brush with oil, fold in half crossways and arrange on a lightly oiled tray. Loosely cover with oiled cling film and leave in a warm place for 1–2 hours or until well risen.

Meanwhile, cut out 12 squares of baking parchment slightly bigger than the folded buns. Have ready a large steamer basket set over boiling water. Arrange the buns in the basket on their paper mats in a single layer, in batches if necessary. Steam for 10 minutes until pillowy, lifting the steamer lid occasionally to stop condensation dripping on to the buns.

Split the buns open and stuff with chunks of pork, cucumber, chopped coriander leaves and spring onion shreds. Add a squirt of sriracha and serve right away.

cook's note
· The best way to roll the dough into ovals is to smack the ball with the palm of your hand and push it away from you. The oval should be thin in the middle and slightly thicker at either end.

italian 00 wheat *flour*

plant source grain
aka farina (Italian)
latin name *Triticum aestivum*
protein/gluten 7–14%
goes with anything
uses biscuits, bread, cakes, pasta, pastry, thickener for sauces

Though Italian '00' flour is increasingly mentioned in cookbooks, magazines and on TV cookery shows, it's not always explained very well. For a start, the Italian grading system is different. In the UK and US, flours are graded by protein/gluten content, which, in turn, indicates how they can be used (see Protein, page 59; Gluten, page 60). Italian flours are graded on how finely or coarsely they've been milled, and the amount of bran and wheat germ removed, i.e. the yield. So, based on milling and yield, they range from *integrale* (wholewheat with all the bran left in), through '2', '1' and '0', down to '00', the finest.

The most confusing difference is that the protein/gluten in '00' flour ranges from a relatively low 7 per cent to as high as 14 per cent. This means that what appears to be the same flour can be used for anything from cakes and pastry, which need a lower-gluten flour, to bread and pasta, which need a higher-gluten flour. If a recipe doesn't specify the type of '00' flour, things could go badly wrong. Fortunately, the flour is packaged according to how it should be used – for example, *per pasta* (for pasta) or *per dolci* (for cakes and biscuits). Helpfully, the wording is usually in English for flour packaged for the UK and US. Even so, it's useful to know a smattering of flour-related Italian. For example, on packets of '00' flour you'll also see *farina di grano tenero*, literally meaning 'flour of tender grain' or soft flour, to distinguish it from *farina di grano duro* or *farina forte* – hard or strong flour.

So far reasonably good, but then it gets more complicated. You'll sometimes see numbers on the packet preceded by 'W' – a guide to flour strength, i.e. protein/gluten content. Roughly speaking, W120–160 is a weak, low-protein flour for baked items that don't rise very much, e.g. biscuits. At the other end of the scale is W310–330, a strong, high-protein flour used for long-fermented items such as sourdough or mile-high cakes such as panettone and pandora.

Also to be reckoned with is the P/L ratio – an indicator of how the protein/gluten in a particular flour behaves in terms of tensile strength (stretchiness) and ability to rise. A low P/L ratio indicates a weak flour producing a sticky, stretchy dough that doesn't rise very much. A high P/L ratio indicates the opposite.

Moving on from technical matters, it's certainly worth trying '00' flour. Even though you might assume it's more or less the same as plain flour, rest assured it makes superior pasta dough – wonderfully thin and quick to cook. Try Tagliatelle with Sage Butter Sauce (see page 241). It's also a must for Spätzle (see page 239) – snippets of tender pasta for mopping up stews or to serve anointed with butter as a satisfying side dish. Pizza crusts are flavoursome, crisp and pleasantly chewy. Pancakes are pillowy, sauces are smoother, and cakes more fragrant. Compare a sponge cake made with plain flour and one made with '00' and you'll see the difference.

The flour is also a pleasure to work with – silky smooth and as fine as baby powder. Just remember to choose the correct type for what you're planning to make.

venison casserole with mushrooms, garlic and rosemary

boneless venison shoulder
1.3kg (3lb), cut into 3cm (1¼in)
chunks
dried mushrooms 35g (1¼oz)
(see Cook's note)
Italian '00' flour or plain flour
3 tablespoons
sea salt ¼ teaspoon
freshly ground black pepper
½ teaspoon
olive oil 3 tablespoons
game stock 450–600ml
(16–20fl oz), preferably
homemade
cubed pancetta 50g (1¾oz)
pickling onions 450g (1lb),
peeled and left whole
garlic cloves 6, peeled and left
whole
tomato purée 3 tablespoons
fresh bay leaves 4
rosemary sprigs 2 good-sized
Spätzle to serve (see page 239)
chopped flat-leaf parsley to
garnish

for the marinade
full-bodied red wine 750ml
(25fl oz)
carrot 1, finely chopped
onion 1 small, finely chopped
celery stalk 1, finely chopped
juniper berries 1 teaspoon,
lightly crushed
black peppercorns ½
teaspoon, crushed

serves 6

A gloriously rich dark stew, popular in northern Italy and Eastern Europe. Tipping my hat to the Italian connection, I've used *doppio zero* (00) to coat the meat and thicken the juices, but you could use plain flour instead. Allow a day or more for marinating the venison.

· · ·

Combine the marinade ingredients in a stainless steel or glass dish. Add the venison, cover and leave in the fridge for 24–48 hours. Remove the venison and set aside, then strain the marinade, reserving the liquid.

Put the dried mushrooms in a bowl and cover with boiling water. Leave to soak for 20 minutes.

Preheat the oven to 150°C/Gas Mark 2. Mix the flour with the salt and pepper, and put in a shallow dish. Pat the venison chunks dry then dredge with the seasoned flour. Heat the olive oil in a large non-stick frying pan over a medium heat. Add the venison and fry for 3–4 minutes, in batches if necessary, until lightly browned. Add a ladleful of the stock if the meat starts to stick. Tip into a large heavy-based flameproof casserole with a lid. Sizzle the pancetta in the same frying pan until just beginning to brown at the edges, then add to the casserole.

Pour the strained marinade into the frying pan. Bring to the boil, scraping up any sediment with a wooden spoon. Pour into the casserole, along with the onions, garlic and soaked mushrooms with their liquid (if using fried mushrooms, add them now – see Cook's note). Stir in the tomato purée. Add the bay leaves, rosemary and enough stock to just cover.

Bring to the boil, cover with a well-fitting lid and put in the oven. Cook for 1½ hours, rotating every 30 minutes, then check to see if there is enough liquid. The juices should be thickened and slightly reduced but not drying out. If necessary, top up with the rest of the stock or some water. Cook for another hour, or until the meat is very tender. Serve with the Spätzle, anointed with plenty of butter and chopped flat-leaf parsley.

cook's note
· Dried mushrooms really intensify the flavour. Otherwise, use a couple of portabello mushrooms, thinly sliced and fried in olive oil.

spätzle

Italian '00' pasta flour 175g (6oz)
freshly grated nutmeg ⅛ teaspoon
sea salt ½ teaspoon
eggs 2, organic or free-range, lightly beaten
whole milk 100ml (3½fl oz)
unsalted butter

serves 6

you will need:
a large, wide colander with plenty of holes in the base for extruding the dough. I used a perforated Chinese skimmer, which did the job beautifully

Light but slightly chewy, these randomly shaped little pieces of dough are perfect for mopping up stew, adding to soups, or simply serving buttered with green vegetables. They're made with Italian *doppio zero* (00) pasta flour, a soft wheat flour that's high in gluten to make it stretchy.

. . .

Sift the flour, nutmeg and ¼ teaspoon of the salt into a large bowl. Whisk in the eggs using a fork. Gradually pour in the milk, whisking all the time to prevent lumps forming. Carry on whisking until you have a smooth dough.

Half fill a large saucepan with water. Add the remaining ¼ teaspoon of salt and bring to the boil.

Position a large colander with plenty of holes in the base over the saucepan. Put a small amount of dough into the colander and use the back of a wooden spoon to press it through the holes and into the boiling water. Stir the water gently to separate the pieces of dough, then boil for 5–8 minutes until tender but still with some bite.

Drain thoroughly, then tip into a warm serving dish. Anoint with butter and serve with the Venison Casserole (see page 238).

flour

tagliatelle with sage butter sauce

Italian '00' pasta flour 250g
  (9oz)
Italian semolina 75g (2¾oz)
eggs 3 large, organic or free-
  range, at room temperature
water 4 litres (7 pints)
sea salt 4 teaspoons
freshly grated Parmesan
  cheese to serve

for the sage butter sauce
unsalted butter 250g (9oz)
fresh sage leaves good
  handful, sliced if large
passata 1 tablespoon

serves 4–6

Cooked in minutes, fresh homemade egg pasta is so much better than shop-bought. It's such a pleasure to make, especially if you have friends or children to help. You will need a pasta machine fitted with cutters for ribbon pasta. Italian *doppio zero* (00) pasta flour is the finest grade and relatively high in gluten – perfect for egg pasta. Semolina (see page 180) gives the pasta a little more texture, which helps it pass through the pasta machine. Italian cookery teacher Ottavia Mazzoni kindly showed me how to roll and knead the dough.

• • •

Put the flours into a sieve set over a large bowl. Muddle with your fingers, then push through the sieve a couple of times until well mixed. Make a well in the centre and crack in the eggs. Whisk lightly with a fork to break up the whites. Keep whisking, gradually drawing in the flour from around the edge.

Once the dough starts to come together, tip on to a large wooden board or a clean work surface. Knead very briefly until all the flour is incorporated. Cover with a bowl and leave to rest for a couple of minutes while you clean your hands and the work surface.

Next, knead the dough. Hold it steady with one hand while folding it over with the fingers of the other hand. Then use the heel of your palm to push the dough away from you. Rotate the dough 90 degrees and repeat the two-part process. Continue for 8–10 minutes, or until the dough is uniform and smooth. Put it in a lightly oiled bowl, cover with cling film and leave to rest for 20–30 minutes.

Uncover the dough and knead briefly to redistribute any oil or moisture that may have gathered on the surface. Flatten into a disc and place on the work surface. Using a long wooden rolling pin, roll the dough from just above the lower edge to just short of the top edge. Rotate 90 degrees and repeat a few times until you have an oval about 5mm (¼in) thick. Slice along the short edge into six strips. Cut away any very curved edges or pointed ends (use the trimmings in a soup). Work with one piece at a time and cover the rest with a clean tea towel.

Set the rollers on a pasta machine to the third notch. Feed the dough strips through twice, arranging them on dry tea towels as they come out of the rollers. Adjust the rollers to the second notch, then roll each piece of dough through twice more. Slice the dough into 30cm (12in) lengths. To make tagliatelle, fit the widest cutters on to the machine, then pass each piece of dough through them. Lay the strips flat on a tea towel as they come out of the machine. Dust lightly with semolina to prevent sticking.

Bring the water to the boil in a large pot. Meanwhile, make the sauce. Sizzle the butter in a frying pan over a medium-high heat. Add the sage leaves and cook for a few seconds until crisp. Stir in the passata and keep warm.

Once the water has boiled, add the salt and then the pasta. Stir to prevent the pasta strands from sticking. Boil for 4–5 minutes, or until 'al dente' – tender, but still with some bite.

Drain through a colander, shaking to remove excess water. Tip into a warm, roomy serving dish and toss gently with the sauce. Sprinkle with Parmesan cheese and serve right away.

flour

chocolate and pepper cake
(pan pepato)

raisins 100g (3½oz)
shelled walnuts 100g (3½oz)
shelled hazelnuts 100g (3½oz)
  without skin
shelled almonds 100g (3½oz)
  without skin
candied citrus peel 100g
  (3½oz) (see Cook's notes)
plain chocolate 100g (3½oz)
  (85–90% cocoa solids)
clear honey 200g (7oz)
unsalted butter 25g (1oz)
sugar 75g (2¾oz)
unsweetened cocoa powder
  4 tablespoons
freshly ground black pepper
  1½ tablespoons
ground cinnamon 1 teaspoon
freshly grated nutmeg
  ½ teaspoon
ground cloves ¼ teaspoon
hot water 100ml (3½fl oz)
Italian '00' flour for cakes (per
  dolci) 150–175g (5½–6oz)

makes 6

I first sampled this cake on holiday in Umbria, and was immediately hooked. It's what I think of as a masculine sweetmeat – dense, chewy and dark, and not particularly sweet. Crusaders apparently carried it in their saddlebags to sustain them on long treks. It's studded with nuts and dried fruit, and intensely flavoured with black pepper and other spices, plus good-quality dark chocolate. I've used *doppio zero* (00) *per dolci* – a special cake flour made from soft wheat. You could use ordinary cake flour instead.

• • •

Put the raisins in a bowl and cover with boiling water. Leave for 30 minutes until they plump up. Roughly chop the nuts and citrus peel. Break the chocolate into bite-sized pieces.

Preheat the oven to 160°C/Gas Mark 3. Measure the honey (see Cook's note) into a heavy-based saucepan and warm over a low heat. Add the chocolate, butter and sugar and stir until melted. Stir in the cocoa, peppercorns, cinnamon, nutmeg and cloves.

Drain the raisins and add to the pan with the nuts and candied peel. By now the mixture will be getting stiff, so slacken it with the hot water. Sprinkle in the flour, a little at a time, stirring with each addition, using enough to bind the mixture. Keep stirring until you have a well-mixed dough.

Tip the dough on to a non-stick baking tray and press into a circle, using a wet palette knife. Slice the circle into six segments. Mould each segment into a ball then flatten into cakes about 2.5cm (1in) thick. Submerge any protruding raisins so they don't burn during baking.

Bake for 20–25 minutes until firm, rotating the tray halfway through. Remove from the oven and leave for 5 minutes, then put the cakes on a rack to cool completely.

cook's notes
• It's well worth using whole chunks of Italian candied peel and dicing it yourself. It has a much better flavour and colour than ready-chopped mixed peel.
• The easiest way to measure clear honey is to pour it directly into a saucepan placed on electronic scales (zero the scale first), rather than using a measuring spoon.

plain wheat *flour*

plant source grain
aka all-purpose flour (US)
latin name *Triticum aestivum*
protein/gluten 9.5–11%
goes with anything
uses batters, binding, biscuits, brownies, cakes, coating for fried foods, cobbler,
crumbles, flatbreads, fritters, muffins, pancakes, pastry, soda bread, thickener for
sauces and stews

Plain flour – so-called to differentiate it from self-raising flour (see page 256) – is what I look on as a background ingredient, always there when needed but not one that inspires experiment or makes you whoop with excitement. That said, it's an indispensable workhorse of the kitchen, or as the Americans fittingly call it, 'all-purpose'. It's the flour most of us reach for to thicken the juices round a roast, or sprinkle on the work surface to prevent dough sticking.

Open a fresh bag of plain flour and you'll immediately get a wholesome wheaty aroma, redolent of mills and bakeries. It feels cool to the touch and clumps slightly when squeezed, unlike strong bread flour that flows more freely. It's a subtle off-white rather than Arctic-white. The bran and the germ have been removed, so the flour is enriched by law with calcium, iron, and the B-vitamins niacin and thiamin, to compensate for nutrients lost during processing (see Roller milling, page 187).

Plain flour is truly multi-purpose. It's used for coating fried food, binding burgers and fritters, thickening batters, sauces and stews, and it's the key ingredient in dough for numerous baked items. It's an essential part of the line-up for egg-and-breadcrumbing fish fillets, chicken breasts and croquettes – see Rice Croquettes with Spinach and Mozzarella, page 252. It creates a protective dry layer around the food to which beaten egg can stick, and also helps prevent tasty juices escaping from the food while it's cooking.

Patiently stirred into a pan of melted butter, plain flour creates the all-important roux that thickens to a creamy béchamel sauce once milk is whisked in – perfect for anointing a dish of cauliflower or macaroni cheese. It also helps thicken crisp tempura-style coating batters – try Tempura Seafood with Wasabi Mayonnaise on page 254 – and it's the flour to use for other batter-based items such as Yorkshire puddings, popovers and pancakes.

As far as the home baker is concerned, plain flour contains a medium amount of gluten (see page 60) – not as much as strong bread flour (see Wheat flour: strong, page 264) or as little as cake flour (see Wheat flour: fine, page 232), but enough for items that need a firm structure and/or a certain amount of rise. It's ideal for biscuits and muffins, a simple sponge cake, or a crumble topping for a fruit dessert. It makes beautifully crisp pastry, including hot water crust, rough puff and shortcrust. Millers achieve the medium gluten content by blending hard wheat varieties with soft (see Gluten, page 60; Wheat and heritage flours, page 262). The aim is to produce a standard product, but brands do vary depending on where it was milled and which wheat varieties were used. You may get different results depending on which one you choose.

Plain flour is easy to find in supermarkets, health food shops and online. My favourites are organic brands that state which wheat varieties have been blended and where they were grown (see Sources, page 280).

Though the flour has a lengthy shelf life, it's worth checking that it's well within the 'best before' date. Your nose will tell you whether or not it's fresh. Keep it in a sealed container in a dry place away from light and heat.

raised game pie with juniper, lemon and gin

plain flour 450g (1lb), preferably
   organic or a heritage variety,
   plus extra for dusting
cornflour 2 teaspoons
sea salt 2 teaspoons
water 175ml (6fl oz)
suet 2 teaspoons
lard 175g (6oz), plus extra for
   greasing

for the filling
boneless mixed game 850g
   (1lb 14oz) such as venison,
   pheasant, rabbit
boneless belly pork 400g (14oz),
   rind removed but not the fat
sea salt 15g (½oz)
freshly ground white pepper
   1 heaped teaspoon
cracked black pepper 1 heaped
   teaspoon
crushed juniper berries
   1 heaped teaspoon
fresh sage leaves 15, stalks
   removed if tough, thinly sliced
lemons finely grated zest of 1½
freshly grated nutmeg
   1 teaspoon

for the egg wash
egg yolks 2, lightly beaten
sea salt good pinch

for the jelly
gelatine leaves 9g (⅓oz) (5 leaves
   depending on size)
good-quality meat stock 300ml
   (10fl oz)
gin 2 tablespoons

serves 10–12

you will need:
an oblong metal raised pie
tin, measuring 30x10x7cm
(12x4x2¾in)

Hot water crust pastry is used here to swaddle the filling and surrounding jelly. The most good-tempered of pastries, it's easy to make and addictively crisp and fatty. The pastry recipe comes from Dorset butcher Lee Moreton, courtesy of his grandfather who was also a butcher. Lee says a touch of suet beefs up the flavour, while cornflour makes the pastry crisper. I've spiked the filling with juniper and lemon, and the jelly with gin, to cut through the richness of the game.

• • •

For the pastry, sift the flour, cornflour and salt into a large bowl. Make a well in the centre and set aside.

Pour the water into a saucepan. Add the suet and lard. Bring to the boil, stirring as the lard melts. As soon as the liquid comes to the boil, remove from the heat and pour it into the flour. Stir constantly with a wooden spoon until cool enough to handle. Gently bring the pastry together to form a paste-like dough. Cover with a clean cloth and leave until completely cold, then chill for at least 30 minutes.

For the filling, cut the game and the belly pork into 1cm (½in) cubes. Spread in a single layer on freezer-proof trays and freeze for about 25 minutes, or until semi-frozen. Tip one-third of the frozen meat into the bowl of a food processor and pulse very briefly (see Cook's notes). Tip the pulsed meat into a large bowl and repeat with the two remaining batches.

Combine the rest of the filling ingredients in a small bowl. Add to the meat, using your hands to mix thoroughly but lightly – the meat should remain chunky – and set aside.

Preheat the oven to 180°C/Gas Mark 4. Grease the sides and base of your chosen pie tin with lard, and line the tin with baking parchment; ensure the parchment hangs over the sides of the tin to help lift the pie out once cooked. Weigh the pastry and cut off one quarter to use as a lid. Dust the work surface and your rolling pin with flour, then roll the pastry lid into an oblong measuring 32x12cm (12¾x4½in), or slightly bigger than the dimensions of the top of your tin. Cover with cling film and leave on the work surface.

Roll out the remaining pastry to an oblong measuring 44x25cm (17½x10in). Drape it over your rolling pin and carefully lift into the tin (see Cook's notes). Press into the base and sides, evening out any thick areas and leaving the excess pastry to overhang the rim. Trim any large uneven sections of overhanging pastry with scissors, leaving 2cm

flour

(¾in) all round for the lid to stick to. Reserve the trimmings for decorations.

Spoon the filling into the tin, levelling the surface. Combine the egg yolks with a pinch of salt, then brush this over the edge of the pastry case. Place the lid on top, press the edges together securely, then trim off the excess pastry. Crimp the edge with a fork or your thumb and make a few small holes along the lid to allow steam to escape.

Gather up the pastry trimmings and roll out thinly. Cut out small leaves, berries, stars – use your creativity here – and stick them to the lid with a dab of egg wash. Then thickly paint the entire lid with egg wash.

Put the tin on a baking tray and bake for 30 minutes. Rotate the tin, then reduce the oven temperature to 160°C/Gas Mark 3. Bake for another 50–60 minutes, rotating the tin every 20 minutes, until the centre of the pie reaches 78°C (172°F) on a thermometer. If necessary, cover the top with foil if the pastry is browning too much. It should be a glossy dark golden brown. Remove from the oven and leave in the tin to cool completely, about 4 hours or overnight.

Meanwhile, make the jelly. Soften the gelatine leaves in cold water for 10 minutes and heat the stock. Drain the gelatine and squeeze dry. Stir into the stock along with the gin. Pour into a jug and leave until almost cool and starting to thicken.

Carefully remove the pie from the tin. Make the holes in the top a little wider and deeper, so you can insert a small funnel. Trickle the jelly, bit by bit, into each of the holes, allowing the liquid to settle before topping up. Chill your pie for 2 or 3 hours to set the jelly, or even overnight if possible.

variation
- If game is out of season, make the pie with pork only. You will need 850g (1lb 14oz) boneless shoulder, 400g (14oz) boneless belly, plus 6 snipped rashers of unsmoked bacon.

cook's notes
- The meat should be minced quite coarsely to give the pie filling texture. Semi-freezing helps prevent the filling from becoming too paste-like when minced, as does restrained pulsing – just four or five times in 2-second bursts.
- There will be thick folds of pastry in the four corners of the tin. Just press with your fingers to even out the thickness. Inspect with an eagle eye to make sure there are no cracks, holes or thin areas – the pastry needs to be sturdy enough to hold the filling and the jelly.

flour

spring lamb and barley pie with lemon, rosemary and mint

pearl barley 100g (3½oz)
rapeseed oil 4 tablespoons
boneless lamb 1.2kg (2lb 12oz), cut into 2cm (1in) cubes, excess fat removed
sea salt
unsalted butter a good knob
banana shallots 3, chopped
Chantenay carrots 3 large, halved lengthways and cut into chunks
rosemary 2 sprigs, leaves picked and chopped
freshly ground black pepper ¼ teaspoon
lemon finely grated zest of 1
plain flour 3 tablespoons, plus extra for rolling out
hot vegetable or lamb stock 850ml (1½ pints)
baby leeks 5, halved lengthways and cut into finger-length chunks
shelled peas 150g (5½oz)
mint leaves small handful, chopped
rough puff pastry 600g (1lb 5oz) (see page 251)
egg 1, organic or free-range, lightly beaten

serves 6

you will need:
a 2-litre (3½-pint) rectangular pie dish with a flat rim

A lovely pie for spring – lamb, leeks and young vegetables, fragrant with lemon and herbs. Plain flour thickens the juices and mops up excess fat. Rough puff pastry makes a superb flaky topping; it's satisfying but time-consuming to make, so use shortcrust pastry instead if that's more convenient.

· · ·

Cook the pearl barley in a pan of boiling water for 30 minutes until tender but still with some bite, then drain.

Meanwhile, heat 2 tablespoons of the oil in a large frying pan. Add the lamb in batches (don't crowd the pan). Season with a little salt, and fry over a medium-high heat for about 10 minutes until brown. Remove with a slotted spoon and set aside. Discard the fatty liquid in the pan.

While the lamb is frying, heat the remaining oil and the knob of butter in a large heavy-based casserole. Fry the shallots and carrots over a medium heat for about 5 minutes until the shallots are soft but not browned. Add the meat to the casserole, and mix. Add the rosemary, ½ teaspoon of salt, the pepper and lemon zest. Sprinkle in the flour and stir to mix. Cook for 2 minutes, then pour in the hot stock. Bring to the boil, then reduce the heat and simmer very gently, uncovered, for 30 minutes, or until the meat is fairly tender.

Add the barley and leeks and simmer for 5 minutes. Stir in the peas and mint, simmer for another 5 minutes, then remove from the heat and ladle the filling into the pie dish.

Preheat the oven to 190°C/Gas Mark 5. Flour the work surface and your rolling pin, and roll out the pastry to a large rectangle about 3cm (1¼in) bigger than the pie dish.

Brush the flat rim of the pie dish with some of the beaten egg. Cut narrow strips of pastry to fit all around the rim, and brush the top of the strips with the beaten egg. Trim the rest of the pastry into a rectangle slightly larger than the pie dish. Place on top of the filled dish, pressing down gently around the edges, and neatly trim the overhang using scissors. Crimp the edges with a fork. Cut holes in the top to let out the steam, and brush the top with egg wash. Place on a baking tray and put in the lower third of the oven. Bake for 40 minutes, or until the pastry is golden and puffy.

rough puff pastry

plain flour 275g (9½oz),
preferably organic, plus extra
for dusting
sea salt heaped ¼ teaspoon
unsalted butter 90g (3¼oz),
firm but not hard, cut into 2cm
(¾in) cubes
lard 90g (3¼oz), cut into 2cm
(¾in) cubes
iced water 150ml (5fl oz)
lemon juice 1¼ teaspoons

makes 600g (1lb 5oz) pastry

Rough puff pastry is time-consuming to make, but it is quicker and easier than proper puff pastry. It holds its shape, reheats and freezes well, and bakes into crisp, flaky layers.

• • •

Sift the flour and salt together in a bowl. Add the butter and lard to the flour, tossing lightly with a round-tipped knife to coat. Don't work the pastry yet or attempt to mix in the fat.

Make a well in the centre. Mix the iced water with the lemon juice and pour into the well. Working quickly and using the knife, mix the water and flour, using a light folding motion and turning the bowl. Do not break up the pieces of fat. Once the ingredients start to come together, gently draw the mixture to a lump with your fingers.

Turn the dough out on to a floured work surface along with any loose flour from the bowl. Do not knead. Shape it gently into an 18x6cm (7x2½in) elongated brick shape – rather like a railway carriage. Wrap in lightly floured greaseproof paper and chill for 20 minutes.

Place on a lightly floured surface. Holding the rolling pin at the ends (so that the pressure is not directly above the dough), make three or four quick depressions across the length of the pastry. Still keeping your hands at the ends of the pin, and using short, even strokes, lightly roll the pastry into an elongated rectangle – the length should be three times the width. It's important to keep the sides straight and the ends square. The pastry will look mottled at this stage Fold up the bottom third. Seal the edges gently with your fingers to trap the air. Fold down and seal the top third in the same way. Rewrap in the greaseproof paper, flouring again if necessary, and chill for 20 minutes.

Flour the work surface and your rolling pin. Position the pastry so that the fold is on your right. Working quickly, make three or four quick depressions and roll out to an oblong again. Fold up the bottom third as before. Seal the edges gently with your fingers to trap the air. Fold down and seal the top third in the same way. Repeat the turning, folding and rolling process three more times, or until the pastry is no longer mottled. Remember to keep your rolling pin and the board well floured throughout. Wrap in greaseproof paper and chill for at least 30 minutes, or up to 8 hours.

rice croquettes with spinach and mozzarella (sicilian *arancini*)

baby spinach 225g (8oz)

sea salt plus sea salt flakes for sprinkling

eggs 2, organic or free-range, lightly beaten

plain flour 50g (1¾oz)

fine dry breadcrumbs 110g (4oz)

mozzarella 85g (3oz), finely diced

vegetable oil for deep-frying

lemon wedges to serve

for the risotto

olive oil 1 tablespoon

unsalted butter 1 tablespoon

shallot 1, finely chopped

risotto rice 200g (7oz), such as Carnaroli

white wine 50ml (2fl oz)

hot chicken or vegetable stock 500ml (18fl oz)

sea salt

freshly ground black pepper

freshly grated Parmesan cheese 20g (¾oz)

Makes 10

Said to resemble little oranges (*arancini*), these deep-fried croquettes are fun to make and an excellent way of using up leftover risotto (see Cook's notes) and other bits and bobs for the filling. I tried every variety possible on a recent trip to Sicily. Here's my favourite: tender spinach with unctuous melted mozzarella – an appetizing contrast to the crunchy crust. Flour plays an essential role here by making a layer between two separate coatings of beaten egg, which, in turn, help the breadcrumbs stick.

. . .

If you don't have any leftover risotto (see Cook's notes), make it at least 2 hours before you want to prepare the arancini. Heat a wide high-sided frying pan over a medium heat. Add the oil and butter and fry the shallot until soft. Stir in the rice, and keep stirring until the grains are shiny. Sprinkle in the wine, stir until absorbed, then add a ladleful of stock. Keep stirring and adding ladlefuls of stock until the rice is just al dente – tender but slightly firm in the middle. Season with sea salt and freshly ground black pepper, then stir in the Parmesan. Tip into a shallow bowl and leave to cool. Chill thoroughly before making arancini (see Cook's notes).

Meanwhile, cook the spinach, sprinkled with a little sea salt, in a steamer for 4–5 minutes until tender. Drain in a sieve, using the back of a large spoon to press out as much liquid as possible. Once it's cooled, use your hands to give it an extra squeeze. You should end up with about 125g (4½oz). Chop finely and divide into ten portions. Set aside on a plate.

Line up the beaten eggs, flour and breadcrumbs in separate bowls ready for dipping the croquettes.

Now for the fun part. Divide the chilled risotto into ten portions, wetting the palms of your hands when they get sticky. Roll into balls about the size of a golf ball. Holding a ball in the palm of one hand, push the thumb of the other hand into the ball. Stuff the hole with a portion of spinach and a small piece of mozzarella. Mould the rice over the stuffing, making sure there are no gaps, and shape it into a ball again. Repeat with the rest of the rice and filling.

Pour the vegetable oil into a high-sided frying pan (see Cook's notes) to no more than half full. Heat to 170°C (340°F), or until a cube of stale bread browns in 20 seconds.

Dip the arancini first into the beaten egg, then in to some flour, back into the egg and finally into the breadcrumbs. Fry

flour

in batches for 8–10 minutes, turning with tongs, until dark golden brown and cooked through (see Cook's notes). Drain on paper towels, then put in a warm serving dish. Adorn with lemon wedges and a sprinkle of sea salt flakes, and serve right away.

cook's notes

- If using leftover risotto, you will need about 550g (1lb 4oz).
- It's really important that the risotto is chilled, otherwise the rice grains won't stick together when you mould the balls. If you're short of time, spread the cooled risotto out on a tray and put in the freezer for 5 minutes.
- I find it easiest to fry just three or four arancini at a time. I use a relatively small, deep pan (20x8cm/8x3¼in) that doesn't need vast quantities of oil for deep-frying.
- Check that the oil temperature remains constant throughout the frying. It should be around 170°C (340°F) – hot enough for the heat to reach the centre without the crumb crust burning.
- To check that the arancini are cooked, open one up and make sure it's hot in the middle.

tempura seafood with wasabi mayonnaise

mixed cooked seafood 400g
  (14oz) packet
sea salt flakes
lemon or lime wedges to serve

for the batter
plain flour 175g (6oz), plus extra
  for dredging the seafood
cornflour 1 tablespoon
sea salt ½ teaspoon
freshly ground black pepper
  ¼ teaspoon
vegetable oil 1 tablespoon,
  plus extra for deep-frying
sparkling mineral water 250ml
  (9fl oz)
egg whites 2

for the wasabi mayonnaise
piece of fresh wasabi root 6cm
  (2½in) (see Cook's note), or
  wasabi paste ¼–½ teaspoon
good-quality mayonnaise
  8 tablespoons

serves 4

Mixed with sparkling mineral water, good-quality plain flour makes a delectably crunchy tempura-style batter – perfect for seafood.

• • •

First make the batter. Tip the flour, cornflour and salt into a sieve set over a bowl. Muddle with your fingers, then push through the sieve. Add the pepper, then lightly whisk in the oil and mineral water. Set aside for 30 minutes to rest.

Next make the wasabi mayonnaise. If using fresh wasabi root, peel and grate it finely, then immediately mix with the mayonnaise and put in a small serving bowl. It will quickly lose its pungency if exposed to the air. Otherwise, mix the wasabi paste with the mayonnaise.

In a clean bowl, beat the egg whites until almost stiff, then fold into the batter.

Pour enough oil into a heavy-based pan to come to a depth of 5cm (2in). Heat over a medium-high heat until very hot but not smoking – 180°C (350°F) on a thermometer, or until a cube of bread browns in 1 minute.

Have ready a shallow dish of flour for dredging the seafood. Gently stir the batter. Using tongs, dip the seafood in the flour, shake to remove any excess, then dunk in the batter. Lift up and let the batter drip back into the bowl, then drop the seafood into the hot oil. Fry for 2–3 minutes until golden and crisp.

Drain on paper towels and tip into a warm serving dish. Sprinkle with sea salt flakes and garnish with lemon or lime wedges. Serve with the wasabi mayonnaise for dipping.

cook's note
• You can buy fresh wasabi root online from wasabi.uk.com or in oriental grocers'. Better still, you can grow it yourself in a pot. It's really useful having fresh wasabi to hand.

dutch baby pancake with bacon and maple syrup

plain flour 60g (2½oz)
whole milk 125ml (4fl oz),
    preferably organic
eggs 3, organic or free-range
sea salt ½ teaspoon
unsalted butter 2 tablespoons
dry-cured streaky bacon
    6 rashers, grilled until crisp
maple syrup to serve

**makes 1 large pancake to
    serve 2–4**

you will need:
a 23–25cm (9–10in) ovenproof
frying pan

Sometimes called a German pancake, a Bismark or a Dutch puff, this magnificent pancake is neither small nor Dutch. It's an American invention dating from the 1900s, and the name is apparently derived from a mispronunciation of the word 'deutsch'. Puffed like a Yorkshire pudding, it makes an impressive Sunday brunch.

• • •

Whizz the flour, milk, eggs and salt in a blender for about 20 seconds. Leave to rest for 30 minutes.

Preheat the oven to 220°C/Gas Mark 7. Melt the butter in a 23–25cm (9–10in) ovenproof frying pan over a medium-high heat. Swirl the pan so the butter coats the sides as well as the base.

Give the batter a stir, then pour it all into the pan, tilting so that the liquid runs evenly to all sides.

Put the pan in the oven and bake for 10–15 minutes until hugely puffy, brown round the edges and cooked through.

Serve straight from the pan, taking care not to burn your fingers. Top with crispy bacon rashers and serve with maple syrup.

variations
• For a sweet topping, serve the pancake with fresh fruit and honey instead of bacon.
• You could also give it an Indian twist – season the batter with cumin seeds and serve with chutney or fresh pickle.

cook's note
• The batter can be left for several hours while you enjoy a Sunday morning walk.

self-raising wheat *flour*

plant source grain
aka self-raising flour
latin name *Triticum aestivum*
protein/gluten 8–11%
goes with anything
uses cakes, dumplings, muffins, pancakes, scones, sponge puddings, suet pastry

As a child, I always wondered how a flour could rise without help. Sadly, my mother was unable to explain this culinary miracle, or why she sometimes used self-raising flour rather than plain. It was only by close scrutiny that I saw that self-raising flour went into sponge cakes but not all cakes, and that it was used for certain puddings but not pastry. It was several years before the reason became clear.

Self-raising flour is plain or wholewheat flour mixed with a raising agent. The raising agent is usually baking powder, though some brands use a combination of bicarbonate of soda and cream of tartar. Once mixed with liquid in a dough or batter, the raising agent produces bubbles of carbon dioxide that expand when heated, thus producing the miraculous rise.

The flour comes in handy when you want to quickly rustle up a batch of fairy cakes or a sponge cake – what I call medium-lift items. It's also good for quick breads such as banana bread or fruity tea bread. For heavier items, the flour sometimes needs extra help. I combine self-raising flour and baking powder to make suet pastry, as in Citrus and Raisin Suet Puddings (see page 259). I also use this belt-and-braces approach in a cake that might otherwise be somewhat leaden – Welsh Curd Cake with Raisins and Apples (see page 261).

The raising agent does give the flour a faintly tangy flavour. This isn't noticeable in baked items, as other ingredients will absorb it, but in a sauce or gravy it causes a slightly 'off' flavour. For the same reason, it's not a good idea to use self-raising flour to dust the inside of cake tins or your work surface when rolling out dough.

Compared with plain flour, self-raising flour has a short shelf life. The raising agent loses its oomph after a few months, so it's best to buy in small quantities, check the use-by date and store in the fridge or another cool dry place.

You can of course make your own self-raising flour as and when you need it. The recommended ratio is usually 2 level teaspoons of baking powder to 225g (8oz) plain flour. Alternatively, use half a level teaspoon of bicarbonate of soda and 1 level teaspoon of cream of tartar to 225g (8oz) of plain flour. Be sure to sieve the ingredients thoroughly to get an even mix. Another option is to substitute plain flour with cake flour. It's lower in gluten and produces a softer bake.

There's an interesting history to self-raising flour. Bristol-based baker Henry Jones patented it in 1845, with the befitting slogan 'It towers above them all'. The flour was a runaway success for the simple reason that it did away with yeast as a raising agent. This meant that housewives could produce an acceptable loaf without kneading and proving, or repeatedly having to replace yeast that had gone off. (Bear in mind that only fresh yeast was available in those days, and domestic fridges had yet to be invented.)

Another important outcome was that yeast-free bread could now be easily made on-board ship during long voyages. This, in turn, meant that sailors no longer had to survive on unpalatable hard-tack biscuits. Strangely, it took several years before the Admiralty were persuaded that fresh bread would be a nutritional benefit.

flour

citrus and raisin suet puddings

self-raising flour 350g (12oz)
baking powder 1½ teaspoons
sea salt ⅛ teaspoon
shredded suet 160g (5½oz)
water 225–250ml (8–9fl oz)
plain flour for dusting
thick cream or very cold vanilla
    ice cream to serve

for the filling
large raisins 75g (2¾oz)
orange liqueur such as
    Cointreau 5 tablespoons
unsalted butter 60g (2¼oz), cut
    into small chunks, plus extra
    for greasing
granulated sugar 50g (1¾oz)
sweet, juicy clementines 3–4
    unpeeled, cut into chunks no
    bigger than 1.5cm (⅝in)

makes 6 individual puddings

you will need:
six 150ml (5fl oz) foil pudding
bowls, plus six sheets
each of baking parchment
and kitchen foil measuring
18x20cm (7x8in), and six
pieces of string long enough
to wrap around the bowls to
tie the paper and foil in place

A fortifying winter suet pudding based on the traditional Sussex pond pudding – named after the UK county of Sussex and the pond of buttery citrus juices that appear when the pastry is cut open. My recipe is for small individual puddings rather than the usual single large one. Suet pastry can be somewhat leaden, but the combination of self-raising flour and baking powder gives it the necessary lift. The pudding is usually made with lemons, but I have used clementines spiked with liqueur-soaked raisins for a sweeter flavour. Make sure the clementines are sweet and juicy.

• • •

To make the filling, soak the raisins in the liqueur for 1 hour or longer until nicely plump. (Use boiling water if you don't have any liqueur.)

Thoroughly grease the six pudding bowls and set aside.

For the pastry, sift the flour, baking powder and salt into a bowl. Stir in the shredded suet with a fork. Gradually stir in the water – just enough to make a soft, slightly sticky dough. Knead briefly until it comes away from the sides of the bowl.

Weigh the dough, then divide into six equal-sized pieces. Form into balls, then press into flat discs.

Lavishly dust your work surface and rolling pin with flour. Using a saucer or small plate as a template, roll out the discs into very thin 18cm (7in) circles. Trim the edges if necessary. Once you have a perfect circle, cut out a segment (one-third) and set aside to use as a lid.

Line the pudding bowls with the larger piece of pastry, overlapping the edges to seal, pushing it up the sides and slightly over the top. Make sure the pastry at the bottom is as thin as the pastry up the sides. Press out any uneven thickness. Trim the edge level with the top of the bowl.

Put a small chunk of butter in the bottom of each bowl and sprinkle with a little sugar. Drain the raisins and mix with the chopped clementines. Fill each bowl with the mixture, then top with the remaining butter and sugar.

Roll the reserved pastry segments into balls and then into circles to form lids. Place on top of the bowls, trim the edges and crimp with a fork to seal.

Place a piece of foil on top of a piece of baking parchment (see above). Holding the two sheets together, make a pleat down the middle to allow for expansion. Repeat with the rest of the sheets. Cover each bowl with a pleated pair of sheets (parchment side down, foil side up), then tie in place with the string.

Place the bowls on a trivet in a large deep saucepan. Pour in enough boiling water to come almost to the top of the trivet. Cover and steam for 1¼ hours on a rolling boil, topping up the water regularly.

Remove the bowls from the pan with tongs. Leave to settle for 5 minutes before removing the string and coverings. Loosen the edge of the pastry with the tip of a knife, then invert the bowls on to warm serving dishes and slice the puddings open to let the hot citrusy juices flow. Serve immediately with cream.

cook's note
· The fruit is cooked with the peel intact, so wash it well under warm running water.

welsh curd cake with raisins and apples

vegetable oil for greasing
self-raising flour 110g (4oz)
baking powder 2 teaspoons
Caerphilly cheese 225g
   (8oz), coarsely grated (see
   Variations)
curd cheese 225g (8oz), broken
   into lumps (see Cook's notes)
light muscovado sugar 110g
   (4oz)
vanilla extract 1 teaspoon
eggs 3, organic or free-range,
   lightly beaten
raisins 110g (4oz)
dried apples 85g (3oz), finely
   chopped (see Cook's notes)
icing sugar for dusting

makes one 28cm (8in) cake

Crumbly Caerphilly cheese combines with tangy curd cheese and fruit in this piquantly flavoured cake – a Welsh take on cheesecake. Self-raising flour lightens the texture.

. . .

Preheat the oven to 180°C/Gas Mark 4. Grease the base and sides of a 20cm (8in) cake tin. Line the base and sides of the tin with baking parchment, then grease the paper too.

Sift the flour and baking powder together into a bowl.

Put the cheeses, sugar and vanilla extract in the bowl of a food processor. Pulse a couple of times, then gradually add the eggs. Whizz until smooth, scraping down the sides of the bowl now and again.

Tip the mixture into a large bowl. Stir in the raisins and apples, then fold in the flour. Spoon into the prepared cake tin, levelling the surface with a wet palette knife.

Bake for 50–60 minutes, rotating the tin halfway through. When a skewer inserted in the centre comes out clean, remove from the oven and leave to settle in the tin for 10 minutes. Turn out on to a wire rack. Leave until completely cold then dust with icing sugar.

variations
• Replace the Caerphilly cheese with another moist, white crumbly cheese. Wensleydale would be a good choice.
• For a boozy cake, replace the vanilla extract with rum or brandy.

cook's notes
• Curd cheese is similar to cream cheese but is lower in fat and lighter textured. It is sometimes called medium-fat soft cheese.
• If you don't have any dried apples, use 200g (7oz) of raisins instead of 110g (4oz).

wheat and heritage flours

Referred to as the mothership of flour, wheat dates back thousands of years to the Stone Age. It had its beginnings in the Eastern Mediterranean and Middle East, and was one of the first crops to be domesticated. Since it could be stored for long periods, wheat was crucial in giving rise to a more settled way of life for nomadic tribes; they were able to switch from hunting and gathering food to actually producing it. Wheat is also unique in providing the world with leavened bread, thanks to its gluten-producing proteins that create an expandable dough when mixed with water (see Gluten, page 60).

Wheat grows in temperate regions throughout the world, from Canada to Australia and India to Italy, and is second to corn in terms of world production. As the World Wheat Market 2016/17 statistics show, the amount we are producing is on the up, though as the late Alan Davidson interestingly points out in *The Oxford Companion to Food*, more people rely on rice as their staple food since some of the total wheat grown is used as animal fodder.

Wheat is an annual plant belonging to the grass family *Poaceae*. The most important species is *Triticum aestivum* (from the Latin *Triticum* meaning threshing or bruising, and *aestivum* meaning summer) or bread wheat. There is also *T. durum* (meaning hard) or semolina wheat, and related species such as einkorn (*T. monococcum*), emmer (*T. dicoccum*) and spelt (*T. spelta*). (See individual entries for detail.)

Until I embarked on this book, most wheat looked the same to me. As I evolved as a grain groupie, however, I started to notice nuances in colour, texture and structure. It became hard to drive past wheat fields without stopping to pluck a few ears and inspect them more closely. The variations are fascinating. Glumes – the bracts at the base of the ear or flower head – may be loose or tightly enclose the grains. Some varieties have elegant upward-sweeping awns or whiskers projecting from the glumes; others are awnless. The way the grains grow around the stem varies too; some grow in well-defined columns, some zigzag and overlap.

Viewed under the microscope, a section through a typical wheat grain reveals four main components: the germ, endosperm, aleurone layer and the bran or seed coat. Working from the inside outwards, the minuscule germ or embryo lies deep within the grain. It's rich in fat, protein, B-vitamins, vitamin E and iron to nourish the growing seed. The bulk of the grain consists of the starchy endosperm. This contains the storage proteins glutenin and gliadin, plus albumins and globulins – proteins that affect water absorption and mixing properties (see Protein, page 50; Gluten, page 60). Surrounding the endosperm is the nutrient-rich aleurone layer that separates the endosperm from the fibrous outer coating of bran.

Classification There are reputedly over 30,000 wheat varieties worldwide. These can be broadly classified according to growing season, protein/gluten content and grain colour.

Spring wheat is sown in mid-spring for harvesting in late summer/early autumn. Winter wheat is sown in late summer/early autumn, becomes dormant during the winter, then resumes growth in spring and is harvested early the following summer.

The protein/gluten content (see Gluten, page 60) determines whether wheat is classified as hard or soft. Depending on variety and the growing conditions, hard wheat contains 12–16 per cent gluten and is used mainly for bread flour. Soft wheat contains 7–9 per cent gluten and is generally used for cake and pastry flour.

Breeders and farmers also classify wheat by bran colour – it may be reddish-brown, white or amber. In the US, colour classification is somewhat confusingly combined with seasonal classification. Red wheat may be 'hard red spring' and 'hard red winter', both of which are high-protein and used mainly for bread and firm-textured baked items, or to boost protein in weaker flours. It may also be 'soft red winter', a low-protein type used for cakes, muffins and pastry. There is also 'hard white' and 'soft white', respectively medium- and low-protein, with a milder flavour than red wheat. Durum wheat, the hardest variety, has amber-coloured bran and a yellow endosperm that give pasta and semolina (see page 180) their characteristic colour.

Wheat renaissance As California-based hunter/cook Hank Shaw writes, 'We live in a world of debased grains fed to indifferent people … wheats bred for yield, not flavor.' Farming journalist Kristan Lawson comments along similar lines: 'For centuries, society has considered wheat a faceless "commodity" like iron ore or cotton, every sack anonymous and interchangeable'. The good news, as both writers go on to point out, is that a slow but powerful wheat renaissance is under way.

Experts attending the annual Grain Gathering (a US-based summit of top-level bakers, millers, grain scientists and industry people) are collectively striving to make whole grains so flavoursome that any doubting Thomas will want to reconsider. Led by wheat geneticist Doctor Stephen Jones, in charge of the Washington State University-affiliated Bread Lab, these experts are putting their heads together to develop promising varieties of wheat that could potentially replace the standard flours routinely sold by retailers.

Thanks to initiatives like this, more chefs, food writers and clued-up consumers are discovering that wheat has a *terroir*, just like wine. As a result there is a growing awareness of flavour nuances – that a variety of wheat tastes different to the same variety from another area. Community Grains, a California-based consortium has spearheaded what it calls an 'Identity Preserved' initiative in which grains are given a detailed CV and are fully traceable from seed to table. There are increasing numbers of dedicated small companies such as US-based Grist and Toll, and Maine Grains, supplying freshly milled flour to discerning enthusiasts.

In the UK, the Wheat Improvement Strategic Programme (WISP), a collaboration of research institutes and universities, has been set up to address food security issues and sustainability of the UK's wheat crop. The consortium is conducting breeding trials aimed at producing new wheat varieties that can tolerate extreme weather conditions and provide increased yields.

Heritage grains Patrick Thornberry of UK niche supplier Bakery Bits (see Sources, page 280) defines heritage grains as a somewhat controversial term for flour milled from grain that lacks the characteristics required for industrial milling. Controversy arises because some millers consider grains growing as recently as the 1970s as heritage, while others define them as those growing pre-industrialization. Controversy aside, studies show that flour made from heritage grains, or heirloom grains as they're called in the US, is generally more nutrient-rich. Heritage grains are also environmentally more sustainable because, unlike modern wheat varieties, they require relatively little or no fertilizer. As Vanessa Kimball, sourdough diva and Bakery Bits consultant, aptly states, 'Modern varieties need to be pampered, to have everything they need brought to them, from water to nutrients.'

It's certainly worth bearing in mind that all domesticated wheat, both heritage and modern, is human-dependent for survival. Unlike ancient wild wheat, it no longer has the ability to sprout and reseed itself, and without farmers to plough the ground and sow the seeds, bucolic fields of undulating golden grain would disappear from our landscape.

strong wheat *flour*

plant source grain
aka bread flour, hard wheat flour, plain strong flour, extra-strong bread flour
latin name *Triticum aestivum*
protein/gluten 12–16%
goes with anything
uses babas, bagels, batter, bread, buns, croissants, crumpets, doughnuts, flatbreads,
gingerbread, pastry, pizza, rich fruit cakes, tea bread

As the name suggests, strong flour is well endowed with gluten (see page 60); levels range from 12–16 per cent compared with 9.5–11 per cent for plain flour. This means that the flour produces dough with the necessary bounce and elasticity to hold its shape when kneaded, to rise and trap the carbon dioxide bubbles produced by yeast, and to firm up around the bubbles as it cooks. Strong flour is therefore a must for yeasted baked items that need an open texture – bread, babas and doughnuts, for example – or even non-yeasted items such as Yorkshire puddings and puffy pancakes or flatbreads.

The UK climate isn't hot and sunny enough to produce high-gluten wheat, so the flour is a mixture of home-grown wheat and strong varieties from elsewhere – often Canada, or even the former Soviet republic of Kazakhstan. Super-resilient Canadian very strong wheat flour has a gluten content of around 15 per cent. This is the one to use for bread that needs lengthy fermentation. It's also a useful partner for low-gluten flours such as rye flour or wholemeal when these are used for bread. It helps them rise and keep their shape.

There are wholemeal versions of both strong and very strong flour, containing the bran layer and the oily germ (see Wheat and heritage flours, page 262). The bran limits gluten development somewhat, so dough made with these doesn't have quite the same oomph as dough made with strong white flour. On the other hand, they contain significant amounts of dietary fibre, iron and B-vitamins. A 50:50 mix of strong wholemeal and strong white is the best of both worlds.

In terms of appearance, strong white flour is as you would expect: pale creamy white with a fine, free-flowing texture. Unlike plain flour it doesn't clump when pressed between your fingers. Open a new bag and you'll get a clean, mildly wheaty aroma.

Strong wholemeal flour is creamy white flecked with light brown husks. Even when sampled raw, freshly milled good-quality flour has a delightfully warm, nutty flavour. You can almost taste the husks.

Strong flour is primarily used for bread-making, particularly for artisan-style loaves where structure, crispness and chew are important. Because of the high gluten content it's more absorbent than plain flour, which means you'll need to add a little more liquid to produce a pliable dough that can be kneaded without tearing. This is particularly necessary when you're using strong wholemeal flour.

Compared with flour sourced directly from a mill (see Sources, page 280), off-the-shelf strong flour can be rather bland. I sometimes perk it up by adding crushed seeds or spices to the dough. I especially like those with an Eastern European flavour such as dill or caraway – they seem to go well with bread. Acclaimed Australian baker and food writer Dan Lepard suggests deepening the flavour with up to 10 per cent wholemeal flour – or you could try a larger amount of strong wholemeal flour instead.

Though strong flour is mainly used for bread and other yeasted baked items, this isn't set in stone. Dan recommends strong flour for rich, dense fruit cakes and gingerbread. I occasionally mix it with plain flour in pastry where it's important to have layers and air pockets – puff, rough puff or flaky pastry, for example.

Though I wouldn't choose strong flour for tender sponge cakes, it's the flour to use for sweet items such as doughnuts and babas. Mixed with yeast and caster sugar, it creates a beautifully light and fluffy dough that rises well and is the ideal texture for soaking up alcohol-spiked syrup. Try my recipe for Limoncello Babas with Figs and Fennel on page 266.

Strong flour is easy to find in supermarkets, but you're likely to find more interesting choices in health food shops and farm shops. If you're a keen bread-maker, it's also worth investigating watermills and windmills that produce their own unique brands (see Sources, page 280).

Strong white flour has a lengthy shelf life, but it's worth checking that it's well within the 'best before' date. It gets progressively sourer as it ages, so let your nose be your guide. Strong wholemeal flour contains the oily germ that becomes rancid within a few months. Keep it in a sealed container in a cool dry place, preferably the fridge.

limoncello babas with figs and fennel

unsalted butter for greasing

strong white bread flour 110g
(4oz)

caster sugar 2 teaspoons

fast-action dried yeast
1½ teaspoons (about 5g/⅕oz)

sea salt pinch

tepid milk 100ml (3½fl oz)

egg 1 large, organic or free-
range, at room temperature

lemons 2 teaspoons freshly
grated zest

unsalted butter 55g (2oz),
melted and cooled slightly

fennel seeds crushed or fennel
pollen

figs 3 plump ripe, sliced
lengthways into six segments
(see Variations)

for the lemon syrup
caster sugar 125g (4½oz)

water 125ml (4fl oz)

lemon 3 strips zest

limoncello liqueur 3
tablespoons (see Cook's
notes), plus extra for
sprinkling

for the Chantilly cream
whipping cream or double
cream 300ml (10fl oz),
preferably organic

caster sugar 1½ tablespoons

vanilla extract 1 teaspoon

makes 6

you will need:
six 11cm (4¼in) metal baba
moulds with a central hole
(see Cooks' notes); and a
piping bag fitted with a large
plain nozzle

These sweet, sticky babas take on sunny Neapolitan flavours with limoncello liqueur, plump fresh figs and aniseed-flavoured fennel seeds – all said to help digestion. Allow plenty of time for the dough to rise and for the babas to soak up the syrup once cooked. If necessary, soak them the day before, and fill them just before serving.

. . .

Thoroughly grease the baba moulds with butter.

Sift the flour, sugar, yeast and salt into a large bowl. Make a well in the centre and pour in the milk, the egg and the lemon zest. Stir with a small whisk or fork, gradually drawing in the flour from around the edge. Using an electric whisk, beat for 5 minutes until the dough is very smooth and starting to cling to the beaters. Beat in the melted butter, making sure it's thoroughly mixed in.

Carefully spoon the dough into the moulds – to no more than half full. Cover with a clean tea towel and leave in a warm place for 50–60 minutes to rise.

Meanwhile, make the syrup. Put the sugar, water and lemon zest strips into a small saucepan. Bring to the boil, then simmer for a few minutes. Remove from the heat and stir in the limoncello.

Preheat the oven to 200°C/Gas Mark 6. Put a baking sheet in to heat.

Carefully move the risen babas in their moulds on to the heated baking sheet. Bake for 12–15 minutes, rotating the sheet halfway through, until golden, and a skewer inserted in the centre comes out clean.

Leave in the moulds for 5 minutes to settle, then turn out into a shallow dish large enough to take them in a single layer. Arrange them with the crusty topside uppermost. Pour over the syrup and leave to soak for 30 minutes. Turn them over, so the spongy bottom is now on top. Sprinkle with more limoncello if you like, then leave for 30 minutes more, or until all the syrup has been soaked up.

To make the Chantilly cream, beat the cream in a large metal or glass bowl until the beaters are starting to leave a trail when lifted from the bowl. Beat in the sugar and vanilla extract, then carry on beating until fluffy.

strong wheat *flour*

Spoon the cream into a piping bag fitted with a large plain nozzle. Pipe a small coil of cream into the middle of the babas (see Cook's notes). Just before serving, put the babas on individual plates. Sprinkle with a few fennel seeds or a pinch of fennel pollen, then arrange three fig segments attractively on top.

variations
- Experiment with flavoured sugars for adding to the flour: lemon verbena, bay or fennel sugar would all be delicious.
- Instead of figs for the topping, use a ripe peach or nectarine sliced into thin segments.

cook's notes
- If you don't have baba moulds, you could use small metal 11cm (4¼in) pie dishes instead, but you will have to cut a hole in the middle of the cooked dough for filling.
- If you don't have limoncello, try anise-flavoured sambuca or herb-fragrant strega instead. Both are said to be good for the digestion. Failing these, traditional rum would be fine too.
- Honour your babas by piping the Chantilly cream into the centre rather than trying to spoon it in. Piping not only looks good but forces air into the cream and makes it lighter.

flour

native american frybread with black bean and red pepper salsa

strong white bread flour 250g (9oz), plus extra for dusting
baking powder 1½ teaspoons
sea salt 1 teaspoon
tepid water 150ml (5fl oz)
lard or oil for deep-frying (see Cook's notes)
sliced avocado to serve
soured cream to serve

for the salsa
cooked black beans 275g (9½oz) (about 140g/5oz dried beans)
red onion 4 tablespoons, finely chopped
roasted red pepper 1, skin and seeds removed, flesh diced
raw or roasted green or red chilli ½ –1, deseeded, skinned and finely diced
lime juice of 1
coriander 4 tablespoons chopped leaves
sea salt flakes ½ teaspoon

makes 4

This iconic frybread has been made for centuries by generations of Native Americans. It's a very simple flour and water dough, kneaded and rolled to a thin circle, then fried in bubbling lard. It comes out of the pan splendidly puffy and golden, crisp on the outside and chewy inside. I first ate it at a chilli festival in New Mexico, expertly fried by Pueblo cooks who topped it with a fiery salsa.

• • •

Sieve the flour, baking powder and salt into a large bowl. Make a well in the centre and pour in the tepid water. Stir with a fork, gradually drawing in the flour from around the edge. Tip on to a floured work surface and knead to a soft dough that isn't sticky. Cover with a damp tea towel and leave to rest for 1 hour.

Combine all the salsa ingredients in a serving bowl. Leave at room temperature while the dough is resting.

Sprinkle the work surface and your rolling pin with flour. Divide the dough into four equal chunks and roll into smooth balls. Roll out very thinly to 13cm (5in) circles. Cut a small triangle in the middle of each circle.

Put enough lard or oil (see Cook's notes) in a non-stick frying pan to come to a depth of 4cm (1½in). Heat over a medium-high heat until very hot but not smoking – 180°C (350°F) on a thermometer, or until a cube of bread browns in 1 minute. Carefully drop in a piece of dough – the dough will whistle and the fat will bubble and splatter. Fry for 2–3 minutes, or until golden on the underside. Flip over and fry for 1–2 minutes more, until golden and puffy. Drain on paper towels and keep warm in a low oven while you cook the rest.

Serve the frybreads with the salsa, topped with avocado and a dollop of soured cream.

cook's notes
· Lard gets a bad press, but do try and bring yourself to use it now and again. Good-quality lard adds a subtle meaty flavour and is perfect for frying at high temperatures. Use groundnut oil as an alternative to lard.
· I use a 20cm (8in) diameter, 8cm (3¼in) deep pan for frying. It's perfect for frying one frybread at a time.

whole wheat *flour*

plant source grain
aka whole wheat flour (US), wholemeal flour (UK)
latin name *Triticum aestivum*
protein/gluten 10%
goes with bananas, cheese, chocolate, coconut, dates, dried fruit, ginger, muscovado
    sugar, mushrooms, oranges, seeds, spices, tomatoes
uses biscuits, brownies, bread, cakes, flatbreads, muffins, pancakes, pastry, scones,
    soda bread

As is sometimes the case with certain flours, nomenclature can be confusing. Whole grain wheat flour is certainly one that needs clarification. It's called 'whole wheat' in the US and, less precisely, 'wholemeal' in the UK. Since any flour can be ground to a meal – corn for example – it would be clearer to call it 'wholemeal wheat flour', albeit somewhat ponderous. Not to be confused with wholemeal flour is 'wheatmeal' flour, aka brown flour, which is plain white flour to which bran has been added, usually about 10–15 per cent. To add to the confusion, in the US there is also 'whole white wheat' flour. This is whole grain flour milled from a type of wheat that has a white layer of bran as opposed to the usual brown. It has a milder flavour and smoother texture than ordinary wholemeal flour.

Semantics aside, whole grain wheat flour, or any other whole grain flour, contains the bran layer, the inner germ and the starchy endosperm (see Wheat and heritage flours, page 262), all a source of important nutrients – dietary fibre, iron and B-vitamins to name a few. It's made by grinding the wheat grains by roller milling or, traditionally, stone grinding.

Roller milling (see page 187) is a high-speed process during which the bran and the germ are separated from the endosperm, and then put back at the end. Some people object to roller milling on the grounds that it generates heat that damages the enzymes in the grain, or that separating and then returning the nutritious components to the flour makes a nonsense of the grain concept.

Stone grinding (see The miller's tale, page 187) is the traditional method in which wheat grains are crushed between two stones, one slowly rotating, the other static. The bran and the germ are left intact, producing flour that remains one hundred per cent wholemeal throughout the process. The flour isn't subjected to heat, it retains the nutrients and has more flavour. Understandably it's the method preferred by bread enthusiasts.

Those of a certain age may have best-forgotten memories of leaden wholemeal pastry, a must-have during the 1970s wholefood movement. Wholemeal flour and products made with it are a very different matter today, thanks to a growing band of expert bakers, millers, grain scientists and farmers who are collectively striving to raise the bar in this respect (see Wheat and heritage flours, page 262).

I experienced an epiphany when I opened a bag of freshly milled wholemeal flour from a local organic farm. It can only be described as the Rolls Royce of wholemeal flour. It was beautiful in every way – an attractive creamy white, marled with flecks of acorn-brown husks, and it had a wonderfully wheaty aroma and notably nutty flavour with a pleasant creamy aftertaste.

If you find the idea of wholemeal flour a bit too – how shall I put it – wholesome, it's worth putting such thoughts aside. The flour adds welcome colour and earthy flavour to all kinds of baked items – not just bread, but scones, muffins, cakes and even croissants. Improved flavour comes at the expense of rise, however, so you'll usually need to add baking powder or bicarbonate of soda to help with the necessary lift.

Wholemeal flour behaves a bit differently from plain flour; it takes longer to absorb liquids, for example. It's a good idea to rest your dough or batter before baking to give it a chance to hydrate. A ten-minute rest will be fine for quick-cook items such as muffins and scones, but bread dough will need two or three hours at least.

A useful rule of thumb is to substitute up to 50 per cent wholemeal flour for plain flour, especially for pastry and pancakes. If you're new to wholemeal flour, it's best to start off with a recipe specifically created for it. Try the Tamarisk Wholemeal Spice Cake with Ginger Glaze on page 273.

It's worth tracking down the very best wholemeal flour you can find. My favourites are organic brands that state which wheat varieties have been blended and where they were grown (see Sources, page 280). Health food shops and the better supermarkets are good hunting grounds.

Wholemeal flour has a relatively short shelf life since it contains the oily germ which goes rancid once exposed to air. Keep it in a sealed container in a cool place, preferably the fridge.

flour

tamarisk wholemeal spice cake with ginger glaze

vegetable oil for greasing
wholemeal flour 250g (9oz),
   preferably a heritage variety or
   freshly milled
baking powder 1 teaspoon
bicarbonate of soda
   ½ teaspoon
ground cinnamon 1 tablespoon
mixed spice 2 teaspoons
unsalted butter 125g (4½oz)
golden caster sugar 200g (7oz)
plain yogurt 250ml (9fl oz),
   preferably organic
eggs 4, organic or free-range,
   lightly beaten
syrup from a jar of preserved
   ginger 4 tablespoons
preserved ginger 2 knobs, very
   thinly sliced into rounds

makes one 20x20cm
   (8x8in) cake

I'm not normally a fan of wholemeal flour – too many toe-curling memories of leaden pastry, brown rice and Birkenstocks. That said, this wholemeal flour, milled in small batches by local organic farm Tamarisk, bowled me over. The cake was fresh-tasting, light and – dare I say it – wholesome. If you decide to make it, do use the very best wholemeal flour you can lay your hands on – preferably a heritage variety (see Sources, page 280). This recipe is loosely based on one by Canadian food writer and fellow grain enthusiast Naomi Duguid. Naomi recommends using wholemeal flour for shortbread too.

• • •

Preheat the oven to 200°C/Gas Mark 6. Grease a 20x20cm (8x8in) square cake tin. Line the base and sides of the tin with baking parchment, then grease the paper too.

Put the flour, baking powder, bicarbonate of soda, cinnamon and mixed spice into a sieve set over a large bowl. Muddle with your fingers, then shake through the sieve. Sieve once or twice more until well blended. Mix the bran left in the sieve back into the flour mixture.

Using an electric whisk, beat the butter and sugar in another large bowl for a few minutes until fluffy. Stir in the yogurt, then add the eggs and beat until combined.

Make a well in the centre of the flour mixture, and pour in all the egg mixture. Mix with a fork, stirring from the centre and gradually drawing in the dry ingredients from around the edge. Tip the resulting batter into your prepared cake tin, levelling the surface with a palette knife.

Bake for 10 minutes, then reduce the oven temperature to 190°C/Gas Mark 5. Bake for 25–30 minutes more, rotating the tin halfway through, or until a skewer inserted in the centre comes out clean. Leave to cool in the tin for 15 minutes.

Lift the cake out of the tin and place on a large plate. Pierce with a skewer in several places. Pour over the syrup from the preserved ginger jar, encouraging it to trickle into the holes. Arrange wafer-thin slices of preserved ginger attractively on top. Leave to soak and cool completely before enjoying.

yam *flour*

plant source tuber
aka elùbo, foofoo, fufu, poundo iyan, pounded yam
latin name *Dioscorea* (various species)
gluten none
protein 6–8%
goes with curries, soups, stews
uses binding, coating for fried foods, dumplings, paste, porridge

Though yam flour is not something I routinely buy, it's worth including since the yam itself is an important staple, particularly in West Africa. It's a brown-skinned, white- or yellow-fleshed tuber with numerous varieties ranging from slender finger-like clusters to single monsters growing a metre or more into the ground. (It's worth noting that in the US, orange-fleshed sweet potatoes are also called yams, even though they're from a different botanical family.)

In West Africa, yams are typically eaten as fufu, a surprisingly delicious polenta-like paste served alongside spicy soups and stews. Fufu was traditionally made by laboriously pounding boiled yams with a massive wooden mortar. Nowadays, old-style fufu has been superseded by pounded yam flour and 'instant' fufu, milled from dried yams. My preference is for yam flour rather than instant fufu; it has fewer additives plus the potential for uses other than fufu.

Making fufu is a simple matter of sprinkling the flour into boiling water and stirring 'with vigour', as my Nigerian cookbook instructs, to get rid of any lumps. You'll end up with a pleasant-flavoured satin-smooth paste, which you then shape into a soft warm mound. Each diner tears off chunks, rolls them into small balls and scoops up the soup or stew. If you like mashed potato, you'll like this.

Another option is to mix the paste with finely chopped onion, chilli and seasonings, mould into bite-sized balls and deep-fry until crisp. Serve as a tasty snack, or with rice and vegetables.

Though fufu is the main role for yam flour, there is no reason why it couldn't be used as a coating for strips of fried chicken or fish – dip them in beaten egg first – or to bind fishcakes and bean burgers. If you're tempted to bake with it, bear in mind that it's gluten-free and will need mixing with other flours to make it workable (see Gluten, page 60).

You'll find yam flour and fufu online (see Sources, page 280) and in shops selling African or Asian groceries.

fufu with spicy goat, red pepper and butternut squash soup

goat meat 900g (2lb), cubed
vegetable oil for frying
onions 2, halved and sliced into crescents
red pepper 1 large, deseeded and diced
sea salt ¼ teaspoon
good-quality hot meat stock 600–850ml (1–1½ pints)
chopped tomatoes 250g (9oz) canned (see Cook's notes)
tomato purée 2 tablespoons
peeled and deseeded butternut squash 350g (12oz), cubed
lime juice of 1

for the fufu
water 600ml (1 pint)
pounded yam flour 175g (6oz)

for the spice rub
black peppercorns 1 teaspoon
allspice berries 1 teaspoon
cloves 2
cumin seeds 1 teaspoon
sea salt 1 teaspoon
garlic cloves 2 fat, crushed
onion 1, grated
ginger root 2cm (¾in) chunk, roughly chopped
fresh red chilli 1, deseeded and chopped
fresh thyme leaves 1 teaspoon

to garnish
thinly sliced red chilli
coriander leaves
lime segments

serves 4–6 as a main meal

As comforting as mashed potato, yam flour porridge, aka fufu, is a delightful accompaniment to this hearty soup. Goat meat is rich and gamey, but not that different from mutton or beef. It goes well with the big, bold flavours used here – pungent spices, chilli, ginger and garlic – and benefits from a leisurely marinate in the spice rub.

. . .

First make the spice rub. Grind the dry spices to a powder using a mortar and pestle. Add the remaining ingredients and pound to a paste with the ground spices. Put the meat in a shallow dish and smear all over with the spice rub. Cover and leave to marinate in the fridge for at least 4 hours, or up to 2 days.

Heat 2 tablespoons of oil in a large heavy-based flameproof casserole. Add the onions, red pepper and the salt. Fry over a medium heat for about 10 minutes, or until the onions are just starting to colour.

Meanwhile, heat another 2 tablespoons of oil in a heavy-based frying pan, large enough to take the meat in a single layer. Add the meat, including any spice rub, and fry over a medium-high heat for 10 minutes, or until lightly browned. Add a little stock if the mixture starts to look dry. Tip the meat into the casserole.

Deglaze the frying pan with a ladleful of stock, and pour into the casserole. Stir in the chopped tomatoes, the tomato purée and enough stock to just cover the meat. Bring to the boil, then simmer, partially covered, for 1½ –2 hours, or until the meat is just tender.

Add the cubed squash and, if necessary, a little more stock to cover. Simmer for another 30 minutes, or until the meat and squash are tender. Stir in the lime juice and keep warm.

To make the fufu, boil the water in a kettle. Tip half into a saucepan set over a medium-low heat, and the rest into a jug. Sieve the yam flour into the water in the saucepan, stirring constantly until smooth. Gradually whisk in the water from the jug. Reduce the heat to low and cook for 5 minutes, continuing to stir, until the mixture is thick and smooth. Tip it into a serving bowl.

Ladle the soup into large individual bowls and top with the garnishes. Pull off chunks of fufu to sop up the soup and scrape the bowl clean.

flour

- Goat meat is the most widely eaten of all meats, geographically, because its consumption isn't forbidden by any major religion. It's a favourite in the Caribbean, Africa, India, Middle East and southern Europe, but strangely not in the UK, despite efforts to promote it. I am a great fan, but if goat isn't your thing, it's fine to use mutton or beef instead.
- Replace the squash with the same amount of diced yam. Wash it thoroughly in cold running water to get rid of the slipperiness.

cook's notes
- For the best flavour use whole spices rather than pre-ground.
- Don't be tempted to use a whole can of chopped tomatoes, as they will dominate the soup.

bibliography

Albala, K. *Beans: A History*. Berg, Oxford and New York 2007

Alderson, E. *The Homemade Flour Cookbook*. Fair Winds Press, Massachusetts 2014

Atala, A. *DOM Rediscovering Brazilian Ingredients*. Phaidon Press, London and New York 2013

Atkinson, C., Banks, M., McFadden, C. *The World Encyclopaedia of Coffee*. Lorenz Books, London 1999

Castanho, T., Bianchi, L. *Brazilian Food*. Mitchell Beazley, London 2014

Chamberlain, L. *The Food and Cooking of Eastern Europe*. Penguin Books, London 1989

Cook's Illustrated Magazine, Editors. *The America's Test Kitchen Cookbook*. Boston Common Press, Massachusetts 2001

Corriher, S.O. *CookWise: The Hows and Whys of Successful Cooking*. William Morrow, New York 1997

Dalby, A. *Food in the Ancient World from A–Z*. Routledge, London and New York 2003

Davidson, A. *The Oxford Companion to Food*. Second edition. Oxford University Press, Oxford 2006

Del Conte, A. *The Classic Food of Northern Italy*. Pavilion Books, London 1995

Devlin, N. *Food For a Happy Gut*. Headline, London 2017

Duguid, N. 'Notes From a Grain Junkie' in *Lucky Peach*, issue no. 14, New York 2015

Econopouly, B.F., Jones, S.S. 'The Rewards of (Gluten) Intolerance' in *Gastronomica*. University of California Press, summer 2017

Fajans, J. *Brazilian Food: Race, Class and Identity in Regional Cuisines*. Berg, London and New York 2012

Field, C. *The Italian Baker*. Harper Collins, New York 1985

Food and Agriculture Organization of the United Nations. *Utilization of Tropical Foods: Roots and Tubers*. FAO, Rome 1989

Franklin, S.B. 'Manioc' in *Gastronomica*. University of California Press, autumn 2012

Fussell, B. *The Story of Corn*. Knopf, New York 1992

Goss-Custard, E. *Honeybuns Gluten-Free Baking*. Pavilion Books, London 2012

Guinaudeau, Z. *Traditional Moroccan Cooking: Recipes from Fez*. Serif, London 1994

Hammond, B. *Cooking Explained*. Longman, Essex 1974

Hanneman, L.J. *Bakery: Bread & Fermented Goods*. Butterworth Heinemann, Oxford 1980

Holland, B., Unwin, I.D., Buss, D.H. *Cereals and Cereal Products: Third Supplement to McCance and Widdowson's The Composition of Foods*. Royal Society of Chemistry and Ministry of Agriculture, Fisheries and Food, 1988

Kamozawa, A., Talbot, H.A. *Gluten-Free Flour Power*. W.W. Norton, New York 2015

Kiple, K.F., Ornelas, K.C., Editors. *The Cambridge World History of Food* Vols 1 and 2. Cambridge University Press, Cambridge 2000

Library of Entertaining Knowledge, The. *Vegetable Substances Used for the Food of Man*. London 1832

Lister, T. *A Handful of Flour*. Headline, London 2016

McGee, H. *On Food and Cooking: The Science and Lore of the Kitchen*. George Allen & Unwin, London 1984

Muir, J. *A Cook's Guide to Grains*. Conran Octopus, London 2002

Owen, S. *The Rice Book*. Frances Lincoln, London 1993

Oxford Symposium on Food & Cookery 1989 Proceedings. *Staple Foods*. Prospect Books 1990

Pollan, M. *Cooked: A Natural History of Transformation*. Penguin, London 2013

Ross, R. *Beyond Bok Choy*. Artisan, New York 1996

Saul, R. *Spelt*. Nourish, London 2015

Segnit, N. *The Flavour Thesaurus*. Bloomsbury Publishing, London 2010

Simon, A.L. Editor. *A Concise Encyclopaedia of Gastronomy: Cereals*. The Wine and Food Society, London 1943

Sing, D. *Indian Cookery*. Penguin Books, London 1970

Speck, M. *Ancient Grains for Modern Meals*. Ten Speed Press, New York 2011

Spivey, D. *The Peppers, Cracklings, and Knots of Wool Cookbook*. State University of New York Press, Albany 1999

Thompson, D. *Thai Food*. Pavilion Books, London 2002

Vaughan, J.G., Geissler, C.A. *The New Oxford Book of Food Plants*. Oxford University Press, Oxford 1997

Weinstein, B., Scarborough M. *Grains Mains*. Rodale, New York 2012

Wolfert, P. *The Food of Morocco*. Bloomsbury, London 2011

Zoladz, M. 'Cassava and Tapioca' in *The Oxford Companion to Sugar and Sweets*. Oxford University Press, Oxford 2015

Selected websites

agris.fao.org (Food and Agriculture Organization of the United Nations)

bakerpedia.com

bakerybits.co.uk

bobsredmill.com

cookingforengineers.com

cooksinfo.com

cgiar.org (formerly Consultative Group for International Agriculture Research now Consortium of International Agricultural Research Centres)

eol.org (Encyclopaedia of Life)

fabflour.co.uk (Flour Advisory Bureau)

fao.org (Food and Agriculture Organization of the United Nations)

grains.org

kingarthurflour.com

pea-lentil.com (USA Dry Pea & Lentil Council)

powo.science.kew.org (Plants of the World Online, Royal Botanical Gardens, Kew)

ryeandhealth.org

starch.dk (International Starch Institute, Denmark)

thebreadlab.wsu.edu

thefreshloaf.com

wholegrainscouncil.org

sources

The flours and starches listed here are the more obscure or hard to find ones, or brands that I have found particularly good.

Almond flour
buywholefoodsonline.co.uk
hollandandbarrett.com
kingarthurflour.com

Amaranth flour
bobsredmill.com
buywholefoodsonline.co.uk
healthysupplies.co.uk
kingarthurflour.com

Atta flour
24mantra.com
bakerybits.co.uk (Offley Mill chapati flour)
mattas.co.uk
redrickshaw.co.uk
somayaskitchen.co.uk

Banana flour (green)
naturalevolutionfoods.co.uk

Barley flour
bobsredmill.com
dovesfarm.co.uk
shipton-mill.com

Black bean flour
bobsredmill.com
healthysupplies.co.uk

Buckwheat flour
dovesfarm.co.uk
mainegrains.com
shipton-mill.com

Cassava flour/farinha de mandioca/sour starch/tapioca starch
cubancuisine.co.uk
brasil-latino.de
souschef.co.uk
supermercadoportugal.com

Cassava flour (all-purpose)
tiana-coconut.com
isabelsfreefrom.co.uk

Cassava flour (tapioca pearls, starch)
bobsredmill.com
healthysupplies.co.uk

Chestnut flour
amisa.co.uk

Coconut flour
tiana-coconut.com

Coffee flour
algcoffee.co.uk

Cornmeal (polenta, purple and yellow cornmeal, masa harina, arepa flour)
bakerybits.co.uk (polenta)
brasil-latino.de
casabrasillondres.co.uk
cubancuisine.co.uk
gristandtoll.com (polenta)
mainegrains.com
mexgrocer.co.uk (masa harina)
souschef.co.uk
supermercadoportugal.com
therawfoodworld.com (purple and yellow cornmeal)

Cricket flour
eatgrub.co.uk
kric8.co.uk

Einkorn flour
bakerybits.co.uk

dovesfarm.co.uk
shipton-mill.com

Emmer flour
bakerybits.co.uk
dovesfarm.co.uk
mainegrains.com
shipton-mill.com

Fava bean flour
hodmedods.co.uk

Khorasan flour
bakerybits.co.uk
dovesfarm.co.uk
shipton-mill.com

Lupin flour
santi-shop.co.uk
vitalabo.co.uk

Maida flour
bakerybits.co.uk (Offley Mill chapati flour)
redrickshaw.com
theasiancookshop.co.uk

Millet flour
bobsredmill.com
dovesfarm.co.uk
jalpurmillersonline.com
redrickshaw.com
shipton-mill.com
spicesofindia.co.uk

Mung bean flour
jalpurmillersonline.com

Oat flour
bobsredmill.com
healthysupplies.co.uk
shipton-mill.com

Pea flour
hodmedods.co.uk

Peanut flour
sukrin.co.uk

Potato starch
bobsredmill.com
healthysupplies.co.uk
spicesofindia.co.uk

Quinoa flour
bobsredmill.com
britishquinoa.co.uk
hodmedods.co.uk
kingarthurflour.com

Rice flour, Asian
mattas.co.uk
somayaskitchen.co.uk
souschef.co.uk

Rice flour, glutinous
japancentre.com
mattas.co.uk
orientalmart.co.uk

Rice flour, roasted red
theasiancookshop.co.uk

Rye flour
bacheldremill.co.uk
dovesfarm.co.uk
gristandtoll.com
mainegrains.com
shipton-mill.com
tamariskfarm.co.uk
(collection only, no online
shop)

Semolina, semola
bakerybits.co.uk (Mulino
Marino semola)

mattas.co.uk (semola
rimacinata)
thetapaslunchcompany.co.uk
(Spanish frying flour)

Sesame flour
sukrin.co.uk

**Sorghum flour, sweet
white sorghum flour**
bobsredmill.com
healthysupplies.co.uk
kingarthurflour.com
shipton-mill.com

**Soya flour (Japanese
kinako)**
japancentre.com
souschef.co.uk

Spelt flour
dovesfarm.co.uk
gristandtoll.com
mainegrains.com
shipton-mill.com
stoatesflour.co.uk

Teff flour
bobsredmill.com
dovesfarm.co.uk
kingarthurflour.com
shipton-mill.com

Tigernut flour
thetigernutcompany.co.uk
tigernuts.com

**Waterchestnut flour
(Chinese, Indian)**
spicesofindia.co.uk (Indian,
Singoda flour)
wingyipstore.co.uk (Chinese)

Wheat flour: fine
shipton-mill.com (cake
and pastry flour)
souschef.co.uk (Honour
dumpling flour)
wingyipstore.co.uk (Honour
dumpling flour)

Wheat flour: Italian
bakerybits.co.uk

**Wheat flour: plain,
strong, whole**
bacheldremill.co.uk
bakerybits.co.uk (heritage
flours)
dovesfarm.co.uk
shipton-mill.com
stoatesflour.co.uk
tamariskfarm.co.uk
(collection only, no
online shop)
wessexmill.co.uk

Yam flour
mattas.co.uk

index

a

almond flour 12–13
  Sicilian citrus and almond cake
    with clementine syrup 14–15
almonds
  almond and bergamot Turkish
    delight 83–5
  barley and almond cake with
    cream cheese and orange
    frosting 30–1
amaranth flour 16–17
  cheese and chilli purple
    cornbread 18–19
apples Welsh curd cake with
  raisins and apples 261
arepas 93
artichokes mushroom, artichoke
  and tomato pizza 104–6
atta flour 20–1
  spiced potato puris 22–3

b

bacon
  Dutch baby pancake with bacon
    and maple syrup 255
  goose soup with buckwheat and
    bacon dumplings 38–9
banana flour (green) 24–5
  banana flour pancakes with
    allspice and tangerine
    cream 26–7
bananas banana, walnut and
  raspberry cake 145
barley flour 28–9
  barley and almond cake with
    cream cheese and orange
    frosting 30–1
biscuits
  Alda O'Loughlin's shortbread
    80–1
  black pepper and potato
    oatcakes 140–1
  chocolate-dipped spiced biscuits
    with walnuts and black

pepper 176–7
  frosted lime biscuits 118
  orange, fennel and black pepper
    biscotti 199–201
  salted cacao biscuits 107
  seeded spelt and beetroot
    crackers with smoked salmon
    pâté 210–11
black bean flour 32–3
  black bean and roasted tomato,
    garlic and onion soup 34–5
black beans
  Native American frybread with
    black bean and red pepper
    salsa 269
  oxtail and black bean stew with
    farofa 50–1
blancmange lime leaf-scented
  blancmange with sesame
  brittle 194–5
bread
  bread dough 60
  cheese and chilli purple
    cornbread 18–19
  Ethiopian injeera 219–21
  fava bean flour wholemeal
    bread 110–11
  Native American frybread with
    black bean and red pepper
    salsa 269
  polenta village bread 88–9
  seeded lupin bread 119–21
  seeded rye bread 175
  spiced onion bread 218
brownies triple chocolate
  brownies 76–7
buckwheat flour 36–7
  buckwheat cheese fritters 40
  buttermilk and bay leaf tart with
    chocolate pastry 41–3
  goose soup with buckwheat and
    bacon dumplings 38–9
butter 10
  Alda O'Loughlin's shortbread
    80–1
  tagliatelle with sage butter
    sauce 240–2
buttermilk and bay leaf tart with

chocolate pastry 41–3
butternut squash fufu with spicy
  goat, red pepper and butternut
  squash soup 276–7

c

cacao nibs 10
  salted cacao biscuits 107
Caerphilly cheese Welsh curd
  cake with raisins and apples 261
cake flour 233
cakes
  banana, walnut and raspberry
    cake 145
  barley and almond cake with
    cream cheese and orange
    frosting 30–1
  Chinese water chestnut
    cake 229–31
  chocolate and pepper cake 243
  clementine gateau with whipped
    ricotta frosting 198
  Italian chestnut cake with
    rosemary 55
  paradise cake from Pavia 156–7
  rum-soaked prune and sultana
    cake 96–7
  Sicilian citrus and almond cake
    with clementine syrup 14–15
  tamarisk wholemeal spice cake
    with ginger glaze 272–3
  triple chocolate brownies 76–7
  Welsh curd cake with raisins and
    apples 261
  white chocolate blondies
    with hazelnuts and
    cranberries 170–1
cardamom seeds
  belly dancer's jelly with
    cardamom brittle 82
  Diwali dessert with cardamom,
    nuts and sultanas 188–9
  pear, cranberry and cardamom
    cobbler 114–15
  sweet millet pudding with nuts,
    saffron and cardamom 131

syrup-soaked soya balls
with sultanas and
cardamom 206–7
carrot and cashew samosas with
peas and mint 124–5
cassava flour 44–6
Brazilian cheese puffs 48–9
oxtail and black bean stew with
farofa 50–1
Tropical tapioca pudding with
mango and lime 47
celery and Cheddar scones 212–14
chapati flour *see* atta flour
chapatis griddled soya
chapatis with garlic chives and
turmeric 204
Cheddar cheese
arepas 93
celery and Cheddar scones
212–14
cheese and chilli purple
cornbread 18–19
leek, cheese and peppercorn
tart 215
chestnut flour 52–3
chestnut flour fritters with fennel
and orange 54
Italian chestnut cake with
rosemary 55
pear tart with rosemary and
orange syrup 56–8
chicken Moroccan chicken,
chickpea and tomato soup 224
chickpea flour 62–3
prawns in raincoats 66–7
Sicilian chickpea fritters 64
spiced pancakes with mint, chilli
and apple relish 65
chickpeas Moroccan chicken,
chickpea and tomato soup 224
chocolate 10
buttermilk and bay leaf tart with
chocolate pastry 41–3
chocolate and pepper cake 243
chocolate-dipped spiced
biscuits with walnuts and
black pepper 176–7
chocolate tartlets with ganache

and ginger cream 178–9
triple chocolate brownies 76–7
white chocolate blondies
with hazelnuts and
cranberries 170–1
clementines
clementine gateau with whipped
ricotta frosting 198
Sicilian citrus and almond cake
with clementine syrup 14–15
coconut flour 68–9
coconut flour and lime
pancakes 70–1
piña colada tart with rum
custard and caramelized
pineapple 72–3
coconut milk
coconut flour and lime
pancakes 70–1
rose-scented coconut
custards 135–7
coffee flour 74–5
triple chocolate brownies 76–7
cornbread cheese and chilli purple
cornbread 18–19
cornflour 78–9
Alda O'Loughlin's shortbread
80–1
almond and bergamot Turkish
delight 83–5
belly dancer's jelly with
cardamom brittle 82
lime leaf-scented blancmange
with sesame brittle 194–5
cornmeal 86–7
arepas 93
blue cornmeal tortillas with
tomato, avocado and chilli
salsa 90–2
polenta village bread 88–9
cranberries pear, cranberry and
cardamom cobbler 114–15
cream banana flour pancakes
with allspice and tangerine
cream 26–7
cream cheese
barley and almond cake with
cream cheese and orange

frosting 30–1
Hungarian cream cheese and
orange dumplings 190–1
cricket flour 94–5
rum-soaked prune and sultana
cake 96–7
croquettes rice croquettes with
spinach and mozzarella 252–3
curd cheese Welsh curd cake with
raisins and apples 261
custard
piña colada tart with rum
custard and caramelized
pineapple 72–3
rose-scented coconut custards
135–7

d

desserts
banana flour pancakes
with allspice and tangerine
cream 26–7
belly dancer's jelly with
cardamom brittle 82
buttermilk and bay leaf tart with
chocolate pastry 41–3
citrus and raisin suet puddings
258–60
clementine gateau with whipped
ricotta frosting 198
Diwali dessert with cardamom,
nuts and sultanas 188–9
greengage and cobnut
crumble 163
lime leaf-scented blancmange
with sesame brittle 194–5
limoncello babas with figs and
fennel 266–7
pear, cranberry and cardamom
cobbler 114–15
rose-scented coconut custards
135–7
sweet millet pudding with nuts,
saffron and cardamom 131
Tropical tapioca pudding with
mango and lime 47

dill seeds seeded lupin
bread 119–21
duck Asian-style duck and
noodle salad with peanut
dressing 150–1
dumplings
goose soup with buckwheat and
bacon dumplings 38–9
Hungarian cream cheese and
orange dumplings 190–1
Japanese rice dumplings with
roasted soybean topping 167

e

eggs
banana flour pancakes 26–7
Brazilian cheese puffs 48–9
coconut flour and lime pancakes
70–1
Dutch baby pancake 255
seeded lupin bread 119
Singapore oyster
omelette 168–9
tagliatelle with sage butter sauce
241
einkorn flour 98–9
spiced pumpkin pie 100–1
emmer flour 102–3
mushroom, artichoke and
tomato pizza 104–6
salted cacao biscuits 107

f

farofa oxtail and black bean stew
with farofa 50–1
fava bean flour 108–9
fava bean flour wholemeal
bread 110–11
fennel seeds
chestnut flour fritters with fennel
and orange 54
limoncello babas with figs and
fennel 266–8
orange, fennel and black pepper

biscotti 199–201
flatbread
Ethiopian injeera 219–21
griddled soya chapatis 204
spiced potato puris 22
fritters
buckwheat cheese fritters 40
chestnut flour fritters with fennel
and orange 54
potato and paneer fritters 228
Sicilian chickpea fritters 64
frosting
barley and almond cake with
cream cheese and orange
frosting 30–1
clementine gateau with whipped
ricotta frosting 198
frosted lime biscuits 118
frybread Native American
frybread with black bean and red
pepper salsa 269
fufu 275
fufu with spicy goat, red
pepper and butternut squash
soup 276–7

g

game raised game pie with juniper,
lemon and gin 246–9
gluten 59, 60–1
goat fufu with spicy goat, red
pepper and butternut squash
soup 276–7
goose soup with buckwheat and
bacon dumplings 38–9
greengage and cobnut crumble 163
greens orecchiette with leafy
greens 184–5
gruyère cheese roasted tomato
and gruyère cheese tart 160–2
gua bao buns steamed gua bao
buns with sticky pork and
smashed cucumber 234–5

i

injeera Ethiopian injeera 219–21
Italian 00 wheat flour
chocolate and pepper cake 243
Spätzle 239
tagliatelle with sage butter
sauce 240–2
venison casserole with
mushrooms, garlic and
rosemary 238

k

khorasan flour 112–13
pear, cranberry and cardamom
cobbler 114–15
kimchi pancakes with ginger
dipping sauce 154–5

l

lamb spring lamb and barley
pie with lemon, rosemary and
mint 250
leek, cheese and peppercorn
tart 215
limoncello babas with figs and
fennel 266–7
lupin flour 116–17
frosted lime biscuits 118
seeded lupin bread 119–21

m

maida flour 122–3
carrot and cashew samosas with
peas and mint 124–5
mangoes Tropical tapioca pudding
with mango and lime 47
mayonnaise
deep-fried squid with paprika
mayonnaise 186
tempura seafood with wasabi
mayonnaise 254

flour

milk
  belly dancer's jelly with
    cardamom brittle 82
  Diwali dessert with cardamom,
    nuts and sultanas 188–9
  Tropical tapioca pudding with
    mango and lime 47
  warm ginger and nutmeg
    smoothie 225
millet flour 126–7
  spring vegetable pies with herbs
    and lemon 128–30
  sweet millet pudding with nuts,
    saffron and cardamom 131
milling 187
mozzarella cheese
  mushroom, artichoke and tomato
    pizza 104–6
  rice croquettes with spinach and
    mozzarella 252–3
mung bean flour 132–3
  rose-scented coconut
    custards 135–7
  spicy onion and tomato
    pudlas with mint and
    cucumber relish 134

n

noodles Asian-style duck and
  noodle salad with peanut
  dressing 150–1
nuts, mixed
  chocolate and pepper cake 243
  Diwali dessert with cardamom,
    nuts and sultanas 188–9
  sweet millet pudding with nuts,
    saffron and cardamom 131

o

oat flour 138–9
  black pepper and potato
    oatcakes 140–1
oats
  black pepper and potato

    oatcakes 140–1
  greengage and cobnut
    crumble 163
omelettes Singapore oyster
  omelette 168–9
onions
  spiced onion bread 218
  spicy onion and tomato pudlas
    with mint and cucumber
    relish 134
  oxtail and black bean stew
    with farofa 50–1
oysters Singapore oyster
  omelette 168–9

p

pancakes
  banana flour pancakes
    with allspice and tangerine
    cream 26–7
  coconut flour and lime
    pancakes 70–1
  Dutch baby pancake with bacon
    and maple syrup 255
  kimchi pancakes with ginger
    dipping sauce 154–5
  Moroccan thousand-hole
    pancakes 183
  spiced pancakes with mint, chilli
    and apple relish 65
  sweet green pea pancakes with
    ricotta, honey and apricots 144
paneer cheese potato and paneer
  fritters 228
Parmesan cheese Brazilian
  cheese puffs 48–9
pasta
  orecchiette with leafy greens
    184–5
  Spätzle 239
  tagliatelle with sage butter
    sauce 240–2
pastry 60
  rough puff pastry 251
  see also pies and tarts
pâté seeded spelt and beetroot

crackers with smoked salmon
  pâté 210–11
pea flour 142–3
  banana, walnut and raspberry
    cake 145
  plum and frangipane tart 146–7
  sweet green pea pancakes with
    ricotta, honey and apricots 144
peanut flour 148–9
  Asian-style duck and
    noodle salad with peanut
    dressing 150–1
pears
  pear, cranberry and cardamom
    cobbler 114–15
  pear tart with rosemary and
    orange syrup 56–8
pies and tarts
  buttermilk and bay leaf tart with
    chocolate pastry 41–3
  chocolate tartlets with ganache
    and ginger cream 178–9
  leek, cheese and peppercorn
    tart 215
  pear tart with rosemary and
    orange syrup 56–8
  piña colada tart with rum
    custard and caramelized
    pineapple 72–3
  plum and frangipane tart 146–7
  raised game pie with juniper,
    lemon and gin 246–9
  roasted tomato and gruyère
    cheese tart 160–2
  spiced pumpkin pie 100–1
  spring lamb and barley pie with
    lemon, rosemary and mint 250
  spring vegetable pies with herbs
    and lemon 128–30
pineapple piña colada tart with
  rum custard and caramelized
  pineapple 72–3
pizzas mushroom, artichoke and
  tomato pizza 104–6
plum and frangipane tart 146–7
polenta 87
  polenta village bread 88–9
pork steamed gua bao buns

with sticky pork and smashed
cucumber 234–5
potato starch 152–3
kimchi pancakes with ginger
dipping sauce 154–5
paradise cake from Pavia 156–7
potatoes
black pepper and potato
oatcakes 140–1
potato and paneer fritters 228
spiced potato puris 22–3
prawns in raincoats 66–7
protein 59
pudlas spicy onion and tomato
pudlas with mint and cucumber
relish 134
pumpkin spiced pumpkin
pie 100–1
puris spiced potato puris 22–3

q

quinoa flour 158–9
greengage and cobnut
crumble 163
roasted tomato and gruyère
cheese tart 160–2

r

relishes
spiced pancakes with mint, chilli
and apple relish 65
spicy onion and tomato pudlas
with mint and cucumber
relish 134
resistant starch 205
rice croquettes with spinach and
mozzarella 252–3
rice flour 164–6
Japanese rice dumplings with
roasted soybean topping 167
Singapore oyster omelette 168–9
white chocolate blondies
with hazelnuts and

cranberries 170–1
ricotta cheese
clementine gateau with whipped
ricotta frosting 198
sweet green pea pancakes with
ricotta, honey and apricots 144
rosewater rose-scented coconut
custards 135–7
rye flour 172–4
chocolate-dipped spiced
biscuits with walnuts and
black pepper 176–7
chocolate tartlets with ganache
and ginger cream 178–9
seeded rye bread 175

s

sage tagliatelle with sage butter
sauce 240–2
salads Asian-style duck and
noodle salad with peanut
dressing 150–1
salmon seeded spelt and beetroot
crackers with smoked salmon
pâté 210–11
salsa
blue cornmeal tortillas with
tomato, avocado and chilli
salsa 90–2
Native American frybread with
black bean and red pepper
salsa 269
samosas carrot and cashew
samosas with peas and
mint 124–5
sauces
kimchi pancakes with ginger
dipping sauce 154–5
tagliatelle with sage butter
sauce 240–2
scones celery and Cheddar
scones 212–14
seafood tempura seafood with
wasabi mayonnaise 254
seeds 10–11

seeded lupin bread 119
seeded rye bread 175
semolina 180–2
deep-fried squid with paprika
mayonnaise 186
Diwali dessert with cardamom,
nuts and sultanas 188–9
Hungarian cream cheese and
orange dumplings 190–1
Moroccan thousand-hole
pancakes 183
orecchiette with leafy
greens 184–5
tagliatelle with sage butter
sauce 240–2
sesame flour 192–3
lime leaf-scented blancmange
with sesame brittle 194–5
shortbread Alda O'Loughlin's
shortbread 80–1
smoothies warm ginger and
nutmeg smoothie 225
sorghum flour 196–7
clementine gateau with whipped
ricotta frosting 198
orange, fennel and black pepper
biscotti 199–201
soup
black bean and roasted tomato,
garlic and onion soup 34–5
fufu with spicy goat, red
pepper and butternut squash
soup 276–7
goose soup with buckwheat and
bacon dumplings 38–9
Moroccan chicken, chickpea
and tomato soup 224
soya flour 202–3
griddled soya chapatis with garlic
chives and turmeric 204
syrup-soaked soya balls
with sultanas and cardamom
206–7
Spanish flour *see* semolina
spelt flour 208–9
celery and Cheddar
scones 212–14

leek, cheese and peppercorn
tart 215
seeded spelt and beetroot
crackers with smoked salmon
pâté 210–11
spinach rice croquettes with
spinach and mozzarella 252–3
squid deep-fried squid with paprika
mayonnaise 186
suet puddings citrus and raisin suet
puddings 258–60
sultanas syrup-soaked soya
balls with sultanas and
cardamom 206–7

t

Taleggio cheese buckwheat cheese
fritters 40
tangerines
banana flour pancakes
with allspice and tangerine
cream 26–7
chestnut flour fritters with fennel
and orange 54
tapioca starch 46
Brazilian cheese puffs 48–9
pear tart with rosemary and
orange syrup 56–8
tapioca Tropical tapioca pudding
with mango and lime 47
teff flour 216–17
Ethiopian injeera 219–21
spiced onion bread 218
tempura seafood with wasabi
mayonnaise 254
tiger nut flour 222–3
Moroccan chicken, chickpea and
tomato soup 224
warm ginger and nutmeg
smoothie 225
tomatoes
black bean and roasted tomato,
garlic and onion soup 34–5
Moroccan chicken, chickpea and
tomato soup 224
oxtail and black bean stew with

farofa 50–1
spicy onion and tomato pudlas
with mint and cucumber
relish 134
tortillas blue cornmeal tortillas
with tomato, avocado and chilli
salsa 90–2
Turkish delight almond and
bergamot Turkish delight 83–5

V

vegetables spring vegetable pies
with herbs and lemon 128–30
venison casserole with mushrooms,
garlic and rosemary 238

W

wasabi 11
tempura seafood with wasabi
mayonnaise 254
water chestnut flour 226–7
Chinese water chestnut
cake 229–31
potato and paneer fritters 228
wheat and heritage flours 262–3
wheat flour: fine 232–3
steamed gua bao buns with
sticky pork and smashed
cucumber 234–5
wheat flour: Italian 00 236–7
chocolate and pepper cake 243
Spätzle 239
tagliatelle with sage butter
sauce 241–2
venison casserole with
mushrooms, garlic and
rosemary 238
wheat flour: plain 244–5
Alda O'Loughlin's shortbread
80–1
Dutch baby pancake with bacon
and maple syrup 255
kimchi pancakes with ginger
dipping sauce 154–5

raised game pie with juniper,
lemon and gin 246–9
rice croquettes with spinach and
mozzarella 252–3
rough puff pastry 251
spring lamb and barley pie with
lemon, rosemary and mint 250
tempura seafood with wasabi
mayonnaise 254
wheat flour: self-raising 256–7
citrus and raisin suet
puddings 258–60
rum-soaked prune and sultana
cake 96–7
Welsh curd cake with raisins and
apples 261
wheat flour: strong 264–5
limoncello babas with figs and
fennel 266–7
Native American frybread with
black bean and red pepper
salsa 269
wheat flour: whole 270–1
tamarisk wholemeal spice cake
with ginger glaze 272–3

y

yam flour 274–5
fufu with spicy goat, red
pepper and butternut squash
soup 276–7

acknowledgments and credits

Writing this book has been a privilege and a deeply rewarding challenge that has brought me in contact with so many good-hearted people. Without them the book would not have happened. My sincere thanks to the following:

Jon Croft and Meg Avent of Absolute Press for publishing the book

Food writer Jenny Linford for encouraging me to put forward a proposal

Project editor Emily North for endless patience and encouragement

Marie O'Mara for designing the book so beautifully and art directing the photography

Mike Cooper for stunning photography, fortifying lunches, spacious studio and general calmness

Genevieve Taylor and Danielle Coombs for preparing the food for photography with impressive efficiency and making it look so good

Nic Armstrong and Lisa Waterman for months of patient recipe testing and washing up

Lisa Vipond for scrupulous kitchen cleaning

My husband Ed and all my family for their love and support throughout the project

My friends for understanding my disappearance from the social world

Food writer Hattie Ellis for her enthusiasm and advice

Expert bakers Emmanuel Hadjiandreou and Paul Merry for information and advice

Food writer and friend Lesley Mackley for ongoing support

Clare Marriage of Doves Farm for supplying beautiful ears of emmer wheat for photography

Josiah Meldrum and Nick Saltmarsh of Hodmedods for supplying props, donating generous bags of pea, bean and quinoa flour and for generally promoting non-wheat flours

Oxford Food Symposiasts Sandra Mian and Marcia Zoladz, and Brazilian chef Almir Da Fonseca, for in-depth information about cassava flour

Horticulturists and long-term friends Joy and Michael Michaud for ongoing encouragement and sound advice about crops

Dorset butcher Lee Moreton for helpful advice on the technicalities of raised pies

Siobhan Nolan of Shipton Mill for expert tuition in gluten-free baking

Michael Stoate of Cann Mills for guiding me through the ins and outs of traditional stone milling

James Whetlor of Cabrito Goat Meat for supplying a generous amount of goat meat

I also wish to thank the following for contributing recipes:
Sarah Beattie
Jenny Chandler
Anna del Conte
Naomi Duguid
Roopa Gulati
Carol Kearns
Jenny Linford
Ottavia Mazzoni
Jenni Muir
Marina O'Loughlin
Kay Plunkett-Hogge
Sejal Sukhadwala

. . .

Publisher Jon Croft
Commissioning editor Meg Avent
Art director and designer Marie O'Mara
Project editor Emily North
Home economist and food stylist Genevieve Taylor
Assistant food stylists Christine McFadden and Danielle Coombs
Photographer Mike Cooper
Copy editor Rachel Malig
Proof reader Margaret Haynes
Indexer Cathy Heath